Scholars of the Law

Scholars of the Law

English Jurisprudence from Blackstone to Hart

Richard A. Cosgrove

New York University Press
NEW YORK AND LONDON

New York University Press
New York and London

Library of Congress Cataloging-in-Publication Data
Cosgrove, Richard A.
Scholars of the law : English jurisprudence from Blackstone to Hart / Richard A. Cosgrove.
p. cm.
Includes bibliographical references and index.
ISBN 0-8147-1533-8 (acid-free paper)
1. Jurisprudence. 2. Law—Philosophy. 3. Law—Great Britain—History. I. title.
KD640.C668 1996 95-41782
340'.1—dc20 CIP

New York University Press books are printed on acid-free paper, and their binding materials are chosen for strength and durability.

Manufactured in the United States of America

10 9 8 7 6 5 4 3 2 1

For Loretta

Rosemary	*Joseph*	*David*	*Elizabeth*
Kyle	*Kaleigh*	*Jourdan*	*Courtney*

Contents

Acknowledgments

This work is based primarily upon a reconsideration of texts that have long served as staples of jurisprudential debate. The new edition of John Austin's *The Province of Jurisprudence Determined* (1995) from Cambridge University Press, so ably edited by Wilfrid E. Rumble, has demonstrated anew the continuing appeal of classic works in jurisprudence. My scholarly debts are thus primarily to those individuals treated in the book who remain the giants of legal philosophy in the common-law tradition. Next come the many scholars who, like myself, have succumbed to the intellectual challenge that contemplation of legal history and jurisprudence presents.

I am grateful as well to the staffs of the Bodleian Library, Oxford, and especially the Oxford Law Library for their unfailing courtesy and assistance. In the United Kingdom as well, on a more personal note, for their friendship and hospitality, I record my appreciation to Ann Dykes of Oxford and Enid Shepherd of Forest Hill, Oxfordshire.

For their suggestions in the preparation of the manuscript I would like to thank my colleague at the University of Arizona, J. Robert Vignery, and Richard W. Davis of Washington University, St. Louis. For his perceptive comments on a paper drawn from this work I thank John Orth of the University of North Carolina School of Law.

For financial support of my work I extend my thanks to the Provost's Author Support Fund at the University of Arizona.

Two individuals, Michael Schaller and Helen Nader, served as head of my department during the research and writing of this book and I acknowledge with thanks their strong personal support for my work.

I also wish to record my special thanks to Patricia Foreman, whose computer versatility and endless patience made the manuscript a reality.

Finally, I thank my wife Loretta whose honorary membership in the Western Conference on British Studies has sustained not only me, but many others in the field of British studies. Since the appearance of my last book in 1987, my four children (Rosemary, Joseph, David, and Beth) have now provided me with another generation of family to enrich my life and stimulate my work. These grandchildren (Kyle, Kaleigh, Jourdan, and Courtney), in the Burkean sense, make the transition from generation to generation a joyful experience.

Chapter One

From Jurisprudence to Legal Philosophy

The study of jurisprudence as a specialized branch of intellectual history has matured during the last two decades in conjunction with a renewed interest in legal history. In a letter to American jurist Oliver Wendell Holmes in 1880, A. V. Dicey, soon to revive the Vinerian professorship of English law at Oxford, wrote about the nuances of legal scholarship: "A work on law may, it seems to me, be concerned with any or all of three questions *first* What is the law? (practical lawyer), *secondly* What ought to be law? (Jurist or legislator), *thirdly* What is the history of the law? (legal historian)."[1] Dicey's ruminations anticipated the basic divisions of inquiry into legal phenomena that have prevailed for most of the twentieth century. Many scholars have noted the divorce between legal history and jurisprudence but few have addressed it in systematic fashion. The dichotomy between these two areas of legal scholarship prompted this recent assessment: "Just as Anglo-American legal theory since Bentham and Austin has been notoriously ahistorical—encouraging each generation of theorists to search anew for universal truth untempered by the need to account for historical variation and contingency—so too Anglo-American legal history has been persistently untheoretical."[2] This situation has inevitably divided the audience for such scholarship.

In 1880 as well Dicey opened an article on the contemporary state of legal philosophy with the famous aphorism: "Jurisprudence is a word which stinks in the nostrils of a practicing barrister." Dicey then elaborated this prejudice: "A jurist is, they constantly find, a professor whose claim to dogmatize on law in general lies in the fact that he has made himself master of no one legal system in particular, whilst his boasted science consists in the enunciation of platitudes which if they ought, as he insists, to be law everywhere, cannot in fact be shown to be law anywhere."[3] Appraisals of the common law have usually focused on the unique features generated by judicial legislation, adherence to precedent, and vocational training at the Inns of Court. The respect accorded to philosophical analysis has always been limited. Many years later academic lawyer A. L. Goodhart added to this generalization when he wrote: "English jurists have always been afraid of abstract ideas in the air."[4] Goodhart referred to the aversion of English jurists to grand philosophical structures that characterized the stereotype of their civil law brethren whose legal heritage derived from Roman law. Familiarity with the works of major English jurists shows quickly, however, that civil lawyers have never held a monopoly on abstract legal thought. This division between jurists and practitioners continues to vex their respective enterprises with little sign of reducing the gap between the two; a century later Raymond Cocks wrote: "Modern jurisprudence is largely unconcerned with the problems which are of greatest importance to practitioners. . . . In so far as jurisprudence was concerned with the study of ideas about law it was an odd view of the subject which excluded from consideration the ideas which were regarded as important by those who actually practiced law."[5] The path of English jurisprudence for most of the past two centuries has led back to an assessment of what purposes legal philosophy should serve.

It is the argument of this book that many of the controversies that have beset legal speculation since the time of Sir William Blackstone in the middle of the eighteenth century originated in issues of motivation and audience, not just definition and analysis. Lack of consensus on a definition of jurisprudence itself has plagued the discipline. Perhaps the broadest conception of jurisprudence held that it is the art of the good and the just *(ars boni et aequi)*. This definition has little relevance to attorneys trained in the adversarial tradition of the common law and whose foremost duty is to serve the interests of a client. The difference between the eighteenth- and twentieth-century efforts to work out the implications of this dictum becomes readily discernible when representative definitions of each era are contrasted. On the one hand, for Adam Smith jurisprudence connoted the broadest lines of inquiry, the search for a synthesis of history, analysis, and criticism of law.[6] On the other hand, representative definitions from contemporary jurists have drawn narrower boundaries for jurisprudence. Neil MacCormick, for example, has defined jurisprudence as "the theoretical study of a practical subject";[7] and Richard Posner has written: "By 'jurisprudence' I mean the most fundamental, general, and theoretical plane of analysis of the social phenomenon called law. For the most part it deals with problems, and uses perspectives, remote from the daily concerns of legal practitioners."[8] The latter two definitions echo Dicey in the division between the theoretical and practical elements of jurisprudence.

What has clearly happened over the past two centuries is a fundamental change in the way jurists have envisioned their task. The broad thrust of Smith's triad has given way to emphasis upon one aspect of his conception of law. This has resulted in increasingly complex studies and the consequent diminution of the audience to which they are addressed. To cite another example, whereas Blackstone attempted to comprehend the common law in the *Commentaries*, the treatise writers of the late Victorian era were content to examine one branch of the law in the search for those rational principles assumed to characterize the law that made it worthy of scientific inquiry.[9] In the 1880s this trend culminated in the creation of an academic legal culture that became the primary producer and consumer of legal studies to the detriment of broader social and political analysis. Jurisprudence became identified solely as legal philosophy, separated from more mundane (read practical) aspects of the law. Dicey's original comment of 1880 demonstrated insight, although the reconciliation between legal theory and legal practice that he envisioned has not yet materialized.

In a general sense, therefore, how jurists have conceived jurisprudence, either in broad or narrow fashion, has determined the content of scholarship. The definition of law in English jurisprudence has driven widespread speculation that has yielded little agreement. Whether law merely prescribes rules of conduct (the positivist tradition) or whether law contains other, often ethereal, elements (the natural law tradition) has haunted English jurisprudence for the past two hundred years. The long and sometimes acrimonious debate among jurists about exactly what constitutes law has sometimes served as a proxy for other controversial issues that have attracted the attention of legal scholars since Blackstone.

Two quotations, one serious and one satirical, illustrate the diversity of approach that a definition of law has spawned. Lord Haldane, Lord Chancellor in 1913 and certainly more reflective about the philosophical issues of law than most of those who have held that office, wrote:

> Law, properly so called, whether civil or criminal, means essentially those rules of conduct which are expressly and publicly laid down by the sovereign will of the state and are enforced by the sanction of compulsion. Law, however, imports something more than this. . . . In short, if its full significance is to be appreciated, larger conceptions than those of the mere lawyer are essential, conceptions which come to us from the moralist and the sociologist, and without which we cannot see fully how the genesis of law has come about.[10]

Haldane neatly synthesized both the positivist and natural law traditions without a hint of the intellectual difficulties involved. A more succinct and less favorable appreciation of English law dated from 1909: "The Law is our 'Old Man of the Sea,' cumbrous in procedure, barbarous in phraseology and—even in the most exalted quarters—constantly sacrificing the spirit to the letter."[11] Such widely divergent conclusions in tone and substance suggest the intense disagreements that have marked the history of English jurisprudence since the middle of the eighteenth century. The customary depiction of a triumphant positivist orthodoxy, identified primarily with jurists, does not explain adequately the vagaries of jurisprudential debate characteristic of academic culture, nor does it address the realities of daily practice where little time can be allotted to philosophical issues within the law.

Until recently intellectual historians have generally ignored this argument despite the fact that generations of jurists have engaged in it.[12] Historians have preferred the relatively safer ground of the political argument that has lurked behind the subtleties of legal analysis. For example, historians have focused more on Blackstone's alleged role as apologist for the established order of the 1760s than for his connection to the natural law tradition. The life of Jeremy Bentham has interested primarily those historians eager to sketch the path of administrative reform in Victorian England, not those interested in Bentham as the most enduring of English legal philosophers. His essays in censorial (critical) jurisprudence, whether judged successful or not, have continued to spur evaluation from both critics and admirers of this aspect of his utilitarianism. Certainly political purposes did play a major role in Bentham's motivation, for he sought consciously to generate legal and political change in his day. Historians, who paid scant attention to John Austin until the 1970s, now cite him as often for his defense of existing constitutional arrangements as for his more rewarding, albeit more challenging analyses of law. To be sure, the technical writings of Bentham and Austin present a forbidding body of work; they are not easily accessible, are usually composed in a style that obscures rather than enlightens, and demand specialized training that historians are unlikely to command. That historians have rarely ventured into the complex world of jurisprudence is therefore no surprise. These jurists addressed issues that posterity has tended to ignore, yet as representative figures they provide access to the traditions of English jurisprudence.

Sir Henry Maine has served as a more congenial Victorian subject because his role as a critic of democracy made him a substantial figure in the political controversies of his day, especially in his last years in the 1880s. The more philosophical elements of his work in the critique of the natural law tradition and the benefits of comparative legal analysis have received more significant discussion from scholars in other disciplines. Sir Thomas Erskine Holland, despite a successful academic career at Oxford, has faded into an obscurity so total that his unfamiliarity to historians is not a matter for reproach. Yet, in terms of his influence on the place and content of jurisprudence within the emerging academic culture of the 1880s, Holland has some claim to attention. Finally, the last of the jurists examined in this book, H. L. A. Hart, became an icon of sorts within the field of jurisprudence; beyond the confines of the academy, however, Hart exercised little influence. The evaluation and interpretation of English jurisprudence has to a significant extent gone by default to those scholars who already worked within its traditions.

Charting the history of jurisprudential thought presents special obstacles because the integration of different issues, such as the technical doctrine of tort law or the relationship of the law in general to contemporary society, have no necessary connection to one another: "When the history of academic law in England during the past 200 years comes to be written, the uneven progress of jurisprudence will form an important subplot in the story."[13] The specific issues of legal philosophy constitute a subdiscipline with its own language and tasks. In addition, the political implications of a jurist's legal and/or constitutional texts represent a legitimate field of inquiry for the historian. Finally, more compatible with the traditional goals of historians, the political and social context that produced the style and content of jurisprudential argument has served as a focus for historical interpretation. The fragmented nature of these three endeavors has created a wide body of knowledge, but the narrow areas of discourse have prevented a comprehensive assessment of the major figures who form the nucleus of the English tradition in legal philosophy. It is time, therefore, to make available to other historians the rich intellectual history that legal theory in England has offered. The conjunction of jurisprudence with historical investigation has accelerated since 1970, and "thus it may be that movements in both legal history and jurisprudence are converging towards a common domain; and it may be that the Anglo-American world is about to experience a renaissance of historical jurisprudence."[14] Rebirth may be too strong a word, but this does not detract from the importance of the undertaking.

Central to this quest is the issue of audience. Initially the impulse to unravel the mysteries of the law led jurists to address their conclusions to the educated public. The study of law served as a proxy for social analysis and offered a pretext for a general interpretation of society. This strategy met with varying degrees of success. Blackstone and Bentham certainly established themselves as jurists whose assertions merited serious consideration by those who pondered the fate of England. Austin, however, gained little reputation in his lifetime, and his influence has been almost entirely posthumous. This failure stemmed from Austin's inability to execute the same design as his predecessors, not a deviation from their purposes. In similar fashion Maine hoped his jurisprudence would focus attention on, and offer solutions to, broad questions of social policy. The great transformation in this tradition occurred in Holland's time when the creation of a separate legal academic culture set out to serve a narrower audience and defined its objectives in more limited terms. The result may be seen in the fact that Hart, despite the significant recognition he has earned within university circles worldwide, has remained essentially unknown outside the fraternity of legal philosophers. The fate of these jurists mirrored the jurisprudence they produced, which went from the law as the spacious contemplation of the human condition to a discipline (often not honored within the undergraduate curriculum) within academic culture.

As has already been suggested, the split between the concerns of practitioners and legal theorists has given rise to separate spheres of intellectual labor, even though both groups deplore this outcome and inveigh against it rhetorically. Despite claims of esteem for the goals of jurisprudence, the vocational side of legal education has almost always triumphed in curricular disputes. Changes in legal education over the last century have thus affirmed the dichotomy between the essential purposes of law and jurisprudence. Legal philosophy has remained important only to a shrinking audience within the academy; jurisprudence has succumbed to the academic vice of increasing specialization. As Harold Perkin has written: "In order to preserve their separate function and existence, it became necessary for the university disciplines to emphasize their separation from the professions they served outside the walls and also, inside the walls, from the other university disciplines."[15] The separation of theory from practice, and academic lawyer from practitioner, has followed from the transition of jurisprudence as broad analysis to a discipline intent on more remote issues of public policy.

For the historian who seeks to understand the development of English jurisprudence in appropriate historical context, the focus on academic culture complements the traditional modes of interpreting legal history. What might be termed the law review vision of legal history has assumed (rather than proved) the internal logic of legal development. This approach to the legal history of the common law has rested primarily on assembling the appropriate cases, reconciling any differences among them, explaining away the irreconcilable, and demonstrating that the evolution of legal doctrine was susceptible to scientific inquiry. Indeed, the necessity to prove law a science (and thus take a place within the university community) was an enduring concern for the nascent community of legal academics of the Victorian era, for without it their claim to a place in the academy diminished significantly. The philosophical background to this attitude presumed that legal maturation was internal and rational, and that the judicial function entailed finding the "right" answer to questions of doctrine. According to this theory judges found the law, did not create new law, and simply discovered the correct solution in the pending action. Since the 1870s this belief has served as the primary founding myth that shaped the subsequent path of legal philosophy. For the legal academics of late-Victorian England, symbolized by Holland, the search for the "right" answer meant rationalizing the development of the law; the life of the law was logic. This goal transformed the agenda of academic law forever.

In opposition to this emphasis on the internal determinants of doctrinal growth, other scholars have insisted on the fundamental role of external factors in shaping the course of legal history; as Holmes put it, the life of the law was experience. The nature of these outside influences has varied widely. Marxist scholars, for example, have attempted to analyze the basic socioeconomic elements that have determined legal doctrines and ideas, whether in the formation of property law or in the place of law as a form of social control. In general, so this argument runs, the dynamics of legal change must be sought in broader categories than the simple assertion of legal rationality. The emphasis on extralegal explanations for legal phenomena has echoed throughout the twentieth century from sociological jurisprudence at the beginning to American realism in the 1920s and 1930s and thence to the critical legal studies movement of the 1980s. Despite frequent exhortations to expand the boundaries of legal inquiry, the task has been undertaken more in theory than in action. When the integration of several disciplines has occurred successfully, the result has usually intensified the practitioner's distrust of academic research. The esoteric language—and sometimes the conclusions—of these synthetic efforts has been successful, if at all, only with legal scholars of similar sympathies and beliefs. Despite the great hopes for the expansion of the law's purview held by many scholars in this century, the precise role of social and economic factors in an overall interpretation of the law has remained obscure.

A third major approach to the interpretation of legal history has stressed the importance of legal tradition in the development of legal systems. This interpretive framework for legal history, associated primarily with Alan Watson, holds that "the legal tradition shapes the law that comes out: divisions, classifications, types of remedy, scope of rules and exceptions. . . . The input of the society often bears little relation to the output of the legal elite. . . . Law, then, despite its practical impact, is above all and primarily the culture of the lawyers and especially of the lawmakers. . . . Law is largely autonomous and not shaped by societal needs; though legal institutions will not exist without corresponding social institutions, law evolves from the legal tradition."[16] Watson has made a useful contribution to legal history by his suggestion that the previous two approaches have become such clichés that a fresh examination of the problems of legal history from the perspective of a legal tradition will yield additional insights.

Watson has continued his argument in an extensive series of books and articles that have in common his theme that legal systems "are not always sensitive to wider political, social, and economic issues."[17] Watson has never denied that law interacts with other areas of human endeavor, but he has suggested that its scope has not generally been as extended as other theories of legal change have held. The culture of lawyers has played a significant role in the nature and significance of legal change. The influence of this legal culture varies among legal systems and has not worked in a precise fashion, thereby requiring that each case be evaluated on its own merits.

A new orthodoxy, eclectic in its search for validity, has arisen in the last several decades: "There is a general sympathy with the idea that you cannot really understand law without attending both to its history, and to the way in which the operations of the various legal systems, and the professional culture of lawyers, interacts with what may, for the want of a better term, be called society generally."[18] With respect to the history of English jurisprudence, the genesis of an academic jurisprudential tradition in the 1870s and 1880s marked the crucial transition to its modern state.

To expand on the thesis of this book, whereas Blackstone, Bentham, Austin, and Maine had specific audiences and purposes, the next jurist, Holland, certainly not a figure of comparable stature, symbolized the increasing academic context of legal philosophy. The first four had conceived of jurisprudence as the basic science of society, one whose purpose literally knew no bounds. Academic legal culture changed the nature and intent of jurisprudence dramatically. This new tradition, in its increasingly professional manifestations, took the broad conception of jurisprudence and reduced it to an academic enterprise. The reincarnation of jurisprudence in a new state reached its apogee in the place won by Hart in the Anglo-American academic world, a celebrity deserved by Hart but of a different character than that earned by the members of the earlier tradition.

The revolution in jurisprudence wrought by academic culture was disguised by the continuity of language and by the focus upon many of the same problems that attracted Blackstone and Bentham. Thus there often appears a superficial continuity that masks the deeper transition that has occurred over the last two centuries. From Blackstone forward, jurists have argued that the most pressing task of jurisprudence was the creation of a science of law, but they have reached no consensus about what constituted the scientific nature of law. Debate about the meaning of science has often prevented any agreement beyond one that the law may be studied in a way that provides an ordered body of knowledge. The quest for a science of law has disguised the varied disputes this issue has encompassed.

Another theme that has permeated jurisprudential debate and provided a superficial consistency has involved the endless debate about the relationship of morality to law. The separation of law from morality has sparked controversy since Blackstone. No jurist has proposed a literal divorce between law and the dictates of morality; most have argued that the separation of law from morality was methodological only. The intellectual rigor expected of legal science demanded that confusion between the two be eliminated by their complete divorce; as Sir Frederick Pollock wrote in 1882: "If he [a jurist] feels moved to write on ethics as well as on jurisprudence, he may do it separately."[19] Once again, however, the interminable reviews of this issue give an erroneous picture, for the concerns of academicians turned this issue into something far different than the polemic Bentham had launched against Blackstone.

Perhaps the most general change in English jurisprudence has been the victory of the positivist tradition at the expense of the older natural law theory, of which Blackstone was regarded as the last great representative. The dominant legal tradition of European civilization, natural law theory held among other teachings that a law in violation of moral norms did not bind an individual. Natural law comprised those principles of human behavior that derived from right reason. Thus a law, otherwise passed in accordance with constitutional procedures, might lack validity if it did not conform to moral standards. English legal positivism, clearly the dominant tradition since the time of Bentham, has insisted "that law is properly understood as a system of positive rules endorsed by the state and autonomous from considerations of religion, morality, or natural justice."[20] Thus the moral content of a law in the positivist view had nothing to do with its validity. What seemed a simple formula, the separation of law from morality, in reality has haunted English philosophy since Blackstone and Bentham. Many a jurist has struggled unsuccessfully to produce a precise delineation of the formula. Pollock, in his inaugural lecture as Corpus professor of jurisprudence at Oxford in 1883, straddled the issue neatly: "For Jurisprudence, if it is to be truly and vitally distinct from the empirical collection of matters of fact, must partake of the nature of Philosophy."[21] How to achieve this goal Pollock did not specify. The creation of legal science, the separation of law from morality, and natural law versus positivism are topics that have supplied continuity to English jurisprudence; each generation has sought to resolve them in terms of its own insights.

The definition of jurisprudence as an academic field has had two major results. It has widened the gap between practitioners and legal academics. While jurisprudence no longer stinks in anyone's nostrils, legal theory still searches for its place within the broad framework of legal culture. As Robert Summers has written: "All the legitimate general objectives of a legal theorist can be reduced to two: To try to advance the subject oneself and to induce others to join in. Since law is important, these objectives are important. Insofar as they are achieved, we will understand law better, and, perhaps, make better use of it."[22] The second consequence, the narrowing of the audience to academe, has tended to offset the first, and thus the contradictions of jurisprudence have persisted. The conflict between the practical and the contemplative in the aims of jurisprudence has remained unresolved.

The development of academic law as a university discipline, it might be argued, has worsened this situation since the 1880s. The splintering of broad fields of endeavor into narrow specialties has worked against common discourse within the legal community.[23] The issues of jurisprudence have acquired a special language that makes the answers more remote even from the trained reader, and the view of jurisprudence as the spacious consideration of society that animated Blackstone and his immediate successors has vanished, the victim of that specialization that scholars pretend to abhor but invariably pursue in practice. In the interpretation of modern English jurisprudence, therefore, the advent of academic law has played as dramatic a role as any of the three versions of legal history discussed earlier.

To return to Dicey's tripartite division of legal scholarship, this book does not aim to provide answers to those philosophical questions, past or present, that have attracted the attention of jurists. Nor does it pretend to chronicle, reconcile, or explain specific legal doctrines, the terrain of the law reviews. Nor does it presume to explicate or calendar in novel manner the ideas of the jurists treated in later chapters. Its more modest purpose is to introduce historians to those jurists whose names are usually well known, but whose place in the intellectual history of modern jurisprudence is rarely understood. The transformation of jurisprudence from the Enlightenment ideal of a search for the basic laws that governed human society into a subset of legal studies far removed from public concern marked an important element of the process that historians have termed "professionalization." From Blackstone to Hart, with intervals of dormancy, English jurisprudence has compiled an enviable record of intellectual achievement. This work has rarely gained the attention of historians because legal and constitutional issues in the world after the Glorious Revolution lacked the political relevance they had enjoyed in the seventeenth century. The emphasis on legal and constitutional history as a major ingredient of the English past has suffered on two counts: the belief that the Glorious Revolution "settled" the constitution, and the shifting trends of academic scholarship that have emphasized the claims of social history in the past few decades. What was once regarded as perhaps the primary rationale for the study of English history, the knowledge of its legal and constitutional development, has declined as its world power has ebbed.

The focus on issues of interest to historians to the exclusion of others that fascinate practitioners and legal philosophers is not meant to slight the importance of those concerns; it is the price paid to demonstrate to historians the relevance of past and contemporary legal theory to the wider currents of English intellectual history. As Morton Horwitz has written: "We must become more self-conscious about legal historiography and the ways in which controversies over political and legal theory influence legal historical inquiry. It is time for us to bridge the chasm between legal theory and legal history."[24] This book is intended to contribute to the reunion of legal theory with intellectual history in order that historians may understand better the place of jurisprudence in academic legal culture and in the more general concerns of society. The fundamental premise of the work is, as others have recognized, that "common law thought cannot be understood without taking a long historical view."[25] Only from this perspective can the great change in the purposes of jurisprudence gain proper appreciation.

Chapter Two

Sir William Blackstone The Intersection of Positivism and Natural Law Theory

For much of the period since his death in 1780 Sir William Blackstone has fallen into that special category of intellectual whose works, although widely popular in his lifetime, gradually decline in influence in succeeding decades. This fate has befallen intellectuals from all disciplines and eras. In the passage from one generation to another their reputations hang increasingly upon mere phrases, and their complex arguments become trivialized. Whereas historians of modern Britain know of Blackstone's most famous work, the *Commentaries on the Laws of England,* as well as the fame it commanded, few intrepid scholars have examined the four volumes in detail (usually some 2000 pages). For historians without specific legal training, the

Commentaries, or at least the greater proportion of them, have represented a monument of scholarship that did not invite close scrutiny. The recapitulation of doctrine as it existed in the middle of the eighteenth century covered many topics that time has rendered obsolete.

Despite this drawback Blackstone has remained an instantly recognizable figure, one who exercised undeniable authority and earned a reputation rivaled by few and exceeded by none. His role as the source of legal education for generations of common lawyers ensured his prominence, yet this influence also led to the dismissal of his importance for English jurisprudence. For many decades Blackstone served as a convenient symbol, a name to which ritual obeisance was directed but whose work no longer seemed compelling: "The thought of William Blackstone is often casually dismissed in our day as being irrelevant to the systematic study of jurisprudence."[1] In the 1980s scholars took Blackstone seriously again, and his ideas and conclusions have once again become the subject of serious discussion. This agenda was directed in part to "dispose of many myths created by Bentham's caricature of the Vinerian professor."[2] The revival of interest in Blackstone is merited because the great Commentator was the Janus of English jurisprudence, looking backward to the natural law tradition and forward to legal positivism and the beginnings of modern English jurisprudence.

Some jurists and historians have evaluated Blackstone primarily to determine whether his attachment to the natural law tradition of jurisprudence was genuine or simply a matter of following convention. Others have looked to him for his treatment of specific doctrines of constitutional law such as the sovereignty of Parliament or the theory of judicial interpretation in relation to the role of the legislature. A few scholars have debated whether Blackstone wrote to inaugurate a new science of law or to reform the system of English legal education. Historians have also assessed the extent to which Blackstone defended existing legal arrangements and opposed unwise alterations in the English constitution, thus serving as a bulwark of the status quo and contributing to the complacency of eighteenth-century jurisprudence. Over the last decade Blackstone's intellectual achievement, for historians at least, provides a specific test of changing interpretations of Hanoverian history. The scholarly goals of jurists and historians are not mutually exclusive, but these broad divisions help to establish the setting against which Blackstone's place in English jurisprudence must be judged.

Blackstone was born in London on 10 July 1723. In spite of family tragedies, he received a strong secondary education through the efforts of an uncle. His initial academic success led to matriculation at Pembroke College, Oxford, in 1738, where he compiled an enviable record. He won election as a fellow of All Souls College in 1743, earned the bachelor of civil law degree in 1745, was called to the Bar in 1746 at the Middle Temple, and eventually took the doctorate in civil law at the precocious age of 27.[3] Blackstone never enjoyed any real success at the Bar, and he quickly returned to the more congenial university atmosphere at Oxford. He served as bursar of All Souls from 1745 to 1753 while he nurtured more ambitious plans. In 1753 Blackstone sought but did not gain selection for the regius chair of civil law at Oxford. This setback occurred because of his political views (or perhaps his refusal to modify them appropriately at the behest of the Duke of Newcastle), although most university observers conceded that he offered the best credentials and potential for the post. In the aftermath of this disappointment Blackstone presented a series of lectures on English law at Oxford, the blueprint for the *Commentaries* later published from 1765 to 1769. His purpose was political as well as scholarly, for Blackstone knew that a bequest by Charles Viner for a new chair in English law was in the offing.[4] Blackstone's calculations paid off in 1758 when he secured election as the first Vinerian professor, the first professorship in English law at Oxford, a position he retained until his resignation in 1766. His greatest work was accomplished in Oxford by virtue of his "great powers of mind and character, a capacity to exercise influence over friends and colleagues, a passion for order and efficiency, and an immense capacity for hard work, which gave him pre-eminence in the small and closely-knit society in which he found himself."[5] The *Commentaries* have remained his crowning achievement.

Outside the academy Blackstone enjoyed a political career as well, entering Parliament as a member for Hindon in Wiltshire in 1761 through the encouragement of Lord Shelburne. In 1768 he became M.P. for Westbury in Wiltshire by the patronage of Lord Abingdon.[6] Then in February of 1770 Blackstone began a judicial tenure with his appointment as a justice of the Court of Common Pleas; after a brief interlude at King's Bench he returned to Common Pleas until his death. Blackstone's work at the

Bar was sporadic and unrewarding when compared to his achievements at Oxford, making him a major example of the complaint that academic law in England employs those who cannot attain distinction in court. His political career was not distinguished, for Blackstone never acquired an important place in the House of Commons. His limited oratorical skills accounted in part for this outcome because his infrequent speeches failed to hold the attention of his colleagues. The significant point of this profile, however, was the public role Blackstone played, despite the failure to achieve fame or power in the process. Unlike other members of the English jurisprudential tradition, Blackstone participated actively in the political life of the nation; he could claim more practical political experience than any of his successors. If his political life never made him a major force, he was at least part of the system.

Much the same can be said of his judicial career. Blackstone has never ranked among those judges ordinarily thought the most able in the eighteenth century; not even his greatest admirers have suggested that his judicial tenure compared in importance to that of Lord Mansfield. Blackstone was not a bad judge, however, and one sympathetic critic of his performance on the bench noted his ability to refrain from comment in areas beyond his expertise, thus avoiding an intervention to his disadvantage. Blackstone "showed a very firm grasp of every branch which he was called upon to handle. No problem found him wanting in anxious consideration and sensible conclusion."[7] Yet it was clear that his careers as judge and politician paled in comparison to the fame he won as author of the *Commentaries*. Blackstone enjoyed a full life of practical work, so he hardly qualified as an impractical dreamer of the academy.

Before examination of some issues raised in the *Commentaries,* the historiography of Blackstone's reputation must be placed in chronological perspective. The first and, even after more than two centuries, the severest attack on Blackstone came as early as 1776 when Jeremy Bentham published his *Fragment on Government,* which introduced what became a standard litany of complaints about the alleged deficiencies of the *Commentaries.* Yet even as subsequent jurists gradually adopted Bentham's objections, the *Commentaries* enjoyed their greatest influence in England and North America from 1770 to 1830.[8] Although the practical legacy of the *Commentaries* never eroded, the deprecation of Blackstone's philosophical failures became common by the time of Bentham's death in 1832. This conventional wisdom prevailed for the next half century. It fell to A. V. Dicey, himself a successor to Blackstone as holder of the Vinerian chair, to reassess the place of his predecessor in English jurisprudence. This task proved the more ironic because Dicey began his own legal career as an avowed admirer of Bentham, and basically remained one throughout his life.

In a thorough consideration of Blackstone in 1909, Dicey stressed the literary virtues of the *Commentaries* as opposed to the less successful philosophical exposition of the common law: "The *Commentaries* live by their style."[9] Blackstone had attempted to expound legal principles in prose accessible to lay people, a goal that Dicey himself had tried to reach as well: "He will remain for ever the eminent lawyer, the perfect professor, the consummate man of letters whose genius claimed and vindicated for English law its high and rightful place in the noble literature of England."[10] Dicey's efforts at rehabilitation did not prove completely successful, and Benthamite distrust of Blackstone persisted. American jurist Oliver Wendell Holmes, reflecting on the intellectual origins of his own book *The Common Law* (1881), recorded that "I think the movement came from within—from the passionate demand that what sounded so arbitrary in Blackstone, for instance, should give some reasonable meaning—that the law should be proved, if it could be, to be worthy of the interest of an intelligent man."[11] Many legal scholars expressed an opinion about Blackstone's reputation, but few offered new insights into his work in the light of changing jurisprudential concerns.

In 1932 Sir William Holdsworth, another successor to Blackstone in the line of Vinerian professors, praised Blackstone's contribution to English jurisprudence by pointing to his extraordinary feat of eliciting from the great mass of legal materials a synthesis of English law unequaled since Bracton.[12] Despite this new recognition of Blackstone's contributions, its impact was lessened because the *Commentaries* no longer had a practical function in either the legal system or legal education; it had become a museum piece. For the next several decades scholarly appraisals of Blackstone appeared infrequently, and his views on jurisprudence attracted little interest. In the 1980s renewed attention to the jurisprudence of Bentham inevitably meant retrospective concern for Blackstone. More serious research on Blackstone's jurisprudence appeared in the 1980s than in any other decade of the twentieth century, with the appreciative conclusions of S. F. C. Milsom a typical example.[13] The older pejorative attitude toward the *Commentaries,* traceable directly back to the triumph of Benthamism, has given way to more favorable estimates. The major positive reappraisal Blackstone enjoyed centered on his ability to convey a sense that the common law stood as a unified whole, a belief that the law consisted of related legal doctrines.[14] Important as they are, broad judgments of Blackstone's work do not serve to locate him specifically in the genesis of modern English jurisprudence. For that task it is necessary to return to the *Commentaries.*

For both jurists and historians, except those bent upon Blackstone's treatment of a particular legal topic, the section of the *Commentaries* most relevant to their concerns is the introductory essay to volume 1. This lengthy prelude reflected Blackstone's jurisprudential assumptions before he examined the substantive materials of the common law. The section was especially relevant to the establishment of a jurisprudential tradition, for this philosophical discourse became the portion of Blackstone that Bentham savaged in trying to stake out a contrary position. Blackstone opened himself to criticism because his language vacillated between the customary arguments for legal validity from natural law, and his anticipation of later assertions that located legal systems only in the positive law of a given society.

When Blackstone published the *Commentaries* natural law theory still held a hallowed place in European thought, particularly in legal theory. Originating in classical antiquity and subsequently incorporated into Christian thought, notably by Aquinas, natural law doctrine held that a law depended upon its conformity to morality for the validity it enjoyed and the obligation of obedience it imposed. It received its modern expression from continental authors of the seventeenth century such as Hugo Grotius and Samuel Pufendorf who specialized in the law of nations. By deduction from nature and right reason that bound all people, universal natural law norms might be discovered. By its tenets specific civil ordinances contrary to the prescriptions of natural law were invalid and could not command obedience. Put another way, an unjust law was no law.

To this philosophical and juristic convention Blackstone adhered, although some critics have attributed a tone of conformity to Blackstone's expression, as if he felt obliged to perform a moral duty in making this homage. Some scholars have supposed that this section was ornamental only, "a mere concession to the stylistic or pedagogical conventions of the age, and without substantial intrinsic relation to the structure or content of the *Commentaries*."[15] If Blackstone intended that the introduction should have only a decorative function he erred badly, for it was upon these passages (really just twenty pages or so) that Bentham focused the heart of his criticism. Other scholars have correctly regarded Blackstone's affinity for natural law as fundamental to his goals, and therefore intrinsic to an interpretation of the *Commentaries*.[16] In fact, the natural law elements in Blackstone do provide important evidence for ascertaining his purposes and were hardly an embellishment.

Perhaps Blackstone's most famous expression of natural law theory came in the following passage: "This law of nature, being co-eval with mankind and dictated by God himself, is of course superior in obligation to any other. It is binding all over the globe, in all countries, and at all times: no human laws are of any validity, if contrary to this; and such of them as are valid derive all their force, and all their authority, mediately or immediately, from this original."[17] Blackstone added to this testament by stating: "Upon these two foundations, the law of nature and the law of revelation, depend all human laws; that is to say, no human laws should be suffered to contradict these."[18] Reaffirmation by positive law did not make natural rights any stronger, for they depended on natural law mandate. While these statements seem clear, it should be noted that Blackstone modified them by also suggesting that on many issues neither revelation nor natural law provided guidance. This left the individual at liberty on these indifferent points, but society found it necessary to place restraints on actions through positive enactments. If Blackstone had stopped with these pronouncements, confusion about his real purposes might never have arisen.

No sooner had Blackstone proclaimed himself a follower of natural law than he began to use the language of the law in a far different manner. In his definition of the several areas of positive law, for example, Blackstone wrote: "Municipal law, thus understood, is properly defined to be 'a rule of civil conduct prescribed by the supreme power in a state, commanding what is right and prohibiting what is wrong.'"[19] If Blackstone subscribed only to natural law ideas, then this passage contained sentiments not ordinarily associated with him. Blackstone elaborated: "For legislature, as was before observed, is the greatest act of superiority that can be exercised by one being over another. Wherefore it is requisite to the very essence of a law, that it be made by the supreme power. Sovereignty and legislature are indeed convertible terms; one cannot subsist without the other."[20] These assertions fit more appropriately into the positivist tradition that has often made Blackstone a particular target. Blackstone reiterated Hobbes's contention that the basic element of law was found in the command of a sovereign,[21] for law always presupposed some superior who made it. Legal positivism has defied precise definition; a historian, in trying to pin down a particular concept, might compare its ambiguities to the protracted battles that have raged around such words as gentry or class. Legal positivism has remained elusive because scholars have placed too heavy a burden on the phrase, asking it to describe too many different issues. Its many meanings would be too difficult to enumerate, although core beliefs would emphasize the legal analysis of the empirical facts of a legal system and stress law as a species of command; speculation about the ultimate nature of law would be simply irrelevant. Thus within the purview of a few pages Blackstone had neatly encapsulated both the natural law and positivist traditions of jurisprudence. Blackstone had struck a neat balance between the mysterious and the scientific dimensions of the common law.[22]

With respect to sovereignty, a staple of discussions about constitutional law, Blackstone wrote: "By the sovereign power . . . is meant the making of laws; for wherever that power resides, all others must conform to, and be directed by it, whatever appearance the outward form and administration of the government may put on."[23] The doctrine was essential to Blackstone, for without it the constitution had no meaning.[24] Blackstone placed parliamentary sovereignty within the triumvirate of king, lords and commons; "Here then is lodged the sovereignty of the British constitution; and lodged as beneficially as is possible for society. For in no other shape could we be so certain of finding the three great qualities of government so well and so happily united."[25] From such a passage, to his critics, came the Blackstone who supported the status quo uncritically and symbolized resistance to legal reform. Although sovereignty meant absolute power and was vested in Parliament, Blackstone argued that this authority could not be exercised arbitrarily, and thus it enhanced rather than threatened civil liberty.[26] The simultaneous embrace of natural law and positivist legal theory produced the Blackstone capable of exciting, widely divergent interpretations by later scholars.

The different intellectual tasks of legal analysis and history have led to different emphases by each discipline when it came to estimating Blackstone's significance. One important debate among jurists has revolved around the apparent contradiction between the language of Hobbesian positive law employed by Blackstone and that of traditional natural theory law as right reason based upon normative moral postulates.[27] Where Blackstone's ultimate intellectual allegiance lay is capable of no definitive answer because he left such mixed signals; the best conclusion may well be that he believed sincerely in both traditions and, unlike later scholars, saw no necessary dichotomy between them. One example, Blackstone's attempt to make reason the heart of the common law, must suffice. Was reason a reflection of God's order for the universe or was reason a natural principle of the common law that produced underlying symmetry beneath its historical development? Blackstone clearly preferred to regard reason as experiential rather than deductive: "The content of law—the custom received as law in England—was an historical artifact. But historical pedigree did not alone determine which customs were received as common law, and the more general ethical bases of human law ensured that nothing 'contrary to reason' would be allowed as law."[28] As a result of this stance Blackstone believed that the "conclusions of reason could be derived from experience."[29] Thus Blackstone managed to combine both modes of argument in pressing his conclusions about the laws of England.

On the issue of the relevance of natural law theory to the *Commentaries,* John Finnis has argued persuasively that this philosophical structure was crucial to Blackstone's intentions and methodology.[30] Finnis maintained that the alleged absolute divide between natural law and positivist jurisprudence in Blackstone did not exist. Blackstone combined the language of the two traditions in a way that has permitted subsequent partisans to stress one or the other, but Blackstone never separated the two in his conception of the *Commentaries.* A similar approach to Blackstone came in the argument that rather than being identical, moral obligation and legal validity were treated by Blackstone as topics that permitted both natural law and positivist ideas: "Blackstone does find a way in his *Commentaries* to explain that men's *moral* obligation to obey positive laws arises from the conformity of these laws to natural ones, and also that their *legal* validity finds its source in the sovereign's will."[31] This emphasis on the separation of law from morality, usually regarded as a major doctrine of legal positivism, made Blackstone not the end of a philosophical era, but more of a bridge to modern legal philosophy. He recognized without difficulty the distinction between acts that were evil in themselves (and bound by conscience) and those that were morally neutral but prohibited by positive law. A sharp division between the Blackstone portrayed as the last gasp of archaic natural law theory and his positivist critics no longer seems tenable, for he "sought to unite jurisprudence and common law practice into one framework.[32] Historians and jurists have often preferred schema that makes generalization possible. Individuals are lumped together in schools or movements, often with little regard for the differences that separated a jurist from contemporary peers. In this sense, therefore, Blackstone cannot be easily categorized.

What might the historian conclude from the debate about the philosophical foundations of the *Commentaries?* Blackstone has enjoyed a restoration of reputation precisely because a close reading of the introduction to the *Commentaries* has produced a more complex author, one who has continued to pose different problems for scholars. For example, the way in which Blackstone classified English law has led to some stress on the role played by civil law in providing Blackstone with a model for this task: "He was attempting to achieve successfully what others had tried to do but failed. This was to combine two methodologies by looking at English law in a Roman way in order to prove that it was a logical structure."[33] The old caricature of Blackstone as a superficial scribbler no longer prevails; a thinker of intellectual complexity has replaced the unsophisticated Commentator who languished in relative obscurity throughout much of the nineteenth century. While many topics treated by Blackstone no longer have any real interest for historians, his legal philosophy continues to repay consideration. It is no lack of scholarly courage to argue that several readings of Blackstone's introduction remain possible. The study of the common law as a fit subject for reasoned exposition rescued the law from the technical works that the public shunned: "For his contemporary readers, moreover, Blackstone's organization and conceptualization of the system of law in England proved a revelation, as the *Commentaries* was found to have furnished reason and erudition where confusion and technicality hitherto obtained."[34] In this sense, therefore, Blackstone sought to reveal the rational principles that would make the law a science similar to other subjects of eighteenth-century inquiry. Within this framework both legal and philosophical motives were at work. His position at the intersection of the two major competing legal traditions will long inspire discussion, but Blackstone's position among the great jurists is now more secure than was the case for generations.

Another issue of interest to historians was Blackstone's discussion of the sovereignty of Parliament. His insistence on strong government in a well-ordered state led to his deserved reputation as the foremost interpreter of this constitutional doctrine in the eighteenth century.[35] Blackstone has remained the one authority who assessed correctly the political/constitutional developments after the Glorious Revolution, and his explanation in the *Commentaries* correctly identified the shifts in political power that followed in the wake of 1688. Blackstone's treatment was more descriptive than analytical,[36] yet as no other writer before him he focused attention on the shifting nature of constitutional theory by the middle of the eighteenth century. The changing nature of historiographical debates about the eighteenth century has challenged some of Blackstone's conclusions, as will be discussed later, although he remains a useful barometer for historians on political trends.

Recently another dimension of Blackstone on parliamentary sovereignty has significantly shifted the interpretation of his work. In his inaugural lecture as Vinerian professor in 1758, Blackstone had stressed that members of Parliament were the "guardians of the constitution" who made, repealed, and interpreted English laws.[37] By checking dangerous innovations and adopting sensible improvements, they transmitted and amended the constitution for the benefit of society. The science of legislation, Blackstone proclaimed, was "the noblest and most difficult" of any occupation.[38] In pondering the implications of a science of legislation, Blackstone regarded Parliament as an instrument of change—the question was, for better or for worse?

David Lieberman has emphasized the importance of understanding Blackstone's attitude toward legislation.

Blackstone, no less than his great critic Bentham, propounded a theory of scientific legislation. Part of the purpose of the *Commentaries* was to show to contemporary and future legislators that the safest path to legislative wisdom led to an acceptance of the fundamental principles of common law: "Enabling English legislators to better inform themselves of the common law was thus made explicit as a central objective for legislative science in England."[39] Despite Bentham's later canards to the contrary, Blackstone possessed a practical theory of legislation that gave coherence to the *Commentaries:* "It was vital to exhibit England's historic system of law as a genuinely rational and coherently organized system in order further to reveal the past damage that resulted from uninformed legislative modifications and in order to disclose the legal structure on which responsible lawmaking might in future occur."[40] Blackstone responded to the common-law tradition that trusted judicial legislation in preference to legislative enactment. Lieberman's account of Blackstone on the art and science of legislation serves as a useful bridge that connects what jurists have studied profitably in Blackstone's career with the issues that historians have found most interesting.

Of all the issues historians have studied in relation to Blackstone's jurisprudence, the most significant has been the manner in which the *Commentaries* acted as a prop to justify existing institutions, encouraging a complacency with contemporary society that discouraged reform. In this scenario Blackstone's work flattered the mid-eighteenth-century world and contributed to the self-satisfaction that characterized English political and social attitudes at that time. One example of this familiar complaint against Blackstone charged that "he had by his lectures endeared himself to those with favors to bestow by displaying a spirit of subservience or, should we say, by playing up to the prejudices of those in power."[41] The original of this allegation came from Bentham as early as 1776 when he called Blackstone "Mr. Every thing as it should be."[42] Chroust argued as well that Blackstone's "sole aim" in the *Commentaries* was to praise constitutional arrangements to a society predisposed to accept his flattering reflections.[43] Another view on Blackstone's purported goal was that his book was "the product of a man who believed in certain social and moral values, and who employed all the ideas he found around him, to convince himself and to persuade his readers that English law, embodying those values, was entitled to reverence and support."[44] This view, redolent of Bentham's original criticism, has not retained the support of subsequent critics who have rejected it as simplistic.

A more sophisticated repetition of this attack on Blackstone has come from Duncan Kennedy, a major figure in the scholarly movement known as critical legal studies. This diverse school of legal interpretation has, like earlier approaches such as sociological jurisprudence and realism, sought to increase the understanding of law and legal structures through utilization of other disciplines: to view the law from outside the legal culture as well as from the inside. In his lengthy examination of the *Commentaries,* therefore, Kennedy stressed certain features that supported the status quo. For example, the *Commentaries* served "as a relatively easy object for the method of discovering hidden political intentions beneath the surface of legal exposition."[45] Blackstone justified the hegemonic activity of the state because "the legal thought denies or mediates with a bias toward the existing social or economic order. It asserts that we have overcome the fundamental contradiction through our existing practices."[46] And finally Kennedy concluded: "He [Blackstone] had accomplished the task of legitimation, in the face of the claim that the institutional system was incoherent, by demonstrating that there was no contradiction in the existence of separate courts of law and equity."[47] Kennedy's study has gained acclaim as a showpiece of critical legal studies methodology, and as such, has reasserted the customary portrait of Blackstone as an apologist for the society in which he lived.

Two issues affect this interpretation of Blackstone and his attitude toward his own society. H. L. A. Hart agreed that the natural law jurisprudence of Blackstone resulted in an uncritical acceptance of legal institutions because it stifled criticism of existing law.[48] Against this view, however, much evidence to the contrary may be presented. While Blackstone certainly did accept the fundamental validity of the legal institutions with which he was familiar, this did not mean that he accepted the entire structure without reservations. Blackstone possessed a reverence for the English constitution, for it embodied both the antiquity of the law and the continuity of constitutional experience. For example, Blackstone questioned the extent to which the death penalty permeated the criminal code of the eighteenth century and suggested that its alleged deterrent effect had no justification in reality.[49] On another topic Blackstone criticized the game laws, a major cornerstone of the aristocratic privileges that Blackstone ostensibly sought to protect.[50] Blackstone also criticized some elements of the political system, although with "restrained censure," as J. C. D. Clark has written, calling for changes in the electoral process, and opposing leniency through indemnity acts toward religious dissenters.[51] One argument has asserted that Blackstone "promoted reform by rescuing the common law from ancient Latin rolls and reports and by exposing it in compact readable form to the view of defenders and reformers alike."[52] Whether in support of or opposition to the institutions of his day, Blackstone can hardly be termed complacent. Finally, in less significant areas, as in his work for Oxford University Press, Blackstone proved himself an adept reformer, revealing a man of practical business sense with no hint of blind acceptance of the status quo.[53] Thus the image of a Blackstone who symbolized an uncritical optimism about his own era has come under fire from several directions.

The hegemonic Blackstone sketched by Kennedy raises the other major issue about the jurist's attitude toward his own era. Historians would be scandalized, for example, at how little historical context Kennedy adduced in support of his contentions. This failing was truly ironic because the critical legal studies movement has emphasized at great length the degree to which the law must be studied in its historical setting. Neither politics nor social structure was considered in any detail by Kennedy; indeed it might be argued that Kennedy's work neatly illustrates exactly those errors that he sought to counter. Nor did Kennedy consider the circumstances of Blackstone's personal history in support of his argument. This most recent attempt to sustain the interpretation of Blackstone as a legalistic camp follower has been termed an "astonishing error" and far too simplistic in its search for ideological motivation: "Legal structures, including the structure of legal treatises, have a strong cultural component which can be uncovered only by historical examination."[54] In addition, J. W. Cairns has made the point that the *Commentaries* "may over all have had the effect of legitimating the common law in the way Kennedy suggests; but it does not seem to me that it necessarily follows that Blackstone *intended* them to have that effect and that he chose his organizational scheme with that end in view."[55] Kennedy has suffered mortal criticisms of his primary thesis, a new version of the older view that Blackstone was little more than an apologist for what he knew best.[56] Blackstone's work does not, alas for the modern historian, fit neatly into classifications such as old Whig, new Tory, or hegemonist, the usual categories into which scholars try to force it.

Directly related to the issue of Blackstone's conservatism was his understanding of history itself. His grasp of the past was imperfect to say the least, and both admirers and critics have found it easy to cite examples where Blackstone came to erroneous conclusions with serious consequences. The connection between Blackstone's beliefs about history and established institutions was examined in a scholarly exchange that focused on his understanding of the term "feudal" and its connection to the constitutional position of the eighteenth-century aristocracy. This apparently arcane subject had broader implications for the debate about Blackstone's intentions. Robert Willman contended that Blackstone's historical description of feudal society worked as a rationalization for the preservation of the aristocracy's constitutional role in the 1760s.[57] Cairns argued in rebuttal that Blackstone's commitment to the common law as a fundamentally English legal system was complete and that "Blackstone's account of the introduction of feudalism and its relationship to the ancient constitution has little if anything to do with a desire to stress the continuity of English law in order to protect the position of the aristocracy."[58] The result of this otherwise minor dispute helped clarify the importance of Blackstone's historical vision to the development of his jurisprudence and what he intended to accomplish by his legal writings.

The structure of the *Commentaries* requires explanation in historical context in order to appreciate Blackstone's intellectual approach. Blackstone was an institutional writer who sought to make the law accessible to the educated classes.[59] Beginning with Justinian, legal analysis had concentrated on classification to bring order to legal systems that became ever more complex and detailed. Blackstone accepted this task, which was complicated by the emergence of nation states in Europe that demanded some rationale for national autonomy through unique legal institutions.[60] His exposition of the common law as the unique law of the English people was "typical of the institutional genre of legal literature."[61] The institutional approach to the common law permitted Blackstone to arrange his legal materials in the form he believed most conducive to the general audience he sought.

Blackstone took as his point of departure the notion of prescriptive rights, with emphasis on those rights that he believed derived their validity from continuity with Anglo-Saxon society. In his historical outlook Blackstone subscribed to the theory of the Norman Yoke, which held that original Anglo-Saxon free institutions had fallen under the control of Norman feudalism at the time of the Conquest. Intervening centuries had brought the gradual emancipation of Anglo-Saxon law from Norman corruption.[62] Constitutional history had comprised primarily the struggle to restore the ancient liberties that the Norman Conquest had eroded. No doubt his readers found this version of constitutional history congenial, and it helps to account for the sycophantic reputation that has dogged him: "Blackstone argued in effect that time and the processes of history are the only tests of true utility, and he believed that time and history had given to the English common law, as long before it had given to Roman law, a prominent position in view of its permanently utilitarian and easily adjustable character."[63] Thus the institutional perspective, understood in its proper setting, fostered an attitude of complaisance that critics have found infuriating: "It is worth noting that institutional writers in general do not seek to criticize and to suggest reforms in the law they expound. Their significance lies in their expounding a whole system of law as a unified national law. In this Blackstone is no different."[64] The rescue of the common law from medieval obscurity in order to explain its vitality and merit to an educated audience in a university setting vindicated the institutional approach because it alone gave to Blackstone the materials for success.

Another feature of Blackstone's work was its strong academic element. Blackstone had gained the clarity of organization that distinguished the *Commentaries* by refining it through successive lecture series. The novelty of lectures on English law at Oxford must be stressed, for only civil law had hitherto been deemed worthy of academic study. Innovation marked the plans Blackstone devised to reach the educated public as well as to make English law a suitable subject for university teaching. Indeed Blackstone called himself an "academical expounder," and the essentially academic tone of the *Commentaries* has added to the confusion in its assessments.[65] The study of the common law, Blackstone stated in his inaugural lecture, was "properly and regularly academical."[66] The aim of the lectures was "to set forth a systematic exposition of English law for teaching purposes."[67] Reform of the common law could occur only when that law was accessible; one could not reform the unknown. The offering of law as a subject at the universities would aid recruitment of socially correct candidates for the law because Blackstone would maintain its social integrity by making a university education a prerequisite: "The Study of law at the universities would recruit the right people for the Bar."[68] At the level of both the university and the nation, Blackstone attempted to deal with practical problems. His target audience existed outside as well as inside the university environs, and it is not surprising that his conclusions have excited such disparate reactions.

The final issue that historians debate and to which Blackstone's *Commentaries* have some relevance is the characterization of the eighteenth century itself. After decades of slumbering in Namierite peace, and frequently described as devoid of exciting political and constitutional developments especially after the upheavals of the seventeenth century, the eighteenth century has become the center of renewed interest, sparked primarily by the controversial theses of J. C. D. Clark.[69] While his conclusions have touched many different issues, perhaps the most fundamental alteration that Clark proposed was his insistence upon continuity rather than change in the period from the Glorious Revolution to the passage of the first reform act. Clark set forth a series of arguments at odds with the prevailing conventions that characterized historical research on the eighteenth century: "My aim throughout has been to re-integrate religion into an historical vision which has been almost wholly positivist; to discard economic reductionism; to emphasize the importance of politics in social history; and to argue against the familiar picture of eighteenth-century England as the era of bourgeois individualism by showing the persistence of the ancien regime until 1828–32, and the autonomous importance of religion and politics in its final demise."[70] Such familiar landmarks as 1760 as the start of "modern" Britain and the industrial revolution have fallen victim to Clark's witty, provocative style. His attacks on traditional schools of interpretation and their conclusions thought more or less sacrosanct a generation ago have reopened evaluation of older issues. His iconoclastic views have drawn substantial criticism, to which Clark has replied forcefully.[71]

What does the life and work of Blackstone contribute, if anything, to this controversy about revisionism in the history of Hanoverian England? Blackstone, of course, did not play a major role in politics, so evidence connected to him could not be decisive. However, Blackstone's lack of sympathy for all non-Anglicans lends support to Clark's emphasis on the importance of religion in daily life. Blackstone's essential approval of existing institutions and the trends of constitutional government might also lend indirect support to Clark's arguments. But Blackstone's critique of some existing legal arrangements showed that his optimism had limits, and that reform must prevail over continuity on certain issues. Blackstone also endorsed quickly those decisions by Chief Justice Mansfield that changed some aspects of the law between 1756 and 1788 and in the process provided the foundations for the modern branches of law such as torts and contracts: "Blackstone, the supposed defender of all accepted legal tradition, almost immediately upon their appearance and even after he had prepared his original lectures, incorporated them into his Commentaries."[72] In the end, ironically, Blackstone's most important role was probably as foil for Jeremy Bentham, who was truly dedicated to the transformation of English society: "If there was to be reform at all, a statement of the actual position of the law was essential; and it is amusing to realize that Bentham secured his first real glimpse of the need for reform from Blackstone's lectures and Blackstone's book."[73] Blackstone helped establish a perception of jurisprudence that encouraged a comprehensive examination of society's problems with a view toward their remedy. On balance, in brief, the enduring effect of the *Commentaries* led in the direction of change.

If, after 1707, the British nation was invented, in the argument of Linda Colley,[74] the *Commentaries* played a role in this process as well. Although Colley did not focus specifically on the patriotic pride British citizens felt for their constitution (indeed, neither Blackstone nor Bentham figured in her analysis), the statement of constitutional glory by Blackstone received such approval precisely because it reinforced accumulating ideas about national identity. The creation of a unified legal perception, combined with the diversity of legal arrangements symbolized by the continuity of the Scottish legal system, contributed to the process of national definition. In this context, therefore, Blackstone joined a dynamic intellectual process and was not an apologist for the status quo. By drawing upon the heritage of the Glorious Revolution and anticipating the glorification of the constitution so frequent in the Victorian era, Blackstone occupied a position in the history of English jurisprudence too complex to fit neatly into classificatory schemes based on later scholarly concerns.

Given his dialectical position in respect to a jurisprudential tradition, Blackstone indeed faced in two directions. His allusions to the natural law tradition marked him as the last in a long line of jurists to do so before the ascendancy of legal positivism. In another sense, however, Blackstone aided in the initiation of a most important function of jurisprudence that stretched far into the future. This issue concerned the audience for whom Blackstone wrote. On one hand, jurisprudence is now considered a theoretical aspect of the study of law.[75] On the other hand, in the eighteenth century jurisprudence was a much broader discipline, dealing with all elements of society's problems; it did not focus narrowly upon specifically legal issues. The *Commentaries* provided a blueprint for both continuity and change; their scope was spacious, their audience was the educated elite, and they were designed to provoke discussion, as they did so successfully, for they "overshadowed all other contemporary legal writing."[76] Adam Smith was another intellectual who recognized the broad role that jurisprudence should play in the discussion of public policy, although political economy eventually became the name for his brand of social investigation. Blackstone's efforts to sustain jurisprudence as the discipline of public discourse were crowned with success, even if many of his successors dedicated themselves to effacing his work.

Even as he worked to make jurisprudence a topic fit for public discussion, Blackstone attempted to begin a revolution in legal education by making it a part of university experience. The *Commentaries* did become a staple of this endeavor, but the legal educational structure, with responsibilities split between the universities and the Inns of Court, remained the same. In this sense Blackstone failed. Eventually he resigned the Vinerian chair in frustration at Oxford's failure to heed his recommendations for changes in the law curriculum.[77] This failure was beneficial to the extent that it did not sidetrack jurisprudence into the restricted arena of academic debate. The place of jurisprudence as the preferred medium of public discourse, the premier social science of the eighteenth century, was assured.[78] Blackstone contributed to defining the boundaries of jurisprudential thought for several generations; he took the tortured maze of English law and turned it into a subject worthy of general discussion, one that examined the foundations of society in broad fashion. In the decades that followed, the idea that jurisprudence provided the best vehicle for social analysis would entice even Blackstone's severest critics. In the history of English jurisprudence, therefore, Blackstone's position as founder of this tradition will remain an honored one.

Chapter Three

Jeremy Bentham
The Light of Utility

Jeremy Bentham took great pains to emphasize his differences with Blackstone. Bentham portrayed himself as the great advocate of legal positivism in opposition to the natural law assumptions of Blackstone. H. L. A. Hart has described the salient traits of Bentham's jurisprudence that mark his radical departure from existing traditions:

> His imperative theory of law according to which laws are the explicit or tacit commands and prohibitions, standardly supported by coercive sanctions, issued by a sovereign legislator or legislative body or their subordinates, and the permissions to act or refrain from acting issuing from these same sources. The second of these two main features of Bentham's thought is his view that law has no necessary or conceptual connection with

morality, although, as he clearly saw, there are many important and often complex contingent connections between them.[1]

Until recently Bentham's claim to have made a sharp break with Blackstone has won wide acceptance, and that fact, combined with Bentham's ascendancy, was chiefly responsible for consigning Blackstone to obscurity: "Bentham's denunciation of the *Commentaries* placed Blackstone's admirers on the defensive ever after."[2] No doubt this outcome resulted in part from Bentham's mastery of invective, and in part from the fact that the elderly Blackstone did not deign to notice the attacks of an upstart critic, much less reply to them. Even the strongest partisans of Bentham have conceded that much of his criticism directed at Blackstone was misplaced, for "it became a sort of obsession, which caused him to descend to abuse which was unworthy of him."[3] In spite of Bentham's efforts, most historians of the relationship have acknowledged that Bentham, despite his implacable hostility, combined relentless criticism with passages of praise that became as famous as some of his barbs. If Bentham thought Blackstone the enemy whose reputation he had to destroy, Bentham also conceded that Blackstone had taught "Jurisprudence to speak the language of the Scholar and the Gentleman."[4] The questions that now seem most appropriate about the intellectual relationship between the two men are: what was the substance of Bentham's objections, and, more importantly, were Bentham and Blackstone as different in legal philosophy as Bentham loved to assert?

Bentham was born in 1748 into a prosperous family

and early displayed equal measures of intellectual precocity and eccentricity. His mastery of languages and early academic excellence led him to matriculate at Oxford in 1763 in order to study law, for his father harbored high hopes for his son's success at the bar. As an undergraduate Bentham listened to Blackstone's lectures prior to the publication of the *Commentaries* and was not impressed. Bentham's incisive mind found Blackstone's arguments misleading, illogical, and, worse, so complacent about the state of the law that the demanding task of reform would be forever postponed. Bentham made law the focus of his early studies and eventually was called to the bar in 1769. As a practitioner Bentham gained no success at all, settling one case out of court and losing another because of his ignorance of a precedent; the experience made him the more certain that his talent for the law would be best realized outside the courtroom.[5] Bentham never married, and although often surrounded by friends and admirers, he spent most of his life in private, if not in seclusion. His great schemes to acquire public influence like the Panopticon for prison reform came to naught, and he never acquired the reputation in England he sought in his lifetime. Indeed, Bentham gained greater importance abroad, particularly with reference to his schemes for written constitutions and codification. His comprehensive strategy for law reform at home never came to fruition, although significant instances of law reform did originate in his suggestions. In Britain at least his greatest influence, such as it was, occurred after his death in 1832, not during his lifetime.

Previous considerations of Bentham's jurisprudence

have concentrated on four major works and the history of each sheds light on the nature of Bentham's contributions. Bentham wrote copiously throughout his life, yet most of what he produced remained unpublished. For an individual who sought a role in the formulation of public policy, Bentham had the unhappy habit of flitting from topic to topic, never quite finishing his intellectual projects. To this day a veritable Bentham industry has continued to make new discoveries among the manuscripts at the University of London.

The increased emphasis on and praise for Bentham's work as a jurist stands in contrast to the status of his reputation among historians. As Martin Weiner has suggested pertinently, it has become a curious situation that Bentham's work has drawn increasing criticism from historians, particularly in the way that Bentham's schemes constituted an expansion of state control.[6] The recent explication, indeed justification, of Bentham's Panopticon scheme by Janet Semple, when due regard is granted for the social and political assumptions of a past age, still strikes the reader as a scary experiment in social engineering.[7] Bentham valued benevolent government in most cases more highly than liberty, and so his name became linked to the growth of government in the nineteenth century. If historians have failed to appreciate the fundamental nature of Bentham's contribution to modern English jurisprudence, it is also the case that legal philosophers have pondered Bentham's work with scant regard for historical context, and have written about his work as if it were devoid of social or political consequences.

From a historical perspective, one might question the

influence of Bentham when many of his ideas never were exposed to public scrutiny. The publication of new studies, based primarily on previously unpublished Bentham manuscripts, has not materially transformed the outlines of his life and work. These works have, at best, helped sort out the chronology and intellectual linkages in Bentham's juristic excursions. Scholarly rummaging in the attic of Bentham's intellect may help in the interpretation of his ideas but cannot aid in the evaluation of whether they mattered in his own day. The paradoxical behavior of Bentham, a person who hungered for public acclaim but would not enter into public discourse, has remained just one of the many quirks of his life beyond satisfactory explanation.

Bentham first attacked Blackstone in 1776 in *A Fragment on Government,* which he published anonymously. Bentham described the public reception of this initial essay as highly favorable, even writing in an 1828 text that the *Fragment* had caused a "sensation," yet the *Commentaries* went through edition after edition, while *A Fragment on Government* did not reach a second edition until forty-seven years later, in 1823. This circumstance indicated clearly that the demand for Bentham's criticism of Blackstone was not exactly overpowering. Much of the waspish tone in the *Fragment* may be attributed to Bentham's youth and the desire for notoriety in attacking a more famous figure. In the period 1774–76 Bentham worked on an additional critique of Blackstone, *A Comment on the Commentaries,* which was in fact never published in his lifetime because he apparently wished to move away from the essentially negative task of criticizing Blackstone toward the more positive goal of constructing a jurisprudence of his own. In 1782 Bentham completed a work now known as *Of Laws in General,* but this too remained unpublished. Not until 1789 did Bentham actually offer to the public the *Introduction to the Principles of Morals and Legislation.* Bentham moved to other projects, and the comprehensive statement of his jurisprudence remained unfinished at his death decades later. Of the Benthamite canon, therefore, only two of the major works on jurisprudence ever appeared in his lifetime, and one was published anonymously. These two had limited success at best.[8] The other two works can have exercised no contemporary influence, for they were not published until the twentieth century.

The indictment Bentham brought against Blackstone has resonated over the last two centuries. A typical verdict concluded that Bentham had exposed the "dismal deficiencies and shoddy performance" of Blackstone in the *Commentaries.*[9] In *A Fragment on Government* Bentham presented the essentials of what he found objectionable in Blackstone's analysis of law. One major issue was Blackstone's attitude toward law reform, which Bentham described as "obsequious quietism," but which, as discussed in the last chapter, did not accord with Blackstone's true ideas in some areas.[10] Bentham accused Blackstone of linguistic imprecision because the Commentator used allusion and metaphor to portray the law, whereas Bentham asserted that only the language of science could succeed as an instrument of legal analysis. Blackstone wrote approvingly of legal fictions, but Bentham argued that their usefulness to the law had long disappeared, and they were now an "encroachment or imposture."[11] Where Blackstone favored judicial legislation as the strongest characteristic of the common law, Bentham regarded this as an usurpation of the legislative function and a charade or "miserable sophistry."[12] On this issue a recent assessment has concluded: "Bentham's hostility to Blackstone seems to have been rooted less in disagreements over substantive policies than in Blackstone's forensically effective defense of a gradualist approach to legal reform that preferred common law interstitial lawmaking to sweeping statutory change and that emphasized both the capacity of the common law to reform and the high incidence of legislative miscarriage."[13] Finally, Bentham denounced Blackstone's assertion of a natural-rights theory (conveniently overlooking those passages where Blackstone had articulated a positivist argument) and eventually delivered the memorable jibe that natural law theory was "nonsense on stilts." In conclusion, Bentham wrote that Blackstone's jurisprudence yielded nothing: *ex nihilo nihil sequitur.*[14]

In terms of intellectual approach Bentham did everything possible to stress the differences that divided him from his quarry. This pose has proved hollow, for Bentham's attempt to establish his credentials as a critical jurist involved semantic tricks of the variety he attributed to Blackstone. By exaggerating the disagreement between them and concentrating his attacks primarily on several pages of Blackstone's introduction, Bentham became a formidable antagonist by the keen focus he brought to his rhetoric. In the process, however, he ignored Blackstone's stated purpose of teaching the law: "Thus many of Bentham's arrows miss their mark."[15] When all the polemical fireworks were over, and as scholars have scrutinized the claims of Bentham more carefully, the similarities of the two jurists claim the attention of posterity more than their differences. As Lieberman has concluded, Bentham effectively distorted the truth when he portrayed himself as a solitary reformer "in a legal setting of entrenched complacency, insularity and obsequiousness."[16] Bentham used Blackstone as a foil to stress the (untrue) innovations of his own work. Bentham, in fact, did not stand alone as a critic of an entrenched establishment except in his own mind. Despite Bentham's protestations to the contrary, the two authors had more in common than the surface disparities Bentham tried so hard to suggest.

The issues that prompt this conclusion are many. Bentham's reputation as a reformer must be carefully qualified, for he rarely joined in public debate and his politically radical views remained largely a matter of private belief. Bentham displayed a hesitancy (or perhaps cowardice) about the expression of his views that belied the notion of an outspoken advocate for change. If a sanguine view of his own day was the criterion, then the fact that Bentham, not Blackstone, wrote the following was noteworthy: "I need scarce remind the reader how happily this alternate state of *authority* and submission is exemplified among ourselves."[17] Bentham's claim that Blackstone believed in the perfection of the British constitution was a debating point of sheer invention.[18] Bentham used Blackstone in many instances as a straw man, a convenient target for a young man anxious to make an impression.

Perhaps the most ludicrous example of Bentham's campaign to make a mark at Blackstone's expense was his criticism of the latter's use of language. In line with the concerns that have characterized the triumphant linguistic emphases of twentieth-century English philosophy, some scholars have praised Bentham for his attention to the meaning of language. Hart, for example, has written that Bentham "believed that the relation of language and so of thought to the world is radically misunderstood if we conceive of sentences as compounded out of words which simply name or stand for elements of reality and thus as having meaning independently of sentential forms."[19] Bentham understood that many difficulties of analysis stemmed from language barriers, particularly in the archaic language of the law. Language had the capacity to elucidate or mislead, and Bentham thought it necessary to concentrate on the relationship among language, the real world, and human beliefs.[20] Language, like the law, lived by fictions, and Bentham regarded part of his mission to remove the distortions of language by cleansing imprecise usages from the province of the law: "His point is that a true understanding of these ideas [duty, power, etc.] involves grasping them as a kind of linguistic shorthand for entities and phenomena which have a concrete existence."[21] Bentham's concern for language may be readily conceded; the issue remains whether design ever became reality in Bentham's jurisprudence. "If clarity in language was the key to the progress of science," it has been argued, "then it was incumbent upon Bentham to suggest ways in which its terminology might be improved."[22] Bentham may have understood the problem, but he certainly did not supply the answer.

The linking of Bentham to clarity of language remains a bad joke to scholars. Bentham invented his own vocabulary, never spared an extra clause, and in general wrote in a style so dense that it is still something of a miracle that anybody makes anything of his nightmarish prose. A sympathetic critic has written: "Bentham may not be the clearest writer, and in his desire to create a new science of morals he could multiply new words and categories in a way very difficult to follow."[23] This excuses Bentham too easily, for he promised he would remedy the language problem. Bentham's abuse of the English language makes him perhaps the most forbidding author in the nineteenth century. He eventually decided that convoluted sentence structure would improve clarity, that sentences should contain only one major idea, and that qualifying clauses should repeat that idea over and over again.[24] The most succinct, and damning, account of Bentham's style has called it "prolix, repetitive, full of obscure devices and conceits of style, and the arguments are made needlessly difficult by a superfluity of subordinate clauses and numerous inversions."[25] Even an admirer such as Semple termed parts of Bentham's writings "repetitions, slovenly, and verbose; at times they descend into turgid circumlocutions that defy meaning."[26] In sum, therefore, for Bentham to complain about Blackstone's style amounted to a common form of intellectual hypocrisy.

Other instances of Bentham's capacity for self-delusion or his penchant for exaggerating his differences with Blackstone exist in some profusion. For example, on the question of the sanctity of property rights, Bentham dismissed with contempt Blackstone's arguments for the natural right of private property: "But what his utilitarianism took away in theory, it gave back in practice, providing an extraordinarily strong defense of private property."[27] Decades ago Boorstin concluded that Bentham, "despite all his rigorousness, and despite all the criticism of the *Commentaries,* . . . presupposed a scheme of social values and a concept of property which were hardly distinguishable from Blackstone's."[28] Whether Blackstone argued from natural law or whether Bentham depended upon the principle of utility, the result was the same: an acceptance of the eighteenth century's emphasis on property as a fundamental pillar of the constitution.

On another topic David Lieberman has traced in precise detail how Bentham came to maturity in an intellectual atmosphere that anticipated his own conclusions about the relative merits of statutory versus judge-made law. His own preference for legislative supremacy over the tradition of judicial decisions was clear, but he was not alone in this choice. Bentham tried consistently to leave the impression that only he had devised plans for substantial reform: "From this perspective, not the least of Bentham's coups in legislative theory was his success in covering his historical tracks—in convincing his followers, along with so many later commentators."[29] In this view Bentham operated in an intellectual milieu so latitudinarian that his later claims for originality cannot be substantiated. Bentham was never the lone voice in the wilderness that formed a major part of his self-proclaimed image.

On political issues Bentham and Blackstone shared positions that belied Bentham's claims of their unalterable opposition. On one subject the two jurists agreed wholeheartedly—their opposition to American independence. Indeed, Bentham thought Blackstone was dangerous because his ideas had helped foment sedition in North America.[30] Bentham's appraisal of Blackstone as a political radical stood in surprising contrast to his usual depiction of the Commentator as hopelessly mired in the optimism Bentham detested. Finally, a conclusion that Bentham would no doubt have hated in view of his image of himself as a radical: "Benthamite reform was safe from the viewpoint of the establishment. The master had had no truck with natural rights. There were no rights of man outside the law. Benthamism enhanced, therefore, the established institutions."[31] Bentham had gloried in the role of reformer: "Bentham regarded his attack on Common Law as falling in the great Enlightenment tradition of rational challenge of established institutions."[32] This conservative portrait resembled remarkably that of Blackstone that Bentham had denounced so virulently as a young man. Given the lack of demonstrable political activity, Bentham's view of himself as a radical alternative to the social order appears just another in a long line of delusions that defined his self-image.

Beyond these specific issues, one crucial element tied Bentham to Blackstone in common endeavor. Whatever else one might conclude about Bentham's grandiose and perhaps even crackpot schemes, throughout his life jurisprudence played the key part in all his plans for reform. His goals presupposed a thorough familiarity with the law, and his objective was fundamental social change: "He became a jurist because he believed, with a long line of earlier thinkers, that law and jurisprudence provided the key to politics and social relations and to the solution of their problems."[33] As in the case of Blackstone, Bentham aimed his jurisprudence at a general audience of educated readers (when he published his work, that is), so that his readers might contemplate the consequences of his arguments and act accordingly. In common with Blackstone, Bentham believed that jurisprudence constituted the proper vehicle for the discussion of public policy: "In Bentham's theory, law plays the social role that Hume assigns to property. Its task is to lay the foundations of society, to *constitute* a people."[34] Only the mastery of jurisprudence permitted the reader to examine the broad questions of social and political reform: "He [Bentham] made it clear that in a comprehensive system of ideas such as his own no single political concept such as liberty, sovereignty, or even political society could be adequately understood in isolation from the web of reciprocal relationships of command and obedience binding men together in any social group."[35] Both Blackstone and Bentham believed that jurisprudence was the discipline most conducive to the debate on public policy to which each wished to contribute. The arguments might differ, but the enterprise remained identical.

The starting point for a review of Bentham's jurisprudence has continued to focus on its foundation, the principle of utility. Historians have grown accustomed to regard Bentham as a nineteenth-century figure, especially when his name dominated controversies such as why the Victorian state developed as it did, or the exact role his beliefs played in guiding the work of those described as Benthamites after 1832. Rarely have they worried about the philosophical foundations upon which Bentham constructed his edifice of reform. Bentham was nothing if not consistent, not to say obsessive, and his explanations of the principle of utility date from his first publications in the 1770s. Bentham's commitment to the utility principle should be interpreted in the context of other Enlightenment attempts to discover the law or laws that governed society, as Isaac Newton had established those that governed the physical universe: "It was Bentham's adaptation of the techniques and principles of natural science to the study of the law which was to draw him to take a stand on other social issues."[36] By reliance on the principle of utility Bentham hoped to create a social science analogous to Newtonian physical science.

From Elie Halevy onward scholars have emphasized this determination to have the doctrine of utility act as the first and universal principle, itself beyond empirical proof, by which all human actions could be calculated: "Given a science of the mind and a science of society which exhibit the qualities both of the experimental and of the exact sciences analogous to the physics of Newton, should it not be possible to found on these new disciplines a moral and legal theory which would be scientific—the achievement of the universal practical science?"[37] Or put another way, Bentham "sought rather the perfection of a neo-Newtonian social physics."[38] The result was as follows:

> Though based on empirical premises, Bentham's utilitarian jurisprudence followed a natural-science model of legislation and judgment and aspired to a wholly quantitative and value-free conception of society—or rather a society whose values were calculable and divorced from questions of practical reason and judgment. Bentham displayed the characteristic Enlightenment scorn for 'prejudice' and 'interest' as well as 'natural rights'—

> categories of jurisprudence which had become factors of theoretical psychology and targets of 'philosophy' and he in effect proposed to establish a social science in terms that were not only empirical but also, in a radical sense, nominalist.[39]

Bentham thought of himself in these terms, so the Newtonian model has not been imposed by later historians contrary to his own self-image.[40] Finally, Bentham "represented in England the spirit that possessed France in the late eighteenth century, the urge to remake the world according to a rational pattern."[41] As a result, Bentham "aimed to be the Newton of the moral world, and his jurisprudence was central to this undertaking."[42] Thus, whatever the effects of his work in the nineteenth century, the basic premises of his jurisprudence were anchored securely in the eighteenth century.

When scholars have rejected the Newtonian model as the dominant influence on Bentham, some other scientific standard has replaced it. Gerald Postema, for example, has argued that it was Carolus Linnaeus, the famous eighteenth-century Swedish botanist, who supplied the scientific impulse for Bentham's conclusions. Bentham's vast classificatory schemes were based on a biological model: "Bentham's idea of the self is that of a rationally self-directed individual, prudently adjusting his actions and plans to the realities of his environment, but always thinking and judging for himself."[43] The principle of utility, therefore, "was meant to serve as the reformer's guide when attempting to rationalize human relationships and reduce the area of conflict they now involved, a doctrine designed to guide a man towards his always behaving in that objective and impersonal fashion in which he is disposed to consider the interests of those who 'are perfect strangers' to him."[44] That Bentham denounced Blackstone for his unscientific language and methodology was not surprising, and that Bentham went further to criticize the common law itself for its unscientific bases should occasion little wonder. Legal reform was crucial to Bentham because in its absence the ancient, unscientific aberrations of the law were perpetuated. Clear rules of public conduct, as opposed to the fictions and untruths of the common law, formed the only reasonable basis for a legal system.[45]

In the four major works on law Bentham constantly stressed the centrality of the principle of utility to his jurisprudence. In *A Fragment on Government* Bentham argued that utility extended to all men and to all societies, so it would serve any country with equal benefit. In his discussion of legal obligation Bentham asserted that the greatest happiness or greatest felicity principle furnished the "sole and all-sufficient reason" and did not depend upon any higher reason. Resolutions of legal disputes should adhere to this guide, for it would resolve most of them and make the grounds of disagreement clearer when a solution could not be found. Only the principle of utility, "accurately apprehended and steadily applied," could direct an individual through the difficult problems with which the law must deal.[46] In the *Comment on the Commentaries* Bentham wrote that "the Principle of utility once adopted as the governing principle, admits of no rival, admits not even of an associate," and its validity could be proved by empirical observation, although Bentham offered no examples in support of this assertion.[47] In *Of Laws in General* Bentham specified that "the common end of all laws as prescribed by the principle of utility is the promotion of the public good."[48] The pursuit of pleasure and the avoidance of pain represented the true guide to human actions, were in fact the "sovereign masters" of behavior, and should determine the content of law.[49] Only the principle of utility could supply a rational, objective basis for the evaluation of human conduct.

The most consistent explication of the utility principle came in *The Principles of Morals and Legislation* (1789). In it Bentham declared that the principle of utility provided the foundation of his work, and he defined it as that principle "which approves or disapproves of every action whatsoever, according to the tendency which it appears to have to augment or diminish the happiness of the party whose interest is in question: or, what is the same thing in other words, to promote or to oppose that happiness. I say of every action whatsoever; and therefore not only of every action of a private individual, but of every measure of government."[50] Bentham then explained the concept of utility: "By utility is meant that property in any object, whereby it tends to produce benefit, advantage, pleasure, good, or happiness, (all this in the present case comes to the same thing) or (what comes again to the same thing) to prevent the happening of mischief, pain, evil, or unhappiness to the party whose interest is considered; if that party be the community in general, then the happiness of the community: If a particular individual, then the happiness of that individual."[51] For the next three hundred pages Bentham relentlessly attempted to build a systematic analysis of law upon his initial definitions, and even his table of contents ran to twenty pages. The first six chapters in particular attempted to establish the principle of utility beyond question. Sympathetic interpreters of Bentham have acknowledged that his jurisprudence, beyond all the verbiage, depended on the principle of utility: "It is . . . clear that he maintained steadfastly throughout his career the absolute sovereignty of the principle of utility."[52] Postema concluded even more decisively that "Bentham, from the very outset of his career, was committed to the principle of utility as the sovereign *decision principle* in the areas of practical life, including adjudication."[53] Bentham's writings, published and unpublished, and the circumstances of his life supported this judgment without qualification.

At this point, however, the historian who seeks to understand the origins of the modern English jurisprudential tradition might well ask: What happens to Bentham when the principle of utility is rejected? Bentham's mechanistic approach to human behavior has suffered fundamental repudiation by the disciplines of both history and psychology. Bentham believed that theoretical decisions, based on rational assessments, characterized every action, and then that action was undertaken in a formal way. This account, in retrospect, strikes the modern reader as oversimplified, misleading, and a highly suspect description of how real people act in the real world.[54] Bentham's conclusions tend now to attract more scorn than respect: "This aspect of Bentham's work does not merit serious consideration today. Modern psychology has yet to find a reliable means of objectively quantifying pleasure or pain.

Certainly this deficiency seriously undermines Bentham's utilitarian foundation for law."[55] A sympathetic interpreter of Bentham such as Semple has conceded that the assertion that human beings were rational in action, not affected by irrational impulses, seems "naive, oversimple, and aberrant, lacking a true insight into the human psyche or a true compassion for the casualties of society."[56]

Recent defenses of Bentham have contained some interesting assertions on the question of utility. Paul Kelly wrote in justification of utilitarian theory about "Bentham's adoption of hedonism as the basis of his psychological theory, which is similar to his justification of the principle of utility as the sole criterion of moral judgment."[57] In a similar vein Dinwiddy argued that Bentham "recognized and explicitly stated, that the principle of utility was a postulate of which the truth could not be *proved.* However, he did set out to devise a theory of morals which *accorded with* the observable facts of human nature (as he saw them), and which did not need any recourse to concepts that were religious or mysterious."[58] These contentions, with their emphasis on the relationship between utility and morality, must be remembered when set against the fact that Bentham's legal reputation was founded on the separation of law from morality. Suffice it to say that his principle of utility has become fraught with difficulties of every sort, and that this must bear upon any assessment of his jurisprudence.

Criticism of Bentham has focused frequently on his philosophical errors. For example, as noted in the previous paragraph, the penchant for definition meant that Bentham assumed what he should have proved. By this method Bentham pushed the ostensibly objective mathematical calculus in the direction he wished. One critic of this philosophical maneuver has observed: "The utilitarians, Bentham foremost among them, who believed that we desire pleasant things on account of their pleasantness, and (more strangely) that pleasure and pain can be measured, would have done well to ask themselves just what pleasure and pain are."[59] The reliance on the principle of utility "involved Bentham in the famously dubious enterprise of articulating a mechanism for measuring happiness and projecting a strictly consequentialist account of the moral content of human actions."[60] In addition, Bentham was guilty of philosophical reductionism as well, for he placed a substantial burden on the principle of utility, that it could provide an answer to all the difficulties of human conduct. That the principle could not sustain this burden soon became obvious: "Because it was derived strictly from one principle, it necessarily ignored many complexities in motives, many differences in degrees of guilt and danger, many social and individual interests for which a less clean-cut system left room. Despite his emphasis on the variety of human life, the possibility that even the most detailed analysis could not completely account for actual human conditions did not worry Bentham."[61] Bentham lent himself to easy caricature because his stress on premeditated calculation ignored so many of the customary, emotional and irrational facets of life. Not for nothing did the word Benthamite become synonymous with a cold, unfeeling approach to human problems, celebrated in literature and contemporary caricature.

Other critics have found in Bentham a vision of society

in which his interpretation of the legal system was vitiated by the rigidity he demonstrated. Although he proposed to construct the basic blueprint for the reformation of society, his means, the principle of utility, proved inadequate to this task: "Bentham's major weaknesses as a thinker were the sponginess of the utility principle in his hands as a guide to policy, his lack of interest in positive or empirical analysis, and his excessive, if characteristically modern, belief in the plasticity of human nature and human institutions."[62] More specifically, the principle of utility offered little to jurisprudence itself: "It is or ought to be the business of legal philosophy not only to consider what law is and why there should be law but to place law in its proper perspective. . . . Bentham's principle of utility has nothing of value to contribute to the first two of these questions and that in the case of the third, that of the perspective, it is positively misleading."[63] The closed nature of Bentham's mind, his detachment from ordinary affairs, his refusal to consider work other than his own, in the end defeated his attempts to gain a major place in the councils of his own day. "It is as if," one critic has written, "very early in his life, he had committed himself to a system of thought which he had found entirely persuasive, totally comprehensive, and, not the least of its merits, uniquely his. Because that system was, for him, so unproblematic, so evidently true and sufficient for all purposes, he felt little need, in his public presentations of it, to take special note of either his forebears or his contemporaries."[64] In view of these difficulties, the historian may well wonder how and why Bentham ever attracted any public attention at all. The reformer who wanted to change the world was in reality so impractical that his major public plan, the Panopticon, never reached fruition.

One answer to questions about Bentham's influence lies in the intensity he brought to his legal writings, a virtue intimately connected to the defects readily recognizable in his work. The constant refrain that he had unlocked the secrets of the law and that he had uncovered the one principle capable of generating effective legal reform gave to Bentham a focus that others lacked: "Bentham was *par excellence* a man dominated by one idea and this was the secret of his success as an influential thinker."[65] His relentless insistence on the inclusive nature of the principle of utility, its ability to furnish remedies for the defects of the law, sustained Bentham through the many disappointments that plagued his efforts to find public acceptance commensurate with the significance of his conclusion. Over the course of his long life and through thousands of pages of detailed analysis, Bentham never lost sight of the one idea that he had used so forcefully to separate himself from his contemporaries. The essential part of this legal science, the principle from which he never deviated, fired Bentham with such enthusiasm that he never wavered from pursuing its triumph.[66]

Bentham also acquired a reputation, to which he was perhaps not fully entitled, from the labors of his disciples, especially James and John Stuart Mill. His followers perpetuated the fame of the master, and so his name acquired a renown beyond his actual accomplishments: "Bentham, *dirigiste* that he was, was all his life flattered by the thought of a band of disciples, bearing his livery and spreading his ideas, and in spite of their differences he liked to say he was the spiritual father of James Mill and Ricardo."[67] His repeated affirmation of the greatest happiness for the greatest number gave to Bentham a celebrity that became seductive; a phrase so widespread must surely have had important consequences. Bentham's influence, once taken for granted, in fact operated within boundaries that have led recent historians to restrict the extent of that influence dramatically: "Perhaps it was inevitable that Bentham's reputation has been made by his fellow intellectuals and only indirectly by nineteenth-century politicians, for it is, by and large, the intellectual and reformer who has read and written about him."[68] In terms of the intellectual history of the nineteenth century, especially as initially delineated by Dicey, Bentham's place became exaggerated to such a degree that only a century later has it been reduced to a more sustainable level. In *Law and Public Opinion,* published in 1905, Dicey offered a model of law reform for the nineteenth century that emphasized Bentham as a fertile source of the changes Dicey admired in that period.[69] This work became the starting point for subsequent attempts to interpret various aspects of Victorian intellectual history, and long exercised an influence that misled as much as enlightened. Whatever enviable reputation Dicey earned as a constitutional scholar, his work in history never reached a comparable level.

If the principle of utility was really a juristic conjuring trick that failed utterly to bring about a legal utopia, Bentham did bequeath a legal legacy—if not as grandiose as he wished—that in fact had profound consequences. His contribution consisted of a knack for raising issues that, whatever the merits of his own answers, have dominated the last two centuries of English jurisprudence. For example, Bentham, despite some of Blackstone's use of similar language on occasion, has prevailed with respect to the command or imperative theory of law.[70] Briefly stated, the command theory of law holds that all laws are expressions of the will of the lawgiver, either commands to do something or prohibitions to desist from a particular act.[71] The command theory has remained a crucial postulate of legal positivism in that all laws are held to have their origin in human agency without reference to an external system of morality. Bentham's formulation has occasioned constant commentary since his death, and has kept his name among the leaders of English jurisprudence. As is characteristic of Bentham's analysis in other areas, the command theory of law has come to be viewed as a little too pat, too simplistic to provide entirely satisfactory answers to the complex questions surrounding law. The renewal of interest in Bentham's legal theory, generated especially by the publication of *Of Laws in General* (1970), has brought Bentham full circle. He enjoys an attention that he never gained in his lifetime. Sympathetic critics have conceded that Bentham's obsession with the principle of utility caused his plans for a comprehensive jurisprudence to fail miserably. His enduring legacy to English legal philosophy has come from his contributions to more specialized topics of juristic debate.

It is now clear, for example, that Bentham, because he never published his views fully in his lifetime, became identified with the command theory of law in a way that did an injustice to the more sophisticated ideas he held.

H. L. A. Hart led the way in trying to recover a Bentham who was his own worst enemy by virtue of his stylistic problems.[72] Bentham apparently did not hold, going against the long tradition of English legal positivism, that all laws must be understood as coercive. He did assert that permissive elements also characterize basic types of law.[73] Despite the stereotype of Bentham's view of law as a crude species of command, Hart argued that "it is plain that the power of imperation as defined by Bentham is an apt description of legislative powers, both of the sovereign lawmaking body and of subordinate lawmaking agencies, at least where the legislation creates legal duties backed by sanctions."[74] The hitherto unsuspected appeal of Bentham's definition of law has returned him to the center of interest in the historical unfolding of legal ideas. The recovery of Bentham's sharper insights has helped to clarify other issues treated by him as well as revise the appraisal of his relations with his intellectual successors.

The command theory of law and the recent discussions of Bentham's articulation of his definition lead directly to his views on the sovereignty of Parliament. One irony of Bentham's career was the similarity of his analysis to that of his great antagonist, Blackstone. As noted earlier, Blackstone had elaborated a theory of parliamentary sovereignty that Bentham found congenial, especially in his long battle to secure the right to build the Panopticon.[75] In this area as well, recent scholarship has discovered a more practical Bentham than the reformer who tried to peddle the principle of utility all his life. The earlier version of Bentham on sovereignty stressed his conception of the doctrine as "total and illimitable,"[76] and this idea stemmed from his oft-asserted belief that the only true law was statutory and judicial legislation represented a primary evil of the common law. Once again, however, Hart has emphasized that Bentham considered the possibility of legal limitations on sovereignty and the division of sovereign powers according to prescribed legal rules.[77] According to this new view, Bentham recognized that the "exercise of sovereignty 'by rule' in a non-autocratic manner required its division into legislative and executive power; and, most important of all, by acknowledging the possible existence—perhaps even probable in most cases—of a power anterior to that of the sovereign: the power or right to invest determinate persons with the supreme power itself."[78] The doctrine of sovereignty as thus described became more flexible and less authoritarian than the usual depiction of Benthamite ideas that had become customary.[79] For the historian, however, the important point is not necessarily what constituted Bentham's real views as derived from unpublished manuscripts; the significance of Bentham on sovereignty is what people believed he taught, even if that has subsequently proven erroneous. In the case of Hart, his discussion of a sophisticated Bentham lent support to his own jurisprudence, and whether Bentham was truly the Hartian forerunner or not remains an open question.

On the specific question of law reform Bentham adhered tenaciously to the solution of codification. One reason for Bentham's lifelong dedication to the cause of codification was his belief that a logical arrangement of the laws, intelligible to lay people, would diminish the role of judges, barristers, and solicitors. Codification would identify those laws that required abolition and would present the opportunity for the passage of new laws.[80] Where Blackstone had seen the common law as the epitome of reason, Bentham found a bewildering, obscure system, replete with procedural technicalities, language that concealed meaning, and a maze of intricacies that permitted the lawyers to carry on their nefarious activities beyond public scrutiny. The chief abuse came from the ancient role played in the law by legal fictions, a practice that infuriated Bentham above all else: "Things were blatantly falsely described, straightforward falsehoods were accepted in court and not allowed to be traversed."[81] Bentham condemned lawyers who utilized a language that only the initiated could understand, although he invented his own language when it suited his purpose. Bentham denounced the sophistries of the legal profession in this fashion: "They can no more speak at their ease without a fiction in their mouths, than Demosthenes without pebbles. Such is the power of professional prejudice to deprave the understanding. They feed upon untruth, as the Turks do upon opium, at first from choice and with their eyes open, afterwards by habit, till at length they lose all shame, avow it for what it is, and swallow it with greediness, not bearing to be without it."[82] Bentham abhorred the artifices of the lawyer's trade, so hostile to setting the law upon a scientific basis. As Hart had written: "He was horrified by these things, but even more horrified by the ease with which English lawyers swallowed and propagated the enervating superstition that these abuses were natural and inevitable, so that only a visionary would dream of their radical reform."[83] Of course these charges did not originate with Bentham, for they had long served as standard fare for complaints about the legal profession. So literally did Bentham take these accusations that only wholesale reform incorporated in a code could restore integrity to the legal system.

The reduction of legal chaos to order fascinated Bentham, for the grand scheme was a form of enterprise that intrigued him throughout his life. For some six decades Bentham worked on a *Pannomion* or comprehensive legal code that would bring order and simplicity to the disorganized mass of the historic common law. This attempt to create a description of the law in all its branches, despite Bentham's attention to it at different times in his life, was left unfinished at his death.[84] Codification entailed the "conversion of jurisprudential or 'judge-made' law (i.e. common law) into enacted or statute law."[85] This process would reflect Bentham's belief that all law should be made by the legislature to ensure its validity. Codification would certify that law existed as a function of the will of the sovereign authority: "Its authenticity should be indisputably established through its emanating from the only valid source of law in the community."[86] For all his good intentions Bentham did not come close to finishing a workable code for the common law: "He left many odd segments of codes, outlines, and unfinished drafts. None of them had the essentials of a workable code; their classifications were complicated and impractical, and they were full of sweeping generalizations."[87] Blackstone was never completely undone, for the common law prevailed in spite of Bentham's strictures, and both men had sought a uniformity in the law that simply did not exist. Lobban has emphasized that the common law had originated as a legal system bent upon providing remedies, and neither Blackstone nor Bentham were prepared to face this fact.[88] Schemes for codification appeared throughout the nineteenth century until the Judicature Acts of 1873 and 1875 reorganized jurisdiction, but the spirit of codification never prevailed. Bentham had failed to accomplish yet another element of the agenda he had pursued for most of his life.

Of all the legal issues inaugurated by Bentham, none has had greater impact than his mandate that legal analysis must separate law from morality, the law as it is must be distinguished from the law as it ought to be. As Hart has written, "In legal theory Bentham's sharp severance in the *Fragment* between law as it is and law as it ought to be and his insistence that the foundations of a legal system are properly described in the morally neutral terms of a general habit of obedience opened the long positivist tradition in English jurisprudence."[89] This quotation expresses perhaps the most conventional interpretation of the history of English jurisprudence. The is/ought dichotomy in legal theory has spurred generations of reflection upon this problem. By the 1870s and 1880s "the separation of law from morals extended also to the separation of law from other 'non-legal' or 'extra-legal' factors."[90] The formal or "analytic" mode in jurisprudence had triumphed, deriving its intellectual energy from the original Benthamite axiom. But, as this chapter suggests, the great divide in English jurisprudence did not come with the Blackstone-Bentham confrontation as Hart argued. The turning point in the modern history of English jurisprudence came later, and for reasons basically unanticipated by either Blackstone or Bentham.

The initial result of the insistence upon the separation of law and morality was a frontal assault on the natural law tradition that Bentham had found so appalling in Blackstone: "He found himself obliged to do battle with those (such as Blackstone) who declared the existence of 'natural law' or 'natural rights'—men with whom he otherwise had much in common—because they tended to submerge this vital and complex subject in clouds of confusion and wishful thinking."[91] One might ask, however, whether Bentham's attachment to the principle of utility merely substituted one form of moral principle for another and replicated the shoddy methodology that he had denounced in his adversaries. In what sense was law to be divorced from morality? The attack on natural law followed the strategy of enhancing legislative power at the expense of the common law: "Statute law did, in terms of form, correspond much more closely than common law to his idea of what law *ought* to be."[92] Bentham's concern with what the law ought to be, of course, sounded suspiciously like the theorizing that he had used as examples of the lack of logical rigor in natural law adherents. Thus the famous formula on the separation of law from morality played a tactical role in the broader campaign against the common law: "Bentham opposed natural law because he wished to keep judging distinct from legislating and not in order to separate law from morality."[93] Successors to Bentham seized upon this prescription and turned it into a verbal talisman that affected English jurisprudence thereafter.

A number of Bentham's critics have pointed out that he simply substituted the principle of utility for traditional natural law theory in trying to ascertain the proper state of relations among individuals in society. Utility for Bentham was "genuinely what the natural law pretended to be—the foundation for both morality and legislation."[94] The attempt to deduce rules of law from the principle of utility established a specifically Benthamite natural law.[95] By employing the principle of utility to serve as the basis for his conclusions about both law and morality, Bentham committed the logical fallacy that he had denounced in others.[96] Because the consequences of the principle of utility could not be empirically demonstrated any more specifically than natural law, it remained a form of moral code not easily distinguishable from natural law.[97] In the long run, therefore, Bentham "was more than willing to make the same sort of judgements that natural law theorists made, to declare some positive laws good and others bad according to a standard outside them."[98] Thus the claim for Bentham's originality must be measured against the sense that he merely repeated the mistakes of his opponents. But if Bentham had erred, the consequences certainly proved fertile.

The separation of law from morality must be understood, therefore, as an analytical tool, another perspective, that originated in Bentham's concern for a science of law. The phrase had a restricted domain because clearly law and morality had always intersected. Laws prescribed all manner of moral imperatives and prohibitions and have continued to do so. The is/ought dichotomy opened up alternative avenues of analysis, but in the process it started a narrowing of jurisprudence's purview that has ultimately altered its essential character. The positivist tradition from Bentham onward has sharpened analysis of the law at the expense of limiting the topics it considered. Bentham did not intend this consequence, yet it was a result for which he must take responsibility.

On these issues crucial to his jurisprudence, Bentham provided significant topics for discussion but never managed to make them instruments for the reform of English society. The principle of utility never became the fundamental axis upon which all law depended. The grand schemes at which Bentham labored all his life never came to fruition, nor were his theoretical premises ever accepted to a meaningful degree. His plans for the restructuring of the legal system failed in the first instance because he never completed the code on which he had worked intermittently throughout his life: "Yet this extraordinary man who invented the word 'codification,' who was its lifelong advocate, and who thought so highly of his own methods, never got within measurable distance of completing a draft, and his attempts seem to show that if he had completed one its over-great particularity and probably its length would have made it hopeless from a practical point of view."[99] In short, Bentham did not realize the total reform of English society to which he aspired.

It was a cruel irony for Bentham that he did have a substantial impact on English law, but this came in the incremental fashion that he loathed because it resembled all too closely the half-hearted efforts he had always denounced in Blackstone. Bentham's contributions to the common law were conspicuous and a legacy in which any reformer could take pride: "Among the changes which accorded with his ideas and which have been ascribed at least in part to his inspiration, one can cite the replacement of fees by salaries in courts of law, the simplification of the law of evidence, the establishment of county courts throughout the country to expedite the administration of justice, and the mitigation of the penal law."[100] Nevertheless, these reforms lacked the totality that Bentham's vision of jurisprudence imposed upon him. He had always desired the complete destruction of Blackstone, but it became partial at best; thus the historian may judge Bentham against his own standards, and by this norm he never acquired that imposing influence that he had desired. With the essential failure of the plans for legal reform, the blueprint for political influence foundered as well.

The question of Benthamite influence in the Victorian era, particularly on the growth of the central administration, has intrigued historians for several decades. The consideration of Bentham's jurisprudence permits the conclusion that if it failed as a general science of society, then inevitably the political consequences he desired never materialized either. In the more specific area of government reform, S. E. Finer offered a model to explain the complex way in which the ideas of an individual have an impact, with Bentham as the specific example of diffusion through irradiation, suscitation, and permeation.[101] This model has worked well, but it might be redefined into categories of primary, secondary, and tertiary importance: "There are those who are rationally persuaded by reading the works of the leading thinkers of a particular school. But they are probably outnumbered by those who, without grappling with the recondite literature, merely adopt the vocabulary as it is purveyed by a horde of less original publicists."[102] Bentham's role as a catalyst in specific historical processes has diminished as historians have shown an increasing reluctance to accept earlier claims for his extensive influence. As Helen Beynon has written, there was little correspondence between what Bentham wanted and what actually transpired in the nineteenth century.[103] In the argument by Anthony Brundage, even the avowed agents of Benthamite change rarely followed the master's ideas to any substantial degree, and they as often directly opposed what Bentham had proposed.[104] For better or worse, Bentham has become fodder for academic discussion, achieving an importance he never gained in life, for champions still enlist in his cause.[105] Where Bentham failed in the grand design for the transformation of society, he did succeed in becoming the central figure of the English jurisprudential tradition as it has flourished in the academic world.

In one respect, however, even academics have treated Bentham unkindly. Many jurists in the past did not credit Bentham with the foundation of the analytic tradition, yielding that position to John Austin, his chief disciple in matters of legal philosophy. This mistaken assessment of the relationship between Bentham and Austin has two explanations. The first involved the cramped manner in which Austin interpreted both the topics for consideration and the doctrines Bentham espoused: "The narrowing of the focus of attention is illustrated by the extraordinary displacement of Bentham by Austin as 'the Father of English Jurisprudence,' a misjudgment that says much about the limitations of English academic law during the first half of this century."[106] Accustomed to a restricted definition of jurisprudence, Victorian jurists naturally (and erroneously) looked to Austin for intellectual guidance. "Austin may have been recognized as the father of jurisprudence, but it was really the bastard child of Bentham."[107]

The second explanation derives from Austin's prominence in the later part of the nineteenth century, which tended to obscure Bentham's place in the pantheon of English jurisprudence. The heyday of Austin in the 1870s and 1880s pushed Bentham into a subsidiary role from which his reputation has only recently escaped. Most legal scholars in the period 1870–1950 assumed that Austin had expanded upon the blueprint drawn by Bentham, and that analytic jurisprudence resulted primarily from Austin's ventures beyond the issues addressed by Bentham. This conclusion was understandable when one recalls that the rehabilitation of Bentham's reputation has depended upon unpublished manuscripts unknown to previous jurists. Austin in fact reduced Bentham's thought to a more rigid system, gaining in analysis what he lost in breadth. On subjects like law as command, sovereignty, and the separation of law and morality, Austin took the Benthamite legacy and narrowed its scope. As Hart wrote: "For like Austin's theory, Bentham's is an imperative theory of law in which the central concepts are those of sovereign and command, and the definitions of both sovereign and command are at first sight very similar in the two authors. But Bentham expounds these ideas with far greater subtlety and flexibility than Austin and illuminates aspects of law largely neglected by him."[108] Much of what became analytical jurisprudence originated in the differences between teacher and student; it did not evolve in a straight line beginning with Austin.

In the final analysis, Blackstone and Bentham, those perpetual antagonists, were linked by their common attempt to provide a general theory of jurisprudence as a proxy for sweeping consideration of social issues. In the long run the former suffered from neglect and the latter from the contraction of his original concerns: "English jurisprudence became the monopoly of legal craftsmen competent and knowledgeable but devoid of greatness because they thought increasingly that legal science could be divorced from legal theory, that the law as it is and the law as it ought to be were two worlds entirely separate from each other and that the lawyer's concern was only with the former."[109] Bentham's emphasis on legislation resulted in increasingly microscopic examination of legal issues:

> The legislator acted indirectly; he established the framework of security through law, a framework whose value was judged initially by the liberty each person had to pursue his own pleasures so long as he did not harm the interests of others. At the level of the civil law, the legislator secured rights to property, prevented interference, simplified titles and judicial proceedings, and enhanced competitiveness in commercial transactions. At the level of the criminal law, he secured the individual

against crime with a rational criminal code and a strong and effective police force and judiciary. At the level of constitutional law, the legislator aimed to provide security against misrule.[110]

This tendency toward legislative activism turned Benthamite jurisprudence into an object of academic concern for its theoretical value only. Bentham's legal theory has triumphed in England but in a venue, the academic world, too limited for his lofty dreams. Bentham fostered the tradition of analytic jurisprudence in England but this fell far short of his design for success.

Chapter Four

John Austin
"The Matter of Jurisprudence Is Positive Law"

If Jeremy Bentham, in one guise or another, is well known to historians, John Austin, his most famous disciple in the field of jurisprudence, has languished in obscurity until recently. This indifference has been undeserved because Austin at one time exercised considerable influence, and he was "the most truly erudite jurist of the nineteenth century."[1] An individual of decidedly modest reputation in his lifetime, Austin enjoyed a posthumous vogue that made him the leading figure in late Victorian jurisprudence. By the 1880s this brief ascendancy had already come under attack, and his reputation languished in the limbo of arcane footnotes until the publication of H. L. A. Hart's *The Concept of Law* in 1961 restored his respectability as a jurist whose work repaid close study. Not until the 1980s did Austin become the subject of major descriptive and analytical studies that have placed him not only in the history of English jurisprudence, but also in the broad context of Victorian intellectual history.[2] The origins and doctrines of Austinian jurisprudence are central to a proper understanding of the English jurisprudential tradition because of the necessity to fix accurately his relationship to Bentham, and to delineate how his own teachings changed meaning in the hands of succeeding jurists. The major influence on the first generation of the academic law professoriate of the 1880s, Austin's writings on jurisprudence has ultimately exercised a fascination for later jurists that would have astounded the author.

John Austin was born in 1790 and nothing remarkable is known about him until he obtained a commission in the army during the Napoleonic wars. His career as an officer did not earn distinction, so he left the service in search of another path to fame and achievement. This set a pattern of high ambition but little accomplishment that dogged Austin for the remainder of his life. He did not achieve the fame and fortune that he sought, and ever after was "haunted with a sense of guilt and worthlessness for not living up to his own exacting standards."[3] He turned to the study of law and was called to the bar in 1818, but, like Bentham, Austin found his experiences in practice profoundly distressing. His few court appearances were disastrous, his career foundered, and eventually he quit the bar in 1825 without appreciable success. In the meantime Austin had met Bentham in 1819 in London, and already familiar with his writings, he succumbed rapidly to the charm of the aged master and joined the inner circle of Bentham's confidants. Austin and his wife Sarah moved to a house in Westminster and became neighbors of Bentham and James Mill. Austin's attention fell upon jurisprudence, the subject to which Bentham had devoted so much time and about which he had written so prolifically. As told in chapter 3, Bentham's diverse interests prevented him from accomplishing all he intended in legal theory, so Austin soon became the heir apparent charged with carrying on the work of his elderly mentor. In a letter to Bentham shortly before his marriage, Austin accepted this role: "I have long revered you, and my deep conviction of the importance of your doctrines has long inflamed me with an earnest desire to see them widely diffused and generally embraced; I shall feel no violent desire for any other object than that of disseminating your doctrines."[4] In 1826 Austin's own intellectual goals altered dramatically upon his appointment as the inaugural professor of jurisprudence at the newly founded University of London.

Austin devoted himself completely to the preparation for his academic career. He journeyed to Bonn in 1826 for two years of study at the university and the opportunity to meet with its famous law faculty. The careful study of civil law provided Austin with a perspective that helped ease him out of Bentham's shadow and gave Austin ideas that distanced him from Bentham.[5] His familiarity with Roman law and contemporary civil law, so unlike the typical insularity of the English bar, has earned him the modern accolade as the "first great lawyer in England since Bracton to be well acquainted with, and influenced by, continental doctrine."[6] While in Germany he prepared the lectures that he hoped would establish his reputation as well as enlighten his students. The German interlude helped start Austin in a direction that would save him from the slavish imitation of Bentham's jurisprudence. At the same time, however, Austin retained the Benthamite mission of transforming the world and contributing to human betterment.[7]

Once again his hopes for success were dashed, for his university lectures undertaken in the fall of 1829, after a year's delay because of his diffidence, were an unmitigated debacle. Detailed to a fault, ultimately boring in the extreme to undergraduates, and marred by the nervous demeanor of the lecturer, his classroom presentations turned an enthusiastic band of students into a despairing few: "Austin thought it a duty to be as dry as Bentham, and discharged that duty scrupulously. The audiences dwindled, and the salary, derived from the fees, dwindled with it. Austin, a poor man, could not go on discoursing gratuitously to empty benches, and gave his last lecture in 1832."[8] When Austin offered his second series of lectures in 1830, not one student took up the challenge. This fiasco, along with lectures at the Inner Temple that met with an equally tepid reception, caused Austin to resign his chair: "He was so scarred by disappointment and humiliation that henceforth he refused even to consider permanent residence in London, as it was the scene of too many memories."[9]

Austin's personal life started on a slide from which it never recovered. After a stint as a law commissioner on Malta from 1836 to 1838, Austin never enjoyed gainful employment for the rest of his life. The Austins lived abroad for extended periods, usually in Germany, where Sarah Austin managed to eke out a living as a translator. They returned to England in 1848 but still refused to live in London, the scene of his greatest disappointment. One assessment of Austin's life has concluded: "Austin was poor, his constitution was weak, he was a failure as a teacher of law, the merits of his writings were unrecognized by all but a few, and, when he died, he was almost unknown amongst lawyers."[10] A more recent interpretation has reinforced this gloomy litany of the personal and professional disappointments Austin endured: "John Austin impressed a small group of contemporaries by his highly original ideas and strong opinions, but he failed to live up to his promise and published so little that he regarded himself as a failure, and he died an embittered man with no apprehension that his name would live."[11] At his death in 1859 Austin seemed a most unlikely candidate for inclusion in the pantheon of English jurisprudence.

Few intellectuals can have enjoyed so remarkable a posthumous shift in fortune than Austin, and the credit for this went to his wife Sarah, surely one of the more notable Victorian wives in the promotion of a husband's reputation. For most of the marriage Sarah had supplied the determination and strength (as well as the income) that had supported Austin in his tribulations. Life with John Austin had always been a trial, for he compounded his fecklessness with frequent bouts of hypochondria, his bitterness at frustrated hopes matched only by his melancholia. In 1832 Austin had published his most significant work, *The Province of Jurisprudence Determined,* and while the book had received a number of favorable reviews,[12] it had not achieved the recognition or financial success that its author had envisioned: "As Lord Melbourne was to say, Austin's *Province of Jurisprudence Determined* (which consisted of some of the lectures Austin had read to his class), was 'the dullest book he had ever read'—and this from someone who read theological books as a pastime."[13] Its relevance to ongoing debates about law and jurisprudence had waned gradually because Austin had failed to publish the subsequent volume on which he labored all his life but never finished. Sarah Austin determined that her husband's ideas should not die with him, and she supervised the republication of *The Province of Jurisprudence Determined* in 1861. She then compiled and published through her reconstruction of notes left by her husband the *Lectures on Jurisprudence* in 1863. This was not, however, the great work upon which Austin labored for decades but never published. The *Lectures* represent the thought of Austin in 1832; he spent the remainder of his life in vain attempts at carrying his work forward. As Sarah Austin wrote: "It seems hardly necessary to repeat, (yet I cannot repeat too often) that this book shows not what the Author had done, but what he intended to do, and in some degree what he was capable of doing."[14] A new generation of jurists and law students discovered in Austin a discussion of legal issues that seemed new and exciting, and his fame was assured. His scholarly reputation has waxed and waned since the 1860s, but it has never slipped back into that obscurity for which Austin seemed destined in 1859.

In turning to the issues discussed in these two major works, the historian should know that Austin suffered from a severe case of Benthamitis; that is, these works are dense, overly technical in many respects, and written in that convoluted style so distressingly reminiscent of Bentham himself. He aimed at a verbal precision that bordered on the obsessive, yet after lavishing so much attention on his writing, "it was stilted and pedantic."[15] These books do not entice the reader as much as present a challenge, for a scholar must *really* possess a commitment to jurisprudence before entering the forbidding world of analytical jurisprudence. No doubt literary deficiencies had contributed to the initial failure of *The Province of Jurisprudence Determined,* and the *Lectures* did not demonstrate much improvement. If Austin's work failed to attract the wide audience he had hoped for, stylistic problems alone would have accounted for his lack of success.

The province of jurisprudence, Austin asserted, was positive law, or law set by political superiors to political inferiors.[16] Positive law was actually in use and its moral content did not affect the fact that it was the proper subject of jurisprudence.[17] Law, properly perceived, Austin defined as a species of command. Positive law alone was the fit topic of jurisprudence for analysis—not divine law, nor laws of morality, nor laws metaphorical or figurative. Other basic concepts of positive law included sovereignty, sanction, and habitual obedience. When put together, therefore, law was a species of command by a superior or sovereign, who was in the habit of receiving obedience, to an inferior, to which disobedience would result in a sanction. This definition would free positive law, thus limited in its scope, from confusion with the moral postulates as expressed in natural law theory. Austin made explicit the necessity to separate law from morality in order for jurisprudence to extend past the old debates and to put law on a scientific basis. Rules of human conduct, such as those that mandated some form of appropriate behavior, could not qualify as law because they lacked the necessary components of law itself. Austin's objective "was nothing less than to elucidate the basic concepts of jurisprudence and the structure of a legal system.[18]

Austin relied heavily on the principle of utility, which he tended to identify with the laws of God or divine law. No paradox dramatizes as well the complex history of the recurring issue of the separation of law from morality in English legal philosophy; no sooner has an individual proclaimed the absolute requirement that law must never be confused with morality in legal analysis than that same individual proposes some alternative religious or moral criterion to act as a legal standard: "According to the theory of utility, the measure or test of human conduct is the law set by God to his human creatures. The commands which he has not revealed, we must construe by the principle of utility: by the probable effects of our conduct on that general happiness or good which is the final cause or purpose of the good and wise lawgiver in all his laws and commandments."[19] Utility and religion were identical (this from the author who had earlier argued that law and morality must never meet): "God himself was a Benthamite."[20] Austin credited Bentham with "clearness and accuracy" in explicating the principle of utility, and with being "the first of all philosophers who has viewed it from every aspect, and has fitted it for practice."[21] Austin enunciated the imperative theory of law that became his most famous legacy and combined it with utility to give his jurisprudence its power.

In *The Province of Jurisprudence Determined* Austin presented his arguments in six lectures. His purpose in the first was to define his terms in a way that would identify laws, properly so called, and rule out those entities that too often masqueraded as law and created confusion in jurisprudence. This was accomplished by a thorough examination of language. Laws, therefore, were a species of command, and the meaning of command was crucial, "since it is the *key* to the sciences of jurisprudence and morals."[22] Lectures 2, 3, and 4 examined the principle of utility in order to specify its importance for jurisprudence. The careful manner in which Austin laid down definitions, constructed his argument, and then attempted to forestall objections recalled in some respects the scholastic approach exemplified best by Aquinas. In lecture 5 Austin dealt with those laws that did not meet the criteria to be called law; such exhortations were not laws because the sanction arose from general opinion only.[23] Finally, in lecture 6, Austin focused his attention on true laws, those that qualified by virtue of the emphasis on command. This lecture is almost as long as the other five combined and represented the capstone to Austin's jurisprudence. His thorough linguistic analysis of major ideas make for slow reading, yet it remained the heart of his approach to law. After all this concentrated contemplation ostensibly in the name of reshaping society, the reader is left without any distinct impression of how this should work. Austin's examples demonstrated even less practicality than Bentham, and this helps explain why the work initially received such an indifferent reception. In an England excited by the reform bill of 1832 and devoted to material progress, Austin's *Province* had little relevance.

In the long run, however, Austin's allegiance to the principle of utility has turned out to be far more complex than originally thought, and his acceptance proved conditional in his later life. For that reason the issue provides a neat study in the way that Austin both accepted and deviated from Benthamite jurisprudence. As indicated in the previous paragraph, many of the early pages of *The Province of Jurisprudence Determined* endorsed utility as the only appropriate "foundation for the moral and political sciences."[24] This circumstance lent credibility to the conventional argument that Bentham and Austin constituted interchangeable parts of the same intellectual heritage. Austin, while accepting utility initially as the basis of his jurisprudence, eventually came to a different view because he became disenchanted with the elaborate calculus that Bentham constructed. While Bentham worked out at great length all the variables in the pleasure and pain calculus and gave specific attention to its theoretical validity, Austin "instead sneers . . . at the competing principles and devotes much time to minimizing the detailed calculations required by emphasizing the extent to which there may be reliance on maxims and rules."[25] Even more pertinent to understanding Austin on utility was the repudiation (or at least a significant downgrading of its importance) after the publication of *The Province of Jurisprudence*

Determined. The trust in rational calculation gave way to a belief in customary political arrangements and emotional ties as the bases of a legal system. Beset by prolonged bouts of depression that crippled his intentions, Austin never published the comprehensive work that would have made this transition plain, and this contributed to the sense of futility that marked the later part of his life: "It must have been a terrible thing for him to realize that his early confidence had been unfounded and that he had sacrificed decades of thought and labour to a science of jurisprudence whose foundations he now recognized to be feeble."[26] Ironically, the Austin who represented analytical jurisprudence to subsequent generations would not have regarded that designation as accurate in his own case.

The discussion of Austin and the evolving nature of his commitment to the principle of utility has introduced perhaps the most crucial issue for the historian: how the changing nature of his relationship to Bentham's teachings affected the later course of English jurisprudence. Despite the tendency of earlier generations to lump the two men together, the recent wave of scholarship has emphasized rightly the disagreements that separated them, especially their "fundamentally different attitudes towards the common law, and different aspirations for their work."[27] Originally Austin had committed himself dramatically to the attainment of Benthamite objectives: "Austin humbly offered to sacrifice worldly opportunities to Bentham's cause."[28] The bonds of utilitarianism that tied the two jurists together in common intellectual enterprise predominated, at least in the beginning, over the relatively minor questions on which they disagreed: "The significance of the relationship that John Austin developed with [James] Mill and Bentham is difficult to exaggerate. To begin with, their ideas strongly influenced the spectacles through which Austin saw much of the world."[29] Austin possessed too independent and inquisitive a mind to settle simply for the role of pupil, however, and gradually differences between the two men appeared, a rare phenomenon for Bentham, who did not welcome dissent from or even discussion of his ideas: acceptance was what he required.

For example, as pointed out earlier, Austin retained a religious basis for his utilitarianism, whereas Bentham rejected any hint of supernatural ethics in his exposition of the principle of utility.[30] The two men had shared the agnosticism common in the circle of Bentham's disciples. Gradually Austin changed his religious convictions: "By the time he gave the lectures on jurisprudence he combined a theological position with his political views; soon afterwards his daughter denied he was an atheist and attributed to him a belief in the importance of religion as a source of morality."[31] This affinity for religious precepts permeated his attempts to modify his own formula for the separation of law and morality. This propensity kept Austin from becoming simply a Benthamite clone: "Austin's use of Divine law also clearly differentiated his ethical theories from either Bentham's or J. S. Mill's."[32] This recognition has helped the argument that the supposed antitheses between natural law adherents like Blackstone and analytical jurists like Austin have been exaggerated, and that the similarities between these two men are more important than their differences. Austin's work must be seen in both its Blackstonian and Benthamite origins.[33] In the context of English jurisprudence, Bentham and Austin carved out separate positions for themselves, and the tendency to regard them as identical does a disservice to both.

On the subject of law in general, whatever disagreements existed on particular points, Austin clung to the belief that Bentham had made outstanding contributions. For this reason the term "analytical jurisprudence" has usually encompassed the work of both men, although it does scant justice to the contributions of either; it has value now only as a historical term, not one germane generally to philosophy or jurisprudence. Analytical jurisprudence took its name from the emphasis of both men, but especially Austin, on the primary task of analyzing legal concepts prior to the examination of any other facet of a legal system. Bentham's stress on proper definitions and his invention of language to accomplish that task tended to portray the analytical school as too rigorously deductive and therefore incapable of breaking away from the closed system he had created. Whether Austin's jurisprudence owed more to inductive or deductive premises has attracted much attention.[34] W. L. Morison has argued strongly for an inductive Austin: "In the manner in which Austin combined a determinedly empirical approach to law with a view that it could be analyzed by means of traditional logic, we see Austin's enduring contribution to jurisprudence."[35] In Austin "the definition 'law is a command of the sovereign' is presented . . . not as a logical postulate from which substantive proportions of law can be analytically deduced but rather as a connotation of the word 'law' in terms of empirical facts."[36] Another version of this interpretation has held that Austin assumed "that all knowledge is ultimately derived from observation and experience."[37] Despite the surface similarities that united Bentham and Austin, their differences now seem the more important for the elaboration of the jurisprudential tradition. Austin eventually went his own philosophical way, with important consequences for the subsequent history of jurisprudence.

The comparison of Bentham and Austin on key issues makes plain that although the subjects under discussion were expressed in much the same language, the conclusions reached were dissimilar. One case in point was the command theory of law, in which Austin defined law as the command of the sovereign, and held that only those rules that proceeded from the will of the sovereign deserved the title of law. Austin did not treat the psychological issues that surrounded the notion of command as fully as Bentham, although Austin was sensitive to the various forms of conduct that the word "command" entailed.[38] He may well have subscribed to an empirical theory of legal analysis, but for intellectual history it was the Austin who stressed definition of legal issues who became of crucial importance to the next generation of legal scholars. His successors, however much in error, regarded Austin as the founder of a theoretical jurisprudence that did not depend upon empirical research. Part of the responsibility for this attitude was due to John Stuart Mill, whose lengthy review article in the *Edinburgh Review* in 1863 brought Austin's name back into the public eye. Mill stressed Austin's facility in the training of precise thought and his skill in the analysis of legal concepts.[39] Mill acknowledged Bentham's role as a teacher but argued that where Bentham wished to demolish, Austin, by virtue of his concern for establishing the bases of law by proper definition, tried to construct a system of knowledge by deductive means. Frederic Harrison gave another articulation of this interpretation in 1878, praising Austin as the jurist in whom "English law found the first clear conception of an abstract jurisprudence; that is, a methodical examination of the general language of law."[40] In this view Austin had already become simply an analyst of fundamental legal ideas without any wider range of interests. Whether this portrayal represented the true Austin became irrelevant, for, in fact, this Austin became enshrined in the jurisprudential tradition. Sir Frederick Pollock in 1872, for example, began the process of making this Austin the target for academic lawyers: "It will be my aim to show that this definition [Austin's law as command] if exclusively insisted on, errs by elevating what is at most one characteristic of law into its essence; that contrawise, by losing sight of what is really an essential constituent, it narrows the proper scope of law and tends to an unsatisfactory view of its operation; and that by putting forward the arbitrary and suppressing the necessary aspect of legislation it seriously obscures the organic relation of law to the community."[41] The conventional interpretation of Austin as a jurist preoccupied with legal definitions at the expense of empirical data was complete.

A similar situation arose with respect to the Austin who was adamant in his insistence upon a legally unfettered sovereign. If such a sovereign authority did not exist, then laws were essentially useless for the regulation of human conduct, and without the power of enforcement the general happiness sought by the principle of utility could not be realized.[42] Specific focus on sovereignty led Austin to define the boundaries of his analysis narrowly, for he thought the purpose of constitutional law was to identify the wielder of sovereign power. Austin asserted that sovereignty did not reside in the customary triumvirate of crown, lords, and commons, but rather in the crown, lords, and the electorate as represented by the commons.[43] Austin as the exponent of an unlimited legal sovereignty has become a cliché, but sovereignty did embody a fundamental concept he sought to establish beyond doubt. His discussion of sovereignty has remained a staple of debate about constitutional law, and the difficulty of locating sovereignty within the legal/political framework has fueled arguments since his death.

As with the definition of law as command, Austin on sovereignty in the end differed in significant ways from Bentham. Bentham had adhered to the traditional view of sovereignty, whereas Austin had made clear his desire to take account of political realities. Austin accepted that sovereignty, to be meaningful, could not have any legal limits on its exercise. Bentham took the view that supreme legislative power might, in fact, be subject to rules governing the operation of that power: "It is one of the ironies of the history of jurisprudence that Bentham in developing his account of the Sovereign's legislative powers came to adopt views at variance with the doctrines both of Blackstone, the target of his fiercest criticism, and John

Austin, his chief disciple among jurists."[44] Once more, therefore, the lumping together of master and pupil obscures the way in which Bentham and Austin ultimately staked out different positions.

Subsequent commentary placed the Austinian analysis of sovereignty in an intellectual category far removed from his original intentions. Frederic Harrison conceded that Austin's relentlessly logical procedure was valid only to the extent that the reader accepted the original assumptions; but examined "as a general proposition of human society, without the prefixed qualifications, in a word, treated as a philosophical principle, it [Austin's doctrine of sovereignty] is quite assailable and not very intelligible."[45] Dissatisfaction with his explanation of sovereignty led Austin to become a favorite straw man for the academic jurists of the 1880s, and what Austin wrote as opposed to what his critics claimed that he wrote helped to create an Austin at odds with his original doctrines. Austin was invariably portrayed as a theoretician whose views on sovereignty had no basis in the real world; the truth was that his last works treated contemporary themes in politics and constitutional arrangements to an extent greater than most of his critics. These later depictions "must not be uncritically identified with the interpretations of subsequent jurists."[46] In this manner the Austin who died in 1859 became distinct from the individual whose name played such a central part in jurisprudential discussion after the posthumous appearance of his books in 1861 and 1863.

On another issue, contemporary politics, Austin's relationship to Bentham affected Austin's reputation among succeeding jurists. Bentham's political views certainly varied over the course of his long life, but in brief outline Bentham eventually (at what precise point scholars of Bentham still disagree)[47] became convinced that his hopes for the role of legislators in the reform of English society along the lines he advocated were doomed because legislators cooperated with the lawyers and judges in sustaining the illusions and failures of the common law. As a result Bentham committed himself to political democracy in order to facilitate the wholesale changes that England required, particularly an end to traditional aristocratic domination of the political world. Just as the argument from tradition failed to justify legal institutions and practices when measured against the principle of utility, so Bentham believed that the argument from history was a fallacy that permeated all English society, and its dire influence must be destroyed.

The circumstances of Austin's life turned him against these tenets of Bentham's political faith. Austin gradually became more conservative, abandoning the Benthamite creed that had originally so excited his enthusiasm, with the result that his political beliefs eventually diametrically opposed those of his mentor. Austin also turned from the reform of the law that had preoccupied Bentham so totally.[48] The conservatism of his political convictions took many years to mature, and it was not until his *A Plea for the Constitution* (1859) that his complete abandonment of Benthamite politics became apparent. In that final political testament he rejected utilitarianism and adopted the argument from tradition as the justification for political order.[49] Austin held that the ordinary citizen was incapable of acting upon the dictates of utility; only the hereditary elite was fully capable of doing so.[50] Austin emphasized the decidedly unBenthamite notion that customary allegiance and constitutional sentiment provided the basis of the political order: "He could no longer uphold the principle affirmed in *The Province of Jurisprudence* that the bond ought to be based on rational appreciation of the superior knowledge of those who enjoyed political authority."[51] So strong was the endorsement of the aristocratic principle as the foundation of society that "it involved a defense of aristocratic power that would have aroused either Jeremy Bentham or James Mill from the slumbers of death, if that were possible."[52] Not only did Austin break decisively with Benthamite politics, the difference provided yet another example of why the conventional linking of the two men no longer carries conviction.

Of all the key ideas elaborated by Austin, none has had such a formidable impact than his assertion that the separation of law from morality constituted the necessary prerequisite for jurisprudential analysis. That Austin himself did not act rigidly on his own suggestion must be distinguished from the power that this formula acquired as a technique for undertaking legal studies. In the latter part of the nineteenth century, so many jurists accepted this aspect of Austinian jurisprudence that the enunciation of its importance became something of a platitude, an incantation that too often suppressed alternative avenues of exploration in jurisprudence. The precise dimensions of Austin's mandate still forms a central element of debate in modern legal theory, so Austin will continue to attract scholarly attention. From the time of Blackstone, no other phrase has generated so much effort from scholars of the law.

In the history of English jurisprudence, however, this issue has had a curious fate. First of all, no contributor to the analytical tradition—neither Bentham nor Austin nor any of their successors—ever took literally the command to separate law from morality even as they pledged intellectual allegiance to the principle. Jurists understood that this axiom was an analytical tool at best, but no one could intend seriously that law must be divorced from morality, for it was patent that law and morality intersected on every level. To speculate meaningfully about law demanded consideration of all manner of moral principles, for law imposed all sorts of moral obligations and itself was suffused with moral precepts. Thus the separation of law and morality turned into a slogan that took on a life of its own, while those who preached the doctrine paid little or no attention to the practical difficulties it raised: "Not one of the early positivist jurists ever disengaged the idea of law from the notion of the ends of law successfully. They all begin by announcing that law and morals are two distinct subjects, that law is simply a command. But within the same treatise they deal with the ends or purposes of law."[53] For the history of English jurisprudence the issue is not the validity of the formula itself; the essential conclusion is that in one way or the other jurists have violated its content by interpreting the original principle to suit their own objectives.

In the generation after Austin, at a time when Austin gained recognition as the founder of a science of law, some jurists recognized specifically that the separation of law from morality was a practical and theoretical impossibility. Sheldon Amos, in a work entitled *The Science of Law,* paid tribute to Austin as the "true founder of the Science of Law" but criticized him for the "laborious and almost painful anxiety" that surrounded his efforts to give the "region of law a scientific character wholly peculiar and distinct."[54] Later Sir Frederick Pollock denied categorically that the separation of law from morality was possible: "The reason of this (unduly neglected by some moderns for the sake of a merely verbal or illusive exactness) is that in the development of the law both by legislative and by judicial processes appeal is constantly made to ethical reason and the moral judgement of the community."[55] In order to escape some of the more troubling aspects of Austin's teaching, jurists scrambled for a means to reunite law and morality without forfeiting the claim to a scientific jurisprudence.

For this reason public opinion loomed large as a unifying factor because this extralegal force lent the support of morality to the legal system. R. M. Pankhurst resolved the Austinian is/ought dilemma by asserting that morality changes over time, and that eventually the law catches up by statutory change; this was, he believed, part of the continuous interaction by which law evolved.[56] B. R. Wise expanded on this point, arguing that "jurisprudence is also closely connected with moral progress, because Law marks the stage of moral growth, by giving a permanent form to the moral ideas already evolved."[57] Public opinion restored in practice the moral backbone to law that Austin had theoretically removed from the study of the law. If law did not express the moral sentiments of society, then the law had no means to command obedience.[58] No Victorian jurist would endorse this latter assertion.

Even more persuasive as to the ritual nature of the invocation of the separation of law and morality is the evidence that Austin himself had no intention of a literal application of the undoubtedly rigid demarcation between the two spheres. The respect given to the principle of utility and the concern for divine law in relation to a legal system afford substantial evidence in support of the contention that Austin never took his own dictum too seriously. The historical significance of Austin's declaration having put the issue in such stark terms has nothing to do with the success of the ideal itself; instead, the true importance comes from the different lines of inquiry it inaugurated. Austin contributed unwittingly to this crucial divergence of purpose. He placed so much emphasis on the exposition of language that he never stressed, as had Bentham, the science of legislation and its impact. His failure to produce the synthetic work about which he brooded for much of his later life left a distorted picture of his own ideas.[59] The theoretical separation of law from morality had the long-term effect of directing legal philosophy into more restricted channels consistent with the creation of an academic culture. As a result of this unintended consequence jurisprudence's domain was narrowed as well.

No matter what judgment one may make about Austin's ultimate intellectual success or what differences separated him from Bentham, the two men shared the goal of making jurisprudence the primary vehicle for social improvement. In this Austin shared the reverence for jurisprudence as the most effective tool for the progress of society with Blackstone as well. In spite of the usual placement of Blackstone at one end of the jurisprudential spectrum and Bentham and Austin at the other, the three jurists agreed that jurisprudence represented the highest form of social commentary. Austin believed that legal analysis and morality were, in fact, inseparable and formed part of a vast intellectual project.[60] One scholar has concluded that Austin "advocated a remarkably broad approach for his time and place."[61] A lengthier assessment in the same vein had made clear the wider vision that animated Austin:

> The modern legal mind with its reluctance to relate any analysis of the law to topics such as theology, finds it difficult to conceive of Austin as a man whose primary concern was not with the minute analysis of legal terms, but rather with their relationship to other elements in a universe dominated by a particular vision of God and the state. The fact that Austin went to such extreme lengths to show what was properly called law should not draw our attention away from his great concern with non-legal issues; the things that were *not* properly called law always fascinated him. In brief he appeared to integrate the legal and the non-legal into a larger understanding of human existence. Later analysts with their concern for the concepts of sovereignty and command would surely have struck Austin's contemporaries as having a most curious obsession with the less adventuresome elements of his lectures. They ignored his quest to explain man's place in the universe.[62]

Jurisprudence represented that instrument for humanistic inquiry uniquely suited for social analysis because it embraced all other disciplines. Despite the breadth of his vision, the Austin who exerted great influence after his death was, in fact, the legal philosopher remembered for a constricted vision of jurisprudence who himself became the subject of increasingly narrow investigation.[63] It was perhaps the final tragedy of Austin's life that the reductionist portrait prevailed: "Not only are laws only metaphorically so called, such as the 'laws' of nature, obviously not in the picture . . . but the law of God, the law of nature, the law of morality, are also outside the range of Austin's jurisprudence, together with what are merely called 'laws' by way of an analogy, such as the laws of good society, or of chess."[64]

Another contribution to the misinterpretation of Austinian thought was the fragmentation of his work by various constituencies that used part of it taken out of context to justify their views. This pruning of his jurisprudence made Austin a respected authority and a target with equal ease. For example, the dictum of law as command had greater attraction for the criminal bar than for those engaged in civil litigation.[65] Austin's theory proved attractive to practitioners because "it was itself an expression of ideas about laws already highly congenial to the bench and the profession. The idea that valid law is something originally laid down by the legislature and the courts, that this law consists essentially of rules, that a sharp line can and should be drawn between the law as it is and the law as it ought to be are all ideas that were already highly congenial to English judges and lawyers in the nineteenth century."[66] This "triumphant Austinianism"[67] clearly gained an ascendancy in some areas of the legal establishment, but not in all.

As an object of academic study Austin's influence was

pervasive but not enduring. The proper interpretation of his jurisprudence still occasions frequent learned commentary: "It is a matter of dispute whether we should view Austin as a wayward child setting modern jurisprudence on a sterile and confused path, or rather as the spokesman for a positivism philosophically come of age."[68] That Austin became a hot topic of academic debate proved the point that his attempt to follow in the tradition of jurisprudence as the broadest of intellectual ventures had failed. Left to the dissection of academic critics, Austin's jurisprudence appeared more limited in scope than he had desired: "For whereas Bentham was celebrated as the great reformer and codifier, the prince of the Pannomion, Austin was to be seen as an educationalist and expositor, who had no desire to transform the substantive legal order, but who was engaged in a definitional and jurisprudential exercise."[69]

The academic appropriation of Austin coincided with the posthumous revival of his writings. Between 1861 and 1880 Austin enjoyed a great vogue in the rapidly evolving world of academic law, but thereafter he came under increasing criticism. His eclipse did not necessarily preclude a continuation of his influence, although it did mean that it lived on in a subterranean fashion that ultimately clouded many of the issues he had raised. The appeal of Austin for academic lawyers had originated in the promise of a scientific jurisprudence. In turn this made for a more accessible subject for university law students, and Austin became a favorite topic for examiners.[70] For law faculties as well, Austin became a symbol of academic trendiness, for his work became the subject of learned glosses and explications. The prestige of science made his work attractive because Austin's devotion to first principles seemed to provide the foundations for a scientific jurisprudence.[71] After 1880 the premises of analytical jurisprudence, at least as interpreted in academic circles, came under increasing attack, so that by 1914, at least for academic lawyers, many of Austin's major doctrines had suffered wholesale rejection. As W. W. Buckland wrote of Austin: "He was a religion; today he seems to be regarded rather as a disease."[72] The vagaries of academic law had brought Austin's reputation to a low point.

This reversal of fortune illustrated the ambivalent nature of the Austinian legacy: what appeared strongest in Austin to some jurists aroused the sharpest criticism from others. For example, the strength of the Austinian analysis had seemed to be its emphasis on the clarity of fundamental concepts and the requirement to define carefully what the study of jurisprudence entailed. After 1880 these presumed virtues turned into liabilities on the ground that Austinian jurisprudence had proved static and that it paid too little attention to the historical sources of law. Frederic Maitland, the greatest of legal historians, reflected this attitude in his belief that "J.A. = O."[73] In an era of vigorous imperial expansion, Austin's conclusions remained "culture-bound," excellent for the analysis of contemporary English society but not applicable to other societies and cultures.[74] This critique of Austin for his lack of historical perspective reinforced the image of a jurist so determined upon his definitions that he had provided no empirical evidence to support his conclusions. Leading academicians eventually rejected Austinianism for its lack of vision: "His static and unhistorical deductions were tellingly ridiculed by Maine, Bryce and Pollock."[75] Only Dicey retained any strong faith that Austin had made positive contributions.[76]

Advances in legal history, especially emphasis on the tracing of doctrinal evolution, made Austin less compelling; the comparative method of legal study pioneered by Sir Henry Maine transformed Austin's analytical methodology into a seemingly obsolete technique without lasting consequences. Sir William Markby, an original Austinian, made a game effort at defending Austin against Maine's criticism, but even he had to concede that Austin could not be protected against charges of legal provincialism.[77] Where Austin had argued, for example, that the customary law of primitive societies could not constitute a legal system because no sovereign existed to enforce the law, a critic like Pollock reversed Austin by writing that "law is enforced by the State because it is law, it is not law merely because the State enforces it."[78] In one sentence Pollock had inverted a basic premise of Austinian jurisprudence. In fairness to Austin, later scholars have not found Pollock's criticism so useful. Alan Watson has offered a defense of Austin's teachings on the validity of customary law—that recognition of customary law by a court amounts to a command of the sovereign—which has restored Austin's reputation on the subject.[79] At the end of the nineteenth century, nevertheless, the impact of Maine's work had turned the leaders of English jurisprudence into caustic critics of Austin.

Austin's reputation suffered as well because, inevitably, reassessments of Austin remarked on the inconsistency of his message to separate law and morality and his failure to make good on his promise to do so: "Austin's second, third, and fourth lectures appear to me to have no business where they are. They are not jurisprudence at all, but ethics out of place."[80] Pollock added to this indictment by suggesting that Austin was really guilty of a natural law approach, and "even regarded it [analytic jurisprudence] as dead and buried by his time."[81] Pollock's dismissal of Austin was typical of academic lawyers: "A dogmatic utilitarian, with no sense of history and small understanding of English or indeed of any law."[82] The dismissal of Austin by academic critics accelerated the process whereby Austin served primarily as the whipping boy of analytical jurisprudence. Oversimplified judgments portended a half century (1900–1950) of scholarly exile for Austin before his work earned serious reconsideration.

The practice of using Austin's jurisprudence only for the scoring of scholarly points added to his reputation as a jurist with a bad case of tunnel vision. The real problem lay with the critics, and not with Austin: "Those, . . . who took a particular interest in Austin's approach from the time when his work was published until the mid twentieth century generally failed to interest themselves in Austin from this point of view because they had no broad philosophical or logical interests."[83] Or put more succinctly: "Austin narrowed down Bentham and Austin's followers narrowed down Austin."[84] The stereotype of Austin as too confused, too prolix, and too deductive seemed to triumph. Many intellectuals have endured the fate of having their ideas trivialized and then having their work caricatured to supply quotations to later scholars who never return to examine the original writings. As a result, for half a century Austin's successors never understood his work: "What emerges is their lack of interest in, or disagreement with, what we regard as most valuable in Austin: the attempt to represent law as concerned with events which are empirical in the sense of being open to ordinary observation and yet constitute a scientific field of study which can be presented systematically by the methods of traditional logic."[85]

The revival of interest in Austin in the last two decades has eliminated much of this misunderstanding; Rumble has provided a judicious perspective on Austin's achievements: "These accomplishments reflected his rare ability for conceptual clarification, his intolerance of cant, his sense of realism, and his commitment to the good of society as he understood it."[86] His commitment to use jurisprudence to foster social benefits placed him squarely in the English tradition. His shortcomings in historical understanding paved the way for the next major figure who undertook to interpret society through the medium of jurisprudence.

Chapter Five

Sir Henry Maine Historical Jurisprudence and Social Reform

Blackstone, Bentham, and Austin, though frequently thought of as so opposed to one another on many crucial issues, shared the belief that legal speculation served as an important medium for extensive social and political theorizing. The study of Sir Henry Maine and historical jurisprudence introduces, so it is usually argued, another significant example of the diversity of law's empire. The conventional interpretation of Maine's relationship to his learned predecessors has argued that an unbridgeable chasm separated the radically different approaches of natural law and of analytical and historical jurisprudence. This assessment specified a relatively simple process by which Maine criticized Blackstone for his reliance on moral arguments, and Bentham and Austin for their lack of historical perspective in reflections upon the nature of law. For example, where Austin sought the universal elements of a legal system, Maine insisted on the contingent and discordant in the historical development of legal systems. In addition, most critics have argued, Maine rejected Bentham's reliance on the principle of utility to the same degree that he attacked Blackstone's connection with natural law theory.

The conjunction of the two remarkable books on jurisprudence published in 1861, the reissue of Austin's *The Province of Jurisprudence Determined* and Maine's *Ancient Law,* appeared at the end of one era and the opening of another. These two pillars of Victorian jurisprudence, Austin and Maine, then competed for dominance, with Austin initially victorious because Maine produced few disciples. In the view of some scholars, what separated Maine from Austin far outweighed the assumptions and conclusions they shared. Whether this assessment retains its validity is a primary concern of this chapter.

The criticisms advanced by Maine rapidly became stock arguments against analytical jurisprudence. Maine insisted that Austin had erred fundamentally in the assertion of the "alleged inapplicability of his conception of a positive law and sovereignty to primitive legal systems."[1] For the lack of these ideas Austin had denied that customary law merited the name of law at all. Maine argued that any legal system should be understood only in its concrete expression as shaped by the full range of extralegal elements in society: "From this perspective the Austinian search for legal forms and the dry calculations of Benthamite utilitarianism had painted a false picture that did not get at the real stuff of social life."[2] Maine further suggested that the elaborate complexities of Austin's attempt to deal with legal issues "too frequently sacrificed the deeper understanding of the actual legal arrangements of diverse societies for mere logical symmetry."[3] Could every society's legal affairs be reduced to a single set of definitions that indicated whether or not it constituted a legal system? Maine did not think so, for "law was the product of time and place, and the theories of Bentham and Austin were themselves products of particular 'limited' historical circumstances."[4] In the end, therefore, Maine held that Austin remained trapped in the social environment that he inhabited: "His conceptions of a positive law and sovereignty are culture-bound. Despite their high degree of validity for contemporary Western European societies, they are inapplicable to primitive societies in general and Indian villages in particular."[5] Thus, while Bentham and Austin had searched for the universal in fixed legal systems, their efforts had failed dismally; some new effort to capture the essence of law was required.

This account of the gulf that separated Maine from his juristic predecessors derived largely from Sir Paul Vinogradoff, in 1903 a successor to Maine in the Corpus chair of jurisprudence at Oxford. Perhaps the jurist who remained most loyal to the tenets of historical jurisprudence, Vinogradoff clearly felt obliged to sustain Maine's reputation as changing scholarly fashion threatened to make his work obsolete or, even worse, irrelevant. It has even been suggested, rather uncharitably, that Vinogradoff "virtually lived off his [Maine's] intellectual capital."[6]

In his inaugural lecture Vinogradoff emphasized how the originality of Maine's historical jurisprudence had opposed the alleged abstract structure of analytical jurisprudence. Although Maine had acknowledged the contributions of Bentham and Austin, Maine was "unable to follow the lead of these thinkers and clearly marks the dividing line between their conceptions and his own. Their mode of investigation is too abstract for him."[7] Vinogradoff believed that the more intellectual distance he could place between Maine and the analytical jurists, the better for the former. No doubt Vinogradoff, whose scholarly work focused on medieval English history, also thought he would benefit if others believed that he remained faithful to Maine's teachings.

Several modern studies of Maine's jurisprudence have reiterated that it rejected the basic conclusions of analytical jurisprudence. Kenneth Bock asserted that Maine's "critical point of departure is . . . to be found in his sense of the inadequacy of Austinian analytic jurisprudence and Benthamite utilitarianism in the study of law and political economy."[8] Later examples of this interpretation that reinforced the differences between Maine and his predecessors called the former's enduring contribution to legal theory his dissent from positivism.[9] By citing only Maine's unflattering references without balancing them with his more sympathetic comments by Maine, scholars have left a distorted picture of his intellectual relationship to earlier jurists. Modern reassessments of Maine's major works have contended that his views changed over time, and that his reaction to previous jurisprudence was more complex than the interpretation Vinogradoff had originally offered in 1903.

This venerable tradition of separating Maine from other British jurists has not prevailed because scholars, in returning to the original writings, discovered that the old classification of Victorian jurists into separate schools was no longer valid. George Feaver, the modern biographer of Maine, noted that Maine and Austin shared important philosophical positions, especially the need for a scientific approach to law.[10] Peter Stein went further, concluding that "Maine's attitude to Bentham and Austin was sometimes equivocal."[11] The latest comprehensive review of Maine's jurisprudence underscored the changing nature of his beliefs. In a number of instances Raymond Cocks stressed that Maine, criticisms notwithstanding, gradually revealed "new respect for the analytical achievements of Bentham and Austin," and Cocks argued that Maine "was not unequivocally set upon the destruction of utilitarian jurisprudence."[12] Wilfrid Rumble has capped this revision by showing that "the nature and significance of the differences between Austin and Maine are best understood against the background of their similarities."[13] In the light of this new emphasis on the issues that brought Maine into a Victorian consensus, the continuity of Victorian jurisprudence through the appearance of *Ancient Law* has become more apparent.

Maine, born in 1822, was the only figure in the jurisprudential tradition to have significant Cambridge associations, for all the others were in one way or another Oxford men. He compiled a brilliant academic record as a Cambridge undergraduate and secured appointment at the age of 25 to the Regius professorship of civil law at his alma mater. He resigned this position in 1854, turning to political journalism, where he espoused a consistently conservative viewpoint. After the publication of *Ancient Law* in 1861 he served as legal adviser to the governor-general's council in India, where he spent most of the 1860s. He returned to England to take the Corpus chair of jurisprudence at Oxford in 1869; he served in that post until 1878, when he was elected master of Trinity Hall, Cambridge. In 1887, one year before his death, he became Whewell professor of international law at Cambridge. Like Blackstone before him, Maine combined notable public service with academic honors, fashioning a career that made him a prominent member of the Victorian intellectual aristocracy.

Maine published four other major books after the appearance of *Ancient Law* in 1861, but none contributed to the study of jurisprudence nor attracted the same degree of scholarly attention as the initial work.[14] *Ancient Law,* rightly, has always been regarded as Maine's masterpiece, the book that established his reputation and elaborated historical jurisprudence most fully. Later interpretations of *Ancient Law* must be understood in the context of those intellectuals who have suffered the reduction of their complex ideas to one formula that distorts or, at best, simplifies the argument. Maine was no exception to this process, for later scholars made the phrase "from status to contract" his trademark. In point of fact, this famous expression did not even make its appearance until Maine had spent some 160 pages in the exploration of other themes. Nor did the pronouncement of social progress involving the movement from status to contract, or the decline of status groups and their replacement by the assumption of individual responsibility, even represent the heart of the book.[15] As Cocks has pointed out, once Maine had introduced this phrase, he made no effort to develop it in a systematic manner.[16] Readers familiar with *Ancient Law* will recall that Maine gave more attention to Jean-Jacques Rousseau on the state of nature and to the long history of natural law theory than to the elaboration of the from-status-to-contract theme: "Maine saw himself as a fighter against pure abstractions and *a priori* assumptions, such as the state of nature and the law of nature."[17] Maine regarded Rousseau as his primary target, for the state of nature represented exactly the sort of notion that destroyed necessary empirical historical investigation.[18] Maine, in fact, ranged throughout the past, looking especially at Roman law, the development of equity in legal systems, and even America's Declaration of Independence. The wide variety of topics treated by Maine suggested the broad purview of his concerns. With respect to the history of English jurisprudence, therefore, *Ancient Law* transcends simplistic sloganeering.

The phrase "from status to contract" acquired cult standing because it provided a succinct allusion to complex legal phenomena. It was additionally an act of faith in inevitable progress and thus served to buttress Victorian assumptions. Finally, the phrase came to be interpreted as one form of a socially scientific law that might fulfill the intellectual quest for such certainties. For Maine, however, it meant the transition "from an early phase of family-based ascriptive status in the law of persons to one in which personal relations were deemed to reflect the free agreement of contracting individuals."[19] In later works Maine left this phrase unamended and never sought to elaborate the most famous of his insights.

Beyond its specific conclusions, *Ancient Law* pioneered the concept of historical jurisprudence. Ordinarily at this point a definition of historical jurisprudence would be in order because different scholars appropriated the term for different purposes. This has proved difficult because Maine himself did not define his usage nor was Cocks able to perform the task on his behalf: "It has not enabled us to discover a definition of historical jurisprudence."[20] Maine apparently took some elements of his concept from German jurists such as Friedrich von Savigny, although not as much as Vinogradoff had believed: "Like Savigny, Maine was concerned fundamentally with reconciling, politically as well as intellectually, law and society; and he rejected the Benthamite and Austinian notion of law as simple command and obligation."[21] Citation of German jurists, and even borrowing from them, certainly increased during the course of the nineteenth century, but this often came to be a scholarly sleight of hand, demonstrating a juristically correct attitude rather than true intellectual exchange. Maine drew upon various sources in an eclectic fashion without relying too heavily on any one influence. Because he never explained satisfactorily the meaning of the phrase so closely associated with his name, he left subsequent scholars free to define it as they pleased, or to use it as an invocation to support conclusions of their own. Maine had written: "But the warning can never be too often repeated, that the grand source of mistake in questions of jurisprudence is the impression that those reasons which actuate us at the present moment, in the maintenance of an existing institution, have necessarily anything in common with the sentiment in which the institution originated."[22] If historical jurisprudence meant only that the law must be studied in its historical dimension, then it would have amounted to little more than cant. Certainly Maine was not the first to draw this elementary conclusion. If Maine had a more perceptive insight about the relation of history to law, he kept it to himself.

Maine used historical jurisprudence as a vehicle for the expression of his thought on the general social condition of contemporary England. His book was entitled *Ancient Law,* but the lessons derived from his study of past law had direct application to his own world:

> One elementary precaution is to remember that all accounts of progress involve, at least implicitly, some characterization of stagnation, retrogression, and decline; and, perhaps a slightly less obvious point, theories of progress are one very effective form of social or cultural criticism in that they are attempts to endow with some kind of scientific or moral authority the discrimination of those current social and cultural developments that are welcome from those that are not.[23]

Maine made his points of social commentary in *Ancient Law,* but its fame became assured when the book gained recognition as a serious work of scholarship.

What historical jurisprudence came to mean for the scholarly community was the comparative method: "the recognition of similarities between the practices and beliefs of contemporary primitive or barbaric peoples and those recorded in the past history of civilization."[24] Although Maine did not invent this influential idea, he gave it a legitimacy in *Ancient Law* that it had not previously enjoyed and offered a tool for further analysis. The comparative method soon became the rote explanation in many fledgling disciplines of Victorian England. "In the 1860s and 70s the map of learning seemed, to many members of the educated class in England, about to be redrawn in an exhiliratingly comprehensive and coherent way," it has been argued, and "the effusion of references . . . pointed to a self-conscious, excited sense of direction and common purpose at work."[25] Reliance on the comparative method became an academic phenomenon, a trendy idea whose implications Maine never explored in systematic fashion.[26] In the end it became a ritual phrase to which academic obeisance was paid, an obligatory footnote by which an individual paid scholarly dues.

What Maine thought he had accomplished by emphasis on the comparative method cannot be described with precision, for he may well have had several objectives in view. Arguments about what he meant by the comparative method may reveal more about posterity than about Maine. For example, Maine and the comparative method affected the perception of imperial duties, especially the necessity of governing diverse customary societies so far removed from English experience: "Since Britain was obliged to make laws for societies scattered across the face of the earth, Maine thought it undeniable that his approach offered the advantage of flexibility."[27] Another contention was that Maine believed that he had provided a key to unlock many of the mysteries that confounded scholars: "Psychologically speaking, he seems to have regarded the Comparative Method as the foundation of a great new science rather than as a last resort."[28] As far as its impact on jurisprudence was concerned, the comparative method provided the "perfect stick with which to beat the Utilitarians for the widely sensed failure of their 'abstract' method."[29] Because Maine left such an ambiguous heritage, all of these interpretations have some support in the available evidence, though not sufficient to establish any one of them absolutely.

Whatever difficulties Maine bequeathed with the comparative method, the impact on English jurisprudence was clear and immediate. One specific illustration of Maine's convoluted legacy emerged in the work of Sir Frederick Pollock. Although he harbored doubts about some aspects of Maine's work, Pollock endorsed enthusiastically Maine's utilization of the comparative method.[30] In common with Maine and his own contemporaries, Pollock never defined exactly what he meant by the comparative method. He used the term for the most part in a generic sense, as a universal methodology valid for all disciplines. At other times he equated the phrase with historical jurisprudence, the best vehicle for the foundation of legal history. On some occasions Pollock used the comparative method to emphasize the value of Roman law. Acquaintance with it was essential because comparison with the common law gave an improved knowledge of English law. Pollock characterized Maine's work in this way: "At one master-stroke he forged a new and lasting bond between law, history, and anthropology. Jurisprudence itself has become a study of the living growth of human society through all its stages, and it is no longer possible for law to be dealt with as a collection of rules."[31] Maine's comparative method, like his phrase "from status to contract," permeated the common discourse of academic culture; it became a shibboleth so pervasive that it turned into a distinctive feature of Victorian academic culture. It eventually "represented a flexing of academic muscles in danger perhaps of pedantic cramp or antiquarian irrelevance."[32] In jurisprudence especially the vogue for comparative law did not lead to the scholarly results promised. For all the praise of that methodology, few jurists actually *attempted* to follow the prescription; Maine popularized the phrase, but he did not found a school that produced significant results. Within jurisprudence the comparative method remained an ideal.

The difficulties in trying to fit Maine properly into his intellectual context did not end there. James Bryce, Regius professor of civil law at Oxford from 1870 to 1893, attempted to distinguish between the comparative method and the separate discipline of history. For Bryce the comparative method meant the habit of investigation "which collects rules and institutions found in every developed legal system, or most of them, [and] notes their similarities or differences."[33] The science of history was not as mechanical, for it had to deal with the contingencies of the human experience. Sir William Holdsworth thought that Maine's influence was the greater precisely because the combination of comparison and history accounted for the great strides in the writing of legal history at the end of the Victorian era.[34] The fact remains, however, that the significant scholarship in legal history in this period was weighted heavily toward the history of English law. It was not comparative in any meaningful sense.

The extent of Maine's specific influence has remained difficult to assess, for he was frequently cited and yet left few followers to carry on his work. All manner of scholars invoked his name, but they did so in support of widely disparate intellectual enterprises. Maine could hardly have sympathized with most of the work ostensibly performed under his inspiration. The conclusion that "the extent and profundity of Maine's influence among the intellectuals would be hard to exaggerate"[35] is surely correct. Maine's undoubted stature has remained undiminished even though his work quickly faded into obscurity after the academic fad of the comparative method had run its course. Maine's place in the jurisprudential tradition has puzzled later generations because he has seemed so out of step, so far afield from the concerns of his predecessors. The relationship to earlier jurists, particularly Bentham and Austin, holds the key to some aspects of fitting Maine into his appropriate place in the history of English jurisprudence.

Maine's original ambiguity toward the analytical jurists makes it difficult to describe his attitude, and the problem is made even more complex by the way in which his own views changed over time. As Maine grew older he altered his perception of himself as primarily a critic of analytical jurisprudence and gradually came to appreciate the questions posed and the answers offered by Bentham and Austin. For example, Maine eventually acknowledged that the principle of utility, originally an object of his scorn, offered a powerful weapon for the critique of existing legal arrangements.[36] The felicific calculus presented a stumbling block because Maine continued to believe that it merely substituted one moral standard for another, thus clouding the issues that jurisprudence sought to clarify.[37] In addition, Maine hesitated to accept as a basis for political reform the principle of utility, in which he saw value as an instrument of legal reform.[38] He wished to extend the insights of the analytical jurists by investing their work with new perspectives.[39] Maine did not repudiate utilitarian jurisprudence, for he wished to turn its conclusions in more productive directions.

On the definition of law offered by Bentham and Austin, Maine thought that the notion of law as the command of a legislator did not accurately portray the situation in past societies, nor did it exhaust the fundamental properties of law. Maine was "suspicious" of the utilitarian argument that law as command represented the only true form of law.[40] He defended the validity of customary law as a legal system suitable for the society in which it existed. The absence of legislation, or positive law, did not make such a society any less responsive to the mandates of customary law. Maine contended that to deny the term "law" to these customary legal rules simply reflected the unhistorical aspects of analytical jurisprudence, although he conceded that Bentham and Austin described accurately the state of English law as it existed when they wrote. Maine believed that the understanding of customary legal systems made it possible to explain the common law with greater sophistication: "Instead of thinking in terms of either commands or red-robed judges, the students of legal theory had to define law as a facet of culture."[41] The analytical jurists had not erred about the nature of law; they had defined it in too restrictive a fashion and without due regard for the historical circumstances that affected contemporary law. Maine wished to build on and expand the insights of the utilitarians, not to reject them because they had nothing to offer jurisprudence.

Maine followed the same line in dealing with the issue of sovereignty. He believed that Bentham and Austin, while not totally wrong, had not explored the subject in all its complexity. In his first consideration of analytical jurisprudence published in 1855, for example, Maine examined the argument that sovereignty consisted essentially of the coercive power of a superior authority to command habitual obedience from the bulk of society.[42] For him the debate on sovereignty had wider repercussions than simply on the domestic sphere, for it affected international law as well. If the Austinian definition of sovereignty were granted, presumably international law could not exist in any significant sense because it lacked the necessary sovereign to enforce its rules. Maine thought this an essentially foolish conclusion.

Maine preferred a more spacious approach to the problem of what might be termed law. While he admired the acute focus of analytical jurisprudence, he argued that it required a greater appreciation of historical context, and that it disregarded many areas of human conduct that had to be taken into account for a true understanding of law: "Abstraction in Austin's hands also ignored the historical antecedents and circumstances under which coercive sovereign power, once established, came to be exercised or moderated or, in fact, excluded from certain areas of action. Opinions, beliefs, sentiments, superstitions, ideas of all kind—in short the historical culture in which sovereignty arose and functioned—were omitted from consideration."[43] The notion of territorial sovereignty so essential to the Austinian analysis "had no application to vast areas of human society."[44] Because it did not possess the cultural component Maine deemed vital, analytical jurisprudence failed to deliver the comprehensive science of law that it had promised.

The same pattern emerged from Maine's consideration of sovereignty as had occurred with law as command. After making trenchant criticisms that would ultimately become standard appraisals of analytical jurisprudence, Maine recognized that Bentham and Austin had considerable merit, particularly in the remorseless application of logic. For Maine, however, logic was not everything in dealing with the law; his critique may well have intended to caution enthusiastic followers of Austin that failure to account for other factors in a legal system might vitiate an analysis.[45] If only enforcement was discussed with respect to sovereignty, then too many other important factors were omitted. In international law, for example, "What we have to notice is, that the founders of International Law, though they did not create a sanction, created a law-abiding sentiment."[46] International law constituted a valid system of law despite the absence of certain aspects of Austin's definition. A nonlegal entity such as sentiment was every bit as crucial to law as the formal categories defined by the analytical jurists. Thus Maine did not destroy the analytical tradition; rather, he attempted to tease out its implications and expand those points that Bentham and Austin had rightly emphasized.

About the relation of law to morality, the congruence of Maine's conclusions with those of Bentham and Austin was even more pronounced. Maine had as little patience as either of his analytical predecessors with the long tradition of natural law theory. The concept of natural law had no historical justification, it rested upon a foundation of imprecise language, and it could supply no empirical evidence for its truth. Maine attributed some of the most pernicious ideas in legal and political theory to the baleful influence of natural law.[47] For Maine the great villain was Rousseau, who had turned natural law concepts upside down by deducing secular political conclusions from moral premises. The Swiss philosopher had worsened matters by invoking the mythical state of nature, his private natural law, to support his idea of political society. Maine devoted substantial space and energy to his critique of Rousseau, and as Cocks has correctly stressed, in *Ancient Law* Maine devoted his sharpest criticisms to natural law and gave far less attention to aspersions on the utilitarian jurists.[48] Maine did not address the separation of law and morality as specifically as his analytical predecessors, but he agreed with the principle, for he also denounced the blending of what the law is and what it ought to be that is so characteristic of natural law.[49] On this point, therefore, Maine supported enthusiastically a major premise of analytical jurisprudence.

Yet, as with his utilitarian predecessors, Maine also urged the separation of law and morality and then turned around and promptly injected moral concerns into his jurisprudence. Maine's attitude toward the law and morality issue reinforced the habit of substituting moral considerations into legal writings. In the same fashion that Blackstone had utilized natural law tenets, Bentham the principle of utility, and Austin the mandate of revelation, Maine turned his arguments into moral imperatives. Thus the signature phrase of "from status to contract" became "not merely an historical truth ('hitherto') but a moral polarity, which no future social development could cancel; a distinction between two moral as well as social worlds: custom set against analysis and intellectual energy, tradition against expediency, dependence against self-reliance, superstitious fear against mutual trust."[50] Maine could not resist the temptation that had also seduced his predecessors.

This agreement on the separation of law from morality led to a more substantial accord on the necessity to make legal study a scientific endeavor for the purpose of placing jurisprudence on a more secure intellectual basis. The multifaceted Victorian understanding of science gave rise to many senses of the word, and to an enduring debate about the proper conception of law as a science.[51] Maine regarded his research and reflections as specifically empirical, with the history of societies providing the source of his experimental evidence. In the Victorian era few jurists troubled themselves about a precise definition of science, and practice generally alternated between the orderly acquisition of knowledge and a strict imitation of one of the scientific disciplines. Maine's work, particularly when he discussed ideas of progress, lent itself to biological analogies, even though Maine himself thought of geology as providing the scientific model he wished to approximate. The layering of the earth's crust seemed to Maine analogous to the many levels of common law created over the centuries.[52] Maine recognized the utilitarian jurists as his forerunners in this pursuit of scientific law, and "may well have concluded that his new approach was essential for realizing the unfulfilled promise of the 'strict scientific process' initiated by Bentham and Austin."[53] In this area Maine once again thought of his work as essentially complementary to that of his scholarly forebears, not as a radical rejection of their contributions.

Finally, the mixed nature of Maine's relationship to the jurisprudential heritage materialized in the evolution of his political beliefs. Where Bentham became more politically radical as he aged, the opposite was true of Austin, and Maine followed the latter's example. The publication of *Popular Government* in 1885, his most avowedly political book, expressed an uncompromising hostility toward many of the political trends affecting the world of the late Victorians. In its implacable aversion to the radical drift of politics, Maine's *Popular Government* resembled Austin's *A Plea for the Constitution.* Maine even quoted approvingly the words of disillusionment written earlier by Austin as an example of political disenchantment caused by the failure of reform.[54] Both works exhibited a strong commitment to political conservatism as understood in each era; Maine cited Austin ("the farthest rebound of a powerful mind from the peculiar philosophical Radicalism of the immediate pupils of Jeremy Bentham")[55] in support of his critique of the march toward political democracy in

Great Britain. Maine disagreed with Bentham primarily on the subject of legislation. Bentham had regarded the legislator as the key to his plans for reform; Maine looked with trepidation at the increasing volume of legislative activity by 1885, and was pessimistic about the results of this frenzy.[56] Political events of Maine's lifetime had called into question political ideas such as the virtues of limited government that Maine had held since youth. As his various political allegiances came under increasing criticism, Maine retreated to a politics of nostalgia that rejected the direction of modern politics.[57] The themes of a lifetime persisted into old age, where in *Popular Government* Maine still felt compelled to question the legacies of Rousseau and Bentham.

Maine denounced strongly the advent of political democracy rounded off by the Reform Act of 1884, and it is this attack for which *Popular Government* is now chiefly remembered. Maine opposed the extension of the franchise in the belief that universal manhood suffrage would lead ultimately to political disaster. He denounced the fatalistic acceptance of the inevitability of democracy as contrary to the record of failure in democratic experiments.[58] Historical jurisprudence enabled Maine to "claim empirical evidence based on strict scholarship—a verifiable past and present" in his rejection of political arguments based on the certainty of progress.[59] He believed in natural elites and protested against the tendency to enshrine political equality at the expense of liberty.[60] For Maine, political progress was rare, fraught with all manner of perils and not nearly as fast or frequent as the proponents of political democracy wished to believe. In the end, from a decidedly different route, Maine had embraced a political creed consistent with Austin's earlier jeremiads.

The apparent paradox of the Maine who criticized and the Maine who admired analytical jurisprudence disappears when the chronology of his work is examined. In 1855 Maine's initial discussion of Austin on sovereignty was most remarkable for the attention paid to a jurist whose name had all but vanished from public view by that time. By the time of *Ancient Law* in 1861, Maine had become more ambivalent about analytical jurisprudence. In *Lectures on the Early History of Institutions* in 1875, after years of service in India, Maine had become more forthright in his acceptance of its strong points.[61] By the end of his life Maine's politics brought a strong identification with Austin's later political fears. Thus Maine's reconciliation to Bentham and Austin was a logical progression when viewed in the context of his personal and political experience. Maine's participation in the jurisprudential tradition should no longer come as a surprise.

In the end, when the intricate maze of support and criticism had exhausted the possible permutations of relationship, one fact remained predominant: Maine had conceived his jurisprudential tasks with the same broad vision that had driven Blackstone, Bentham, and Austin. The introduction of historical perspectives to problems of law permitted Maine to advance opinions about the general evolution of society: "The historical method which Maine practiced required for its logical validation the typically positivist assumption of general laws of social development."[62] Maine shared with his predecessors the belief in jurisprudence as the appropriate discipline in which to address the educated public. In Maine's case the explanation of progress "may be predicted with such certainty as may be found in any scientific law."[63] For Maine, as for the others, jurisprudence provided the best medium for a general commentary on the state of society: "Maine's work provides a very forceful reminder that jurisprudence involves much more than legal philosophy with or without reference to social facts."[64] Maine's jurisprudence tried to impart political wisdom as well as examine legal theory. His signature phrase, from status to contract, gained widespread fame because it became a code for a political viewpoint—"a distinct political theory for Maine, and one which gave his belief in laissez-faire freedom an air of historical inevitability."[65] Maine's Rede lecture in 1875 on India "represents the conviction of an Indian policymaker as much as the credo of an academic historian."[66] The political purpose and content of Maine's jurisprudence placed him squarely on the trail blazed by his juristic predecessors.

Ancient Law attempted to address the jurist, the lawyer, and the educated public, the broad audience that Blackstone, Bentham, and Austin had attempted to reach in order to gain support for their schemes of social and political reconstruction.[67] Bentham had failed because he lacked the personality to enter the world of public affairs. Austin had not drawn a substantial readership because his style had proved too cumbersome. Maine failed because his arguments proved too arcane and his later works did not reflect the beliefs of a majority of his readers; the "blatantly ideological cast"[68] of his writings prevented an appeal to a broader spectrum of the Victorian educated public:

> *Ancient Law* is a complex work partly because, to speak in Victorian terms, it was one in which, as always in Maine, Benthamite rigour and optimism were held in equipoise with a Whiggish sense of the necessary slowness of change and the inescapability of learning by experience, the persistence of the past and the importance of the ripeness of time, and the relative value in their day of institutions and ways of thinking which a more advanced age would find useless or pernicious.[69]

Maine followed in the line of those jurists who made jurisprudence a crucial vehicle for discussion of legal and social theory aimed at a general audience.

Of the four individuals considered so far, especially in the context of academic discussion over the past three decades, Maine's legacy has fallen farthest from the concerns of legal scholarship. The lesser position he now occupies in the gallery of Victorian intellectuals has resulted in large measure from the fact that his work as anthropologist and historian did not survive later scrutiny in the age of academic specialization. The conventional view that Maine was out of step with analytical jurisprudence prevented him from obtaining the attention that he deserved as a speculative jurist. His reputation suffered as his work increasingly became the province of academicians. Both Sir Frederick Pollock and Frederick Maitland, impressive scholars in their own right in the generation after Maine, had significant reservations about Maine's accuracy and perspective. Pollock, despite the effusive nature of his published appraisals after Maine's death, in later life wrote privately about the "odd results" obtained from rereading *Ancient Law,* and the "lapses in detail" that marred Maine's work: "He was certainly no medievalist. I don't think he has a chance of it."[70] Maitland was frequently troubled by the errors that permeated Maine's books: "You spoke of Maine. Well, I always talk of him with reluctance, for on the few occasions on which I sought to verify his statements of fact I came to the conclusion that he trusted much to a memory that played him tricks and rarely looked back at a book he had once read."[71] Maine's historical jurisprudence had too much jurisprudence and insufficient history for Maitland. The rejection in large measure of Maine's work by the succeeding generation created an academic legacy in which Maine occupied a lesser place in the history of English jurisprudence.

In part this occurred because Maine enlisted no disciples other than Vinogradoff, nor did a school form to take his side in scholarly battles and carry forward his work. As even his admirers began to entertain doubts about the efficacy of his work, Maine passed into the second rank of intellectuals, a consignment from which he has never fully escaped. In spite of this, Maine continued to exercise some influence; he attracted the sympathy and admiration of such diverse figures as Pollock, Harold Laski, and the American Justice Oliver Wendell Holmes. This trio agreed that whatever his failings, Maine had possessed the genius to inspire others ("imparting a ferment," Holmes called it)[72] to examine jurisprudence from a different angle. Pollock recorded that "the impulse given by Maine to its intelligent study in England and

America can hardly be overrated."[73] In addition, like Blackstone, Maine possessed the gift of lucid writing. *Ancient Law* may still be read with pleasure even if the reader is unfamiliar with its arguments. Where Bentham and Austin intimidated readers with esoteric vocabularies and rigid classificatory regimes, Maine has remained a literary delight, a jurist who may be read without trepidation. This quality was crucial to realize the dream of a jurisprudence that spoke to the general public. If Maine fell short, it was not for lack of style.

In the end, however, Maine did share with later jurists one effect deleterious to the jurisprudential legacy. In common with his forebears, Maine narrowed significantly the perception of those individuals who had preceded him. Although his attitude toward Austin, for example, was not intentionally hostile, it is now clear that on several important topics he attributed to Austin views that Austin had not held, and that this "may also have influenced the tendency of a number of subsequent jurists to misinterpret Austin."[74] As Cocks concluded: "Maine's failure to provide a convincing synthesis of law, history and philosophy—even of philosophy in the form of the scientific analysis of history—had a very significant legacy for English legal thought. It encouraged a more restricted understanding of what made for legal study; and it limited the scope of such claims as could be made that the legal past contained 'lessons' which could be used directly to improve modern law and standards of legal practice."[75] Maine thus advanced that process by which, even as he proclaimed the most comprehensive aims for his own jurisprudence, his account of his predecessors presented them in a fashion that ultimately restricted the understanding of their work passed down to posterity.

The older depiction of Maine's historical jurisprudence as a mutually exclusive alternative to, and critique of, analytical jurisprudence no longer gives an accurate picture of their relationship. Neat patterns are rare in intellectual history, and the traditional interpretation was terribly misleading about the connection between Maine and his two analytical precursors. Maine was not an aberration from the triumphant utilitarianism of Victorian jurisprudence; he was part of the same enterprise, albeit with different methods and conclusions: "Like Bentham and Austin he was concerned with developing a 'scientific' approach to law through general jurisprudence; like Austin he was primarily concerned with the 'is' rather than the 'ought'—perhaps for political as well as 'scientific' reasons; as with both of them the analysis of what Hohfield called 'fundamental legal conceptions' was central to his concerns; like Austin he regarded Roman law as the exemplar of legal thought in mature systems."[76] Despite the misleading assertions of some later scholars such as Vinogradoff, Maine did not ignore his intellectual antecedents. With respect to Bentham and Austin:

> Maine makes clear his indebtedness to both these thinkers, whose ideas were in important respects the point of departure for his own complementary methods of historical and comparative inquiry. In Maine's view, Jeremy Bentham was essentially a law reformer; and John Austin's consuming interest in the precise analysis of contemporary legal terminology was preliminary to a larger theoretical enterprise aimed at a comprehensive

delineation of the conditions requisite in a formal account of the legal system of a modern state.[77]

The earlier work by his analytical predecessors had lacked Maine's concern for historical development: "Admittedly, Maine was open in his enthusiasm for the methods of the utilitarian jurists in so far as they at least attempted an analysis of law which explicitly related practical matters to a general theory of law; he admired their clarity. But he could never see himself as one of their number because of their failure to integrate historical information and a correct understanding of human nature into their writings on legal change."[78] This omission did not, however, break the intellectual links between Maine and the analytical tradition.

As early as 1861 James Fitzjames Stephen recognized the complementary nature of this common endeavor in a comparative book review of *Ancient Law* and *The Province of Jurisprudence Determined:* "Though analysis is the main purpose of the one and history of the other, each (and especially Mr. Austin) recognizes the necessity to his own inquiries of the line of thought which he does not pursue."[79] What bound Maine to the jurisprudential tradition far exceeded that which separated him.[80] Even as Maine added his personal contribution to this heritage, the transformation of the tradition was foreshadowed before Maine's death; this shift would eventually shape English jurisprudence into a discipline significantly different from that Blackstone, Bentham, Austin, and Maine had envisioned.

Chapter Six

Sir Thomas Erskine Holland The Transition to Modern Academic Law

The central position occupied by Sir Thomas Erskine Holland in the development of modern English jurisprudence may occasion some surprise. Not only has Holland's reputation declined to the point of absolute neglect (indeed, it had suffered precipitously in his own lifetime), he was perhaps the least well known of the Oxford law professoriate that included Sir William Anson, James Bryce, A. V. Dicey, and Sir Frederick Pollock. This group attempted collectively to place English law and jurisprudence on a scientific basis, primarily along the lines first enunciated by Bentham and Austin. Unlike the majority of his Oxford colleagues, Holland had no career in public service and no public forum other than that provided by the occasional letter to *The Times.* He spent most of his professorial career in providing a framework for modern international law, the major principles of which Holland discovered in Benthamite utility rather than the natural law tradition. His sole contribution to legal philosophy came in 1880 with the publication of *The Elements of Jurisprudence,* which continued into a thirteenth edition in 1924, two years before the author's death. About this lone work, however, one contemporary wrote that it was "perhaps the most successful book on jurisprudence ever written."[1] Beyond that one significant work Holland did not venture, for his attention to jurisprudence thereafter seems to have been sporadic at best. *The Elements of Jurisprudence,* long consigned to obscurity, hardly seems sufficient now to merit a place in the jurisprudential canon; yet it is arguable that Holland, no less than Bentham, Austin, or Maine, has shaped the intellectual contours of English jurisprudence for the last century. Holland represented that generation of scholars who defined the analytical tradition for posterity and acted symbolically to transform the course of English legal thought.

Holland did not seem to merit substantial public recognition in his lifetime, so the details of his career remain sketchy. Professor F. H. Lawson left a characterization that did not present Holland as an attractive figure: "rigorous, dogmatic, intolerant, and hard to budge from any position that he had already taken up."[2] Obituaries in the *Law Quarterly Review* gave the impression of a magisterial presence, not an individual. One notice stressed the "serene confidence" that led him to change the *Elements* infrequently in its many editions and to ignore most contemporary critiques of his arguments.[3] The descriptions of Holland as an aloof individual, at least in part, requires some qualification, for his professorial style did not necessarily reflect the inner man.

Holland was born in 1835, attended Magdalen College, Oxford, and thereafter never strayed far from an academic environment. Called to the bar in 1863 at Lincoln's Inn, he later took the bachelor's degree in civil law in 1871 and the doctorate in civil law in 1876 at Oxford. In the meantime he had secured election in 1874 to the Chichele professorship of International Law and Diplomacy at Oxford, a position he held until his retirement in 1910. Holland was knighted in 1917 in recognition of his contributions to the academic study of international law and for his services to the government in the elaboration of naval prize law. Other than reap the honors of an academic career and his knighthood, Holland labored in relative obscurity compared to his more prominent colleagues such as Anson and Bryce, who held seats in Parliament. While the evidence is certainly not conclusive, Holland appears to have suffered from frustrated ambition as a result of the lack of public recognition. Bryce once wrote that Holland possessed the "sense of not having had one's due" and that this made him "more self-assertive."[4] The professorial dignity that his friends noted as his most compelling quality had a different origin than earlier writers have believed.

That Holland raised pedantry to a fine art and thereby exasperated his colleagues and contributed to his failure to gain greater public recognition seems all too apparent. For example, in 1907 A. V. Dicey, although a friend of

Holland's since undergraduate days in the 1850s, hesitated to recommend Holland for a course of lectures at Harvard Law School: "I have no doubt of his knowledge but his excessive insistence on points of form not only, I think, causes a good deal of vexation but is also I think connected with the much deeper defect of inability to pay sufficient deference to the opinion of others."[5] His concern for procedural subtleties led Holland into one quixotic battle after another in university politics. Dicey once recorded with incredulity Holland's remarkable absorption in his own little world: "At the most critical stage of the [Lloyd George] Budget debate, Holland could interest himself in nothing but an amendment ie in the [University] Statutes, which changed the title of the Professorship of International Law, & relieved any future professor from being required to teach Private International Law. As no human being has ever made this demand, I cannot see why we should remove an imaginary peril."[6] This academic fastidiousness especially prevalent in Holland's later years did not always characterize him; as Bryce once observed: "He [Holland] represents to us in the British Academy [to which Holland had been elected in 1902] the acme of captiously nagging persistency. However one ought to attribute it to *morosa senectus:* not thus was he in his young days."[7] Lawson's depiction of a professor pedantic to a fault has always seemed appropriate because it followed from the tactful statement in the *Law Quarterly Review* that Holland's Oxford crusades "made him a well-known figure in University politics, but they generally ranged him on the losing side, for legislators, in the University as elsewhere, tend to be impatient of the points which seemed to him important."[8] Yet the picture is overdrawn.

The issues that need examination are Holland's narrow vision and the inevitable changes that accompanied a long career. Other evidence suggests that Holland was not the epitome of pettiness suggested by the above testimony. Despite the myopic viewpoint Holland exhibited on occasion, Dicey regarded him as second only to Bryce among his friends in academic law. When they were undergraduates in 1858 Dicey had proposed Holland for membership in the Old Mortality society, a short-lived organization of clever Oxford students of the day.[9] Later Dicey designated Holland and Bryce, in the event of Dicey's sudden death, to go through his papers and determine if anything should be published posthumously.[10] Holland clearly had some redeeming traits that inspired such trust and affection over a long period of time. Brierly, for example, wrote of the "real kindliness which lay behind his slight reserve of manner."[11] It seems evident that Holland, rather formal in the discharge of his professorial duties, possessed a warmer side that surfaced in more intimate contact.

Perhaps the best evidence for this humane aspect of Holland's character appeared in a letter to professor Melville Madison Bigelow of the Boston University Law School, at that time a scholar of some repute in medieval English legal history. In response to the tragic death of Bigelow's son, Holland offered the consolation of one who had experienced the same sorrow: "The news of your sad loss has just reached me and fills me with sorrow and sympathy. I can well enter into your feelings, having myself, though after prolonged suspense, had to reconcile myself to the conviction that my younger son had been lost at sea."[12] The advice Holland rendered on that occasion stressed that Bigelow's academic work would provide the "best support and anodyne" for the loss he had endured.

Another issue that illuminated Holland's personality during the period of his professorship was the desirable balance between teaching and research as the ancient universities increasingly embraced the creation of new knowledge as a professional ideal. Holland argued throughout that the professors should bear a significant proportion of teaching responsibilities.[13] Holland, perhaps influenced in part by his own modest publication record after 1880, sought to provide both quality and quantity to undergraduate legal studies.[14] To some extent, therefore, the description of Holland as relentlessly professorial has exaggerated some of his more obvious shortcomings. That he took university affairs too seriously, without a sense of proportion, seems all too clear. Yet he had a more personable side, especially in his championing of undergraduate instruction, that belied the image of the reserved professor. In the age when the profession of law teaching began, Holland found it difficult to adapt to its new demands, caught as he was between the claims of teaching and research. In that trying situation, however, he proved the crucial person in the transformation of English jurisprudence away from its public policy roots and toward the academic discourse it became. More than any other individual Holland symbolized the synthesis of the analytical tradition with the new academic culture of the late Victorian period. In the 1920s he grew frail and lost much of his sight, but even the ravages of old age could not keep him from being, of all the Oxford law professoriate, the "typical academic scholar."[15] His personification of the new culture of academic law made him the perfect vehicle for taking the Benthamite tradition, as modified by Austin and Maine, into uncharted and perhaps disastrous directions.

The initial examples of Holland's scholarship fell squarely within the scope of analytical jurisprudence, the reigning position of which was reinforced by the growing academic prominence of Austin in the 1860s and 1870s. Holland wrote originally under the influence of Austin as representing the new academic trend, in addition to the search for scientific law that characterized the latter half of the nineteenth century. The first fruits of Holland's quest appeared in his advocacy of codification, "Bentham's great panacea,"[16] as a solution to the habitual complaints about the lack of design in the development of the common law. Prior to the preemption by the Judicature Acts of 1873 and 1875, the possibility of a real rationalization of English law acted as a spur to practical and academic ambitions for the generation that would reach professional maturity in the 1880s.

An early article on codification that Holland produced in 1867 contained both the insights and misconstructions that permitted him to shape so significantly the jurisprudential legacy bequeathed to him by Bentham and Austin. Holland acknowledged specifically that his promotion of codification rested on the need for scientific legislation, "which was initiated by the writings of Mr. Bentham and by the lectures of his distinguished follower, Mr. Austin."[17] After a review of the uneven results of the long campaign for law reform since Lord Brougham's speech in 1828, Holland discussed the various objections to a scheme for codification, especially the charge that a code would remove the flexibility long held to exemplify the virtues of the common law. The advantages Holland proposed included a greater public familiarity with the law, better training of lawyers, and the facilitation of legislation. In order to accomplish real codification, Holland argued, the law must undergo a process of expurgation of antiquated statutes, a sifting of the law to identify general principles, and then what remained could be put into the form of a digest. The last stages of the procedure would require consolidation or the synthesis of the law into an organic whole; complete consolidation would lead to codification; and finally revision would allow the code to change in response to new conditions as well as to preserve the benefits already attained.[18] Given the debates of the 1860s for or against codification, Holland offered little that was new or striking to this continuing controversy.

The most interesting statement in the article came in Holland's representation of Bentham as "perhaps the greatest theoretical jurist who has ever lived."[19] This was surely a most curious way to describe the individual who had devoted most of his life, whatever else one thinks of his efforts, to the practical improvement of society. In addition, as has been seen, the works that best illustrated Bentham's legal theory were at this time either unknown or little noticed by posterity. Bentham's place in legal theory has remained secure, but it is worth noting Holland's emphasis on the speculative elements of Bentham's work. Holland's stress on Bentham as a legal theorist anticipated the divorce that Holland would make later between theory and practice in jurisprudence, a separation inimical to Bentham's intentions. "Holland noted that what Bentham had called censorial jurisprudence, criticism of law as it was with a view to its amendment, belonged to the art of legislation, and not to jurisprudence."[20] In other words, Holland already regarded jurisprudence as primarily a topic of academic interest, whereas Bentham viewed his doctrines as essential to, and worthy of discussion by, an enlightened public. This narrow estimate of Bentham's influence was echoed in 1870 when Holland published his *Essays Upon the Form of the Law.* Here Holland stated that the case for codification depended as much upon changes in the form of the law as upon reform of substantive elements.[21] Holland had fastened upon the taxonomy of the law as more intellectually stimulating than its substantive elements. His focus on the formal aspects of the legal system at the expense of the doctrines that affected society most directly started Holland on the road that led ultimately to the conclusions advanced in his major contribution to English jurisprudence.

The Elements of Jurisprudence today has the appearance of a museum piece—so many editions in Holland's lifetime and yet none after his death. To examine it now transports the reader into a past era with intellectual concerns never to be revived. The work did not become a classic treatise that survived the death of the author into another age with a new editor and a fresh generation of law students. When Holland died, the book died with him.

The significance of *Elements,* however, was tied to three questions crucial for the understanding of the transformation in English jurisprudence that Holland symbolized. The importance of Holland's work can best be assessed from the answers to the following questions: why did *Elements* exercise such widespread influence for so long, why did it fade into obscurity so quickly, and what were its consequences for the future of English jurisprudence? To ascertain the answers it is necessary to return to an examination of *Elements,* and to some extent to an appreciation of its arguments.

In the preface to *Elements* Holland wrote about his two great predecessors, Bentham and Austin, and although he made it evident how much he admired their work, he believed it his duty to rectify and clarify where necessary in the continuation of their aims. By 1880 the cult of Austin in academic law circles had about run its course, so the use of Austin as a convenient target had already become a standard element of scholarly writing on jurisprudence. *The Province of Jurisprudence Determined,* Holland wrote, reflected Austin's gift for analysis struggling with "intractable and rarely handled material."[22] To Austin especially, "most Englishmen are indebted for such ideas as they possess of legal method."[23] Austin presented the material he examined in a manner so forceful that the reader could not forget its lessons.

After this high praise for Austin and the analytical tradition came the warnings about its defects. Among the problems Holland noted were the fragmentary nature of the analysis, the labored literary style, and the digressions to such topics as utilitarianism and codification. Austin had strayed too far from the proper domain of the law, Holland charged, and both he and Bentham were "singularly unsystematic."[24] Holland saw himself set firmly along the path of Bentham and Austin, but their work needed improvement by demonstration of their errors in emphasis and analysis. Holland rejected the validity of natural law theory, contemptuously dismissing "'Naturrecht' which may be described as 'Jurisprudence in the Air'."[25] Whatever criticisms Holland might have of the positivist heritage in English jurisprudence, he would not lead the counterrevolution.

The first chapter of *Elements* attempted to define law and to "set forth and explain those comparatively few and simple ideas which underlie the infinite variety of legal rules."[26] This latter goal placed Holland squarely in the middle of the approach to jurisprudence known as classical or formal theory. The classical theorists assumed that the common law, despite its surface diversity or even chaos, ultimately rested upon internally consistent principles that represented the rational arrangement of legal categories.[27] Holland's aim, therefore, was to apprehend and to present those principles that shaped the structure of the common law, and to explicate how those legal rules related to one another. As Holland once wrote to Oliver Wendell Holmes, he rejoiced that "such a scientific jurist as yourself is in a position not only to talk about, but to create, legal principles."[28] The discovery of these elementary postulates became the special vocation of the Oxford professoriate, whether Anson, Dicey, Holland, or Pollock. That such fundamental axioms of the legal system existed at all was taken as a matter of faith, not demonstrated empirically. The basic rationality of the law had to exist, or else all claims to study and to teach law as a science would founder. Because of this imperative, "developing a comprehensive and internally consistent structure of legal categories was a central, if not the central objective of classical legal thought."[29] This predetermination of speculative outcomes ensured that Holland would find his prized principles by restricting the scope of his quest.

When Holland examined law, he defined it as the "formal science of positive law," a phrase that resonated with ideas drawn from his analytical forebears. This definition permitted him to narrow the focus of his inquiry. Jurisprudence was "not the material science of those portions of the law which various nations have in common," but a formal science dependent upon the existing positive laws of a single country.[30] Holland went even further in limiting the philosophical perspective, writing that "the term Jurisprudence is wrongly applied to actual systems of law, or to current views of law, or to suggestions for its amendment, but is the name of a science. This science is a formal, or analytical, rather than a material one. It is the science of actual, or positive, law."[31] The formal science of jurisprudence was differentiated from the broader field of morality, with which it should have no relationship. Holland was adamant in ruling out for consideration "digressions and polemics upon questions lying wholly outside of its appropriate province."[32] Holland fit perfectly Morison's description of the type of successor who altered the Austinian legacy and how it went awry; a legal scholar with little interest in the philosophical springs of Austin's thinking.[33] In the process of deciding the proper boundaries of jurisprudence, Holland removed from its study the broad societal vision so characteristic of Bentham.

Holland defined a law, in the proper sense of the term, as "a general rule of human action, taking cognisance only of external acts, enforced by a determinate authority, which authority is human, and, among human authorities, is that which is paramount in a political society."[34] Holland's use of the word in the previous quotation has remained a remarkable feature only of *Elements,* for it suggests how many topics Holland excluded from his purview. His reliance on the Austinian language of sovereignty for the validity of law focused on one aspect of Austin's work, but he used it as serenely as if Maine's critique had never appeared. It followed from Holland's argument that law in its proper sense could not exist prior to the formation of a state; customary law might amount to prescribed rules of conduct but could not truly constitute law. "It will be sufficient to remark," he wrote, "that until the State is constituted there can be no law, in the strict sense of the term."[35] Once again Holland failed to provide an adequate analysis of the state and sovereignty because he conceived these terms in too narrow a fashion; his account "had come to be more and more generally regarded as an over-simplification of the facts which can no longer be usefully applied to the complex structure of modern States."[36] On this issue, as with so many others, Holland had the effect of limiting the range of discussion instead of expanding it.

The same argument extends to Holland's work on international law, an extension of the conclusions he drew in *Elements.* If law derived from the authority of a state, international law became law only by courtesy. Because international law was "unsupported by the authority of a State,"[37] it did not command recognition as law in the true sense. Holland called international law the "vanishing point of Jurisprudence; since it lacks any arbiter of disputed questions, *save public opinion.*"[38] International law was law by analogy because it represented only the moral code of nations.[39] Given this conception of his subject, Holland's reputation was based on his mastery of detail, not the theoretical exploration of international law itself. Holland wrestled with the implications of Austinian theory for international law most of his life without ever resolving them in a persuasive manner.

In the end Holland's passion for classification also had an inhibiting effect on jurisprudential debate. The emphasis on locating the ultimate rationality of the common law caused Holland to rely on an artificial categorization. The "logical precision" of *Elements* stirred criticism because it did violence to the actual structure of English law.[40] The common law had developed over the centuries without regimentation, so Holland's attempt to impose a theoretical structure would be artificial.[41] The rigidity so characteristic of *Elements* in the end did not stimulate debate so much as close it, and it was here that his personality appeared to affect the nature of his academic work. Holland went from edition to edition, confident in his conclusions, and barely deigning to acknowledge the mounting dissatisfaction with his pronouncements.

It is now possible to answer the questions originally posed about the influence of *The Elements of Jurisprudence.* Its appeal extended to both law teachers and law students.

On its appearance *Elements* earned high praise (usually from other academics) as the definitive embodiment of what legal science was assumed to mean: "Holland moved remorselessly forward from one proposition to another, starting from the nature of the law as a whole and gradually unfolding the various legal questions in greater and greater detail."[42] Holland tried to provide a grammar of the law, carefully distinguished from what law actually existed. What later scholars denounced as excessively formal, Holland's contemporaries regarded as profoundly illuminating. For example, Sir Frederick Pollock commented in an 1882 lecture: "It would not be too much to say that Professor Holland's *Elements of Jurisprudence* is the first work of pure scientific jurisprudence . . . that is, of the general science of law distinctly separated from the ethical part of politics."[43] Pollock also praised Holland's style that improved considerably on the tortured language of Austin: "Professor Holland's is concise without abruptness, flowing without tediousness, and distinct without wearisome repetitions."[44] *Elements* expressed precisely those assumptions of the professoriate, particularly about the existence of fundamental principles at the heart of the common law, and thus made certain its success as an academic endeavor: "It was indeed one of a number of books which appeared in Oxford in the eighties which made sense of English law, and showed that it could be handled as intelligibly and as rationally as the German jurists were doing for the modernized form of Roman law still operating in their own country."[45] It gathered great prestige within the academy at home and abroad but precious little in the wider world.[46] In the expanding world of academic law this achievement was sufficient, and Holland rested on his laurels for the remainder of his career.

Holland's book also flourished because of its utility for law students. Not only did it provide an introduction to the serious study of jurisprudence, it also functioned well as a last review of the law prior to examinations.[47] It served the student at both ends of an academic career, especially after the work had gained professorial approval. "An intelligent student could, when he had finished reading the book," Lawson concluded, "have had no doubt what law was about; and that, at a time when he was expected to read jurisprudence as an introduction to law and not, as now, as the crown of his academic experience, was of no small service."[48] Students, whatever their individual reaction, had to engage this text that their teachers embraced so enthusiastically lest they fail to keep abreast of scholarly fashion. Holland was the first beneficiary of the penchant for academic trends that accompanied the new faculty culture.

The dramatic eclipse of Holland in the world of jurisprudence occurred as a result of several different developments. Holland, having written an enormously successful work, simply abandoned the subject and never returned. After 1880 he devoted himself primarily to the study of international law, a field he had just argued did not amount to law at all. While he eventually acquired a substantial reputation in this area and helped to shape its modern evolution, none of his publications gained the status of *Elements.* Any scholarly treatise ages inevitably, and without Holland's attention to other work in the field, such as the discussion of sociological jurisprudence in the

United States, his book became dated. As the reputation of Austin declined prior to 1914, Holland's work, despite its professed differences, shared in the growing disdain. Even Holland now suffered from denunciation as too general in approach, as opposed to the specialized studies that academic lawyers admired and produced.

Although Holland prospered as a result of the professionalization of law teaching at the universities, his typicality as an academic actually harmed the long-term prospects of his work. Whereas his colleagues at Oxford gained some measure of public recognition, his contributions to naval prize law and other aspects of international law confirmed his standing as an academic authority with no other audience. His letters to *The Times* too often revealed his pedantic side and hurt his stature.[49] That trait, combined with his reluctance to engage critics, rendered his arguments ineffective. This defect caused Holmes to remark that Holland could not sting, Holmes's shorthand for a thinker incapable of writing about fundamental assumptions.[50] Holland fell victim to the prime characteristic of academic culture in the twentieth century: the rapid change in intellectual fashion.

Finally, the reputation of *Elements* waned because its underlying premises became as obsolete as the era they embodied. Holland believed that an enlightened and educated public opinion supplied the necessary moral standards for the functioning of the English legal system. This concern of Holland and other Victorian jurists had shaped the response to criticisms of their approach to private law: public opinion supplied the moral sanction that positive law could not provide, and thus moral precepts acted as laws by analogy without violation of the positivist tradition.[51] In responding to Holmes's famous path of the law article, Holland wrote that "I am especially glad that you make it quite clear the law is differentiated from morality by the public force which lies behind the decisions of the Courts."[52] Public opinion represented the alternative force that gave backing to the prescriptions of private law. As consensus (if one had ever existed) in Victorian public opinion disappeared, it became absurd to explain the practical working of the legal system in such naive terms. The fragmentation of late Victorian society during and after the 1880s made the single standard of middle class opinion woefully inadequate to account for legal phenomena.

The same problems dogged Holland's attempt to define international law as a system of rules whose enforcement came from the moral opinion of the community of nations. Not only did this adhere too slavishly to the original Austinian doctrine that true law could exist only when backed by the authority of a sovereign state, it brought Holland most of the way back to natural law theory, where obligation derived from moral imperatives. From Bentham onward the separation of law from morality had remained a specific aim of positivism, but Holland apparently saw no contradiction between his jurisprudence and his theory of international law. The circularity of Holland's thought lessened its appeal and accelerated its loss of reputation.

With respect to his impact on the subsequent history of English jurisprudence, Holland has played a major, if unacknowledged, role. Perhaps more than any other single work in English jurisprudence, Holland's *Elements* reduced the scope of philosophical inquiry and turned jurisprudence inward as an academic discipline, taking it away from broader public policy discussions. The great practitioners of English jurisprudence had in common the conviction that their enterprise must be aimed at an educated public. Whatever the degree of disagreement among jurists, jurisprudence imposed upon the writer the obligation to investigate the subject in its broadest context. Holland's conceptualization of the analytical tradition transformed the broad sweep of Benthamite speculation into a mere picking at the desiccated skeleton of positivist jurisprudence. The posthumous triumph of Austinian jurisprudence, in the hands of Holland, "led to its atrophying, not because of its logical or empirical problems but because the assumptions which had underpinned its success ceased to hold."[53] Analytical jurisprudence retained its place as the primary methodology for legal philosophy in England, but even there the influence of Holland led to a long period of sterility.

Thus Holland took the fecund legacy of analytical jurisprudence and placed intellectual limits on its doctrines: "Since Holland proposed to use the term 'analytical' as equivalent to 'formal', the effect of his notions on the ideas of his readers concerning what analytical jurisprudence was in Bentham's and Austin's hands was in the highest degree unfortunate."[54] Intellectual leaders in every discipline, of course, have had to endure the work of popularizers or, even worse, the sympathy of critics who distort even as they endorse: "Holland's text applied classical legal scholarship's enthusiasm for systemization, conceptualization and exposition in a manner which was dogmatic, narrow and pedantic."[55] This latter description met neatly, however, the demands of the nascent profession of academic lawyers. After the Judicature Acts of 1873 and 1875, the market for treatises explaining and rationalizing the state of the law increased substantially. Legal reform led to the discovery of principles, not the reverse.[56] As Sugarman also concluded: "In other words, for Dicey, Bryce, Pollock, Anson, Holland, Salmond and other classical law dons, their desired professional legitimacy in the eyes of sceptical universities and a largely hostile profession required the assertion of a special body of expertise which jurists monopolized."[57] If Holland proved one villain of this scenario, he had plenty of support from his academic peers. The conjunction of academic law with jurisprudential speculation became anything but providential.

Equally as important, therefore, in the restriction of jurisprudence's domain was the great alteration in university life now recognized as academic professionalization concurrent with the foundation of modern disciplines. Harold Perkin has made the concept of professionalism the major element in interpreting British history over the last century.[58] Law was no stranger to this process, and Holland symbolized several manifestations of this tendency. The word "professional" has become so elastic that any attempt at unequivocal definition must fail; but, in the context of the late Victorian university, it had several connotations crucial to the direction of academic law. One certainly entailed the establishment of the law curriculum securely within the university.[59] Law had suffered from its ambivalent role as both vocational training and the humanistic contemplation of philosophical questions. As various disciplines proffered agendas for university reform, Holland and the other members of the Oxford law professoriate responded with a program of their own: "To continue to limit the bulk of instruction to Blackstone and Justinian was an anachronism. A strong lobby insisted that the teaching of law at university ought to be based on general principles rather than the rote learning of boundless detail."[60] Holland's *Elements* suited this purpose perfectly by virtue of its severe reductionism. For the law professoriate, alas, reform of the law curriculum to attract more and better students did not succeed, as Bryce conceded in his valedictory lecture in 1893 as regius professor of civil law, which came to symbolize the disappointments of those who had hoped to make law a central feature of undergraduate education.[61] Law made some inroads into the traditional dominance of the classics, but not enough to make a major difference.

A more general process in which Holland and his colleagues participated was the establishment of university teaching as a separate profession.[62] Throughout the nineteenth century university teaching, once characterized by indolence and sinecure, was transformed by the German university model and the missionary impulse of educational optimism. This process meant not only a quest for greater status and more equitable compensation, it also raised questions about the nature and purpose of the university in national life.[63] The task of educating the national elite was no longer a sufficient incentive. For the legal academics, professional advancement suggested an emphasis on research, for the creation of new knowledge became regarded as one test (among many others) of academic success: "As the college tutors became professional academics, research ideals were necessary to differentiate their career from that of schoolmasters."[64] Professionalization affected every dimension of university life, and legal academics attempted to stay abreast of this dynamic process: "The professionalization of academic life was the change most often noted by observers at the time, and highbrow circles generally favoured the changes."[65] The research ideal held out the promise of a golden age for legal academics in their desire to place jurisprudence on a scientific footing.

From the 1880s onward at Oxford the law faculty made numerous contributions to the realization of this new research ideal. Many of their works, however, dealt with separate branches of the law such as torts and contract but rarely with subjects of a broader scope. The research model doubtless helped in the creation of a new legal literature that marked a substantial improvement over its predecessors. Law shared the triumph of the research ideal with the other university disciplines: "Operating with the force of an ideology, the ideal of new knowledge eventually pushed all branches of learning to new levels of achievement."[66] The addition of research degrees such as the B.Litt. and the B.Sc. in 1895 at Oxford showed the new respect that the word "research" commanded.[67] The awarding of research fellowships reinforced this process by passing on scholarly obligations to students. The cycle of professionalization was now complete. Holland was not a forceful advocate of the new research ideal, in part perhaps because his publication record paled in comparison to some of his colleagues. He fought some of his academic battles to retain a balance between teaching and research responsibilities, but, as with his other university goals, in the end he admitted defeat. For Holland, as for many others, the research model eventually triumphed: "The acceptance of research ideals proved to be the only satisfactory rationale for overcoming the problem of 'teaching drudgery' for dons who viewed academic work as their profession."[68] Moreover, professional reputation by the turn of the century became measurable primarily in terms of research; publication had become the road to advancement and academic recognition.

As a practical matter, academic professionalization meant an identification with the prestige of science. Long before Holland's *Elements,* the call to establish law on a scientific basis had an impact on academic law.[69] Part of the problem for Holland and his peers was their general lack of familiarity with science itself, so the word "science" rarely became more than a talisman to hide the difficulties that plagued the endeavor. The standardization of legal knowledge demanded formal methodology, lest personal discretion betray an unscholarly approach.[70] The scientific method also applied to the organization and dissemination of knowledge, not just its creation.[71] The invocation of science became the rallying cry for those academic lawyers who wished to secure a greater status for their work.

Professionalization also imposed the obligation to serve the public by provision of a more satisfactory legal system through organization and explanation of legal principles. To meet this requirement meant an inevitable focus on specific issues to the detriment of law in a wider setting. The embrace of professionalism resulted in "the enormous body of legal scholarship, the rise of a professoriate devoted largely to producing it, the gradual formalization of legal education in a university setting, where it was progressively divorced from practical applicability and dignified with the title of legal science."[72] The result was a separate legal culture that devised its own internal mandates. If the new academic law had actually served the public as envisioned, its fate would have been far different. Ultimately it fell victim to the demands of the academy at the expense of its other self-proclaimed missions.

The most obvious example of the professionalization of academic law was the founding of the *Law Quarterly Review* in 1884.[73] Periodicals aimed at an audience with a specific interest in the law had existed for over half a century, but these were usually vocational in orientation and without the intellectual rigor demanded by academic lawyers.[74] The resolution to the problem lay in the launching of a journal that would meet the needs of academic lawyers, including an outlet for scholarship, service to practitioners, and, it was hoped, guidance to the judiciary.[75] The *Law Quarterly Review* was begun at a meeting in Sir William Markby's rooms at All Souls College, with Anson, Dicey, Holland, and Pollock in attendance.[76] Pollock credited Holland with providing the intellectual leadership of the project, while Markby managed the business affairs of the new venture. Pollock recalled that the *Law Quarterly Review* aimed at the "promotion of legal science without neglect of practice, and devoted chiefly to the Common Law but not disregarding comparative study."[77] From the outset the new journal would embody the desire for scientific law that Holland's *Elements* exemplified. The periodical succeeded beyond the wildest dreams of its proponents, leading shortly thereafter to the *Harvard Law Review* and the consequent proliferation of academic law reviews throughout common-law jurisdictions. It has set a standard of legal scholarship equaled by few and surpassed by none.

It would seem churlish to decry the imposing scholarly record of the *Law Quarterly Review*, but the fact remains that its achievement was secured at the price of increasing specialization. The advent of journals in the twentieth century devoted to a particular field within the law has represented the logical consequence of the founders' underlying assumptions about professionalization. Law reviews quickly came to specialize in technical articles well beyond the layperson, and they advocated dense argument at the expense of the clear communication of ideas.[78] Scholarly expertise became defined in increasingly specialized areas and was measured by publication, so academic respectability expanded to accommodate the narrow fields that emerged. This process was certainly not unique to law, for many other disciplines, including history, experienced the same debate about the scientific nature of its inquiry, elaborated the research ideal, and had approximately the same outcomes.[79] The foundation of the *English Historical Review* in 1886, for example, arose from the same professional concerns that led to the *Law Quarterly Review*. In each case the result was that academics looked inward to their own disciplines, where scholars tended to write for one another.[80] For example, the *En-*

glish Historical Review remained at one thousand subscribers for the next forty years, a monument to the professional ideal with no concessions to the amateur historian or general public.[81]

The demands of professional achievement facilitated the development of the invisible college, "that network of informal relationships and personal acquaintance which links academic men, and particularly researchers in the same discipline but different institutions."[82] Ranging from collaboration to the polite exchange of offprints, such friendships dominated Anglo-American jurisprudence in the era of professionalization.[83] Other innovations such as publishing projects, conferences, and scholarly societies marked the "twin phenomena of professionalisation and specialisation so characteristic of later nineteenth-century intellectual developments."[84] Such professional activities illustrated the dilemma of the academic legal culture, for "the more it succeeded in establishing itself as a desirable form of professional preparation, the more it tended to lose its 'liberal' character."[85]

Holland was but a bit player in these dramatic trends in academic law, and he did not even cultivate scholarly connections as some of his colleagues did. Yet no single career epitomized the consequences of professionalization as did Holland's. Where once jurisprudence had addressed the educated public, Holland's *Elements of Jurisprudence* sought primarily the approval of his learned peers in the academy. As Morison has written of analytical jurisprudence in general during Holland's ascendancy, it "was turning inward upon law and losing the vital and continuing inspiration for it which came from the determination to understand legal phenomena on the basis of a general philosophy of the world in general and the fields of social sciences within it."[86] The generalist had once typified the student of law, the mid-Victorian man of letters in Maine's image, but the new professional jurists did not accept the responsibility this type suggested. The transition to issues of interest only to an academic audience helped set the agenda of English jurisprudence for nearly a century. By sharpening the focus of the law, Holland and his colleagues had narrowed it.

Thus when it came to creating a public role for the academic lawyers and establishing credentials for a substantial influence on policy, Holland and his generation failed signally to gain this objective. The historical development of the common law had occurred almost exclusively through the practical training of apprenticeship, with little contribution from the universities. Part of Blackstone's importance had derived from his call for an academic study of English law. In his inaugural lecture as Vinerian professor in 1883, Dicey thought it worthwhile to ponder the question of whether English law could be taught at the universities at all.[87] The tension between the practical and the theoretical aspects of the common law has proved impossible for academic lawyers to overcome. As P. S. Atiyah has written recently: "I will start with the fairly uncontroversial suggestion that English lawyers are not only more inclined to the pragmatic and somewhat hostile to the theoretical approach, but positively glory in their preference."[88] This attitude troubled academic lawyers not only because it challenged the validity of their labors, but also because many of the academics took this characteristic to be among the glories of the common law, happily far removed from the ethereal speculations of continental theorists. The doubts about legal theory have persisted:

> In the common law "theory" is typically thought of as something set apart from the central concerns of legal scholars or practitioners. "Legal theory" is a distinct subject, an intellectual compartment relatively isolated from other legal studies. Theory itself is contrasted with "practice" and often looked upon with some suspicion by those who see themselves as concerned with the realities of professional legal practice, or with problems of practical reform or doctrinal exegesis.[89]

Academic lawyers have had nobody to blame but themselves for this state of affairs since Holland's era.

Not only did the academic lawyers fail to win the battle between theory and practice, as it turned out the campaign for legal studies on a scientific basis did not have the revolutionary consequences they anticipated. One reason for this result stemmed from the nature of the educational mission the universities had undertaken. One effect of the call to academic seriousness and scholarly rigor was the preparation of students for professional success.[90] Instead of spearheading a radical alteration in legal education, Holland and his colleagues were forced to conclude sadly that the best students still read classics or history before taking their legal education at the Inns of Court. Reformed academic law still could not attract the best students; the universities supplied neither the resources nor the incentive for the victory of the academic lawyers.[91] In addition, the revolution foundered because the changes in law teaching had unanticipated conservative results: "The paradox of later nineteenth-century university reform was that the endowment of research and 'scientific' study could actually reinforce the existing curriculum and abstract it further from modern society."[92] None of the academic lawyers recognized in time that scientific law did not necessarily herald a new age of legal enlightenment.

The best evidence for the failure of the legal academics came from Holland himself. In a letter to Holmes in 1891 he wrote: "It is refreshing to find legal studies spoken of with enthusiasm and respect. The law professors are in this country a feeble folk. The profession in London sneers at us as impractical, while our academical colleagues pity us as narrow-minded Philistines. There are some signs of better days in store for us, but the change of opinion is slow in coming."[93] For Holland the better days never quite materialized. Academic law had nowhere to turn but toward contemplation of its limited horizons. This process accented its support of existing conditions; the relationship of the academic lawyer to the judiciary changed from instruction to approbation. The ultimate result was that "the early legal academics—Maine, Bryce, Dicey, Anson, and Pollock at Oxford and Maitland at Cambridge—did not produce serious successors. Those who came after saw their role as rationalizing the words of the judges rather than questioning them."[94] The abortive coup against traditional legal arrangements left the academic lawyers of the period 1900–50 to define jurisprudence as essentially glosses upon Holland, an intellectual prison from which few escaped. Neither legal history nor jurisprudence flourished. Historians and lawyers drew further apart in their endeavors; and legal theory was trapped within the boundaries Holland had drawn. Writings on jurisprudence were either esoteric or pedestrian, focused almost exclusively on the academic aspects of analytical jurisprudence, and resistant to any return to the conception of jurisprudence as a fundamental part of social analysis: "The modern university no longer possessed a common intellectual language. Instead each specialized academic discipline has its own language that is intelligible in a substantial sense only to its own practitioners."[95] In the case of jurisprudence, the result became legal inquiry that "has contributed little to art, life or law."[96] Not until the professorship of H. L. A. Hart was there a significant attempt to escape from the legacy that Holland symbolized.

The position of the legal academic, defined in the 1880s, has remained basically unchanged in its ancillary role to the legal system. Regulation of legal education has eluded the universities: "Even today there is nothing in Britain to compare with the powerful professional law schools in the United States. Legal education was, and essentially still is, under the control not of the university but of the profession which was dominated by those in practice rather than in academic life."[97] The point is not whether this result has been for the better or the worse, but that it has shaped the jurisprudence that academics have produced. "It is not, I think," Atiyah has written, "unreasonable to suggest that in the English legal system the scholar or teacher is a person with a decidedly inferior status. We are so used to this disparity of status in England that it usually passes without comment, and tends to be regarded as part of the natural order of things."[98] Thus the definition of an academic legal culture did not live up to the expectations of the professors of the 1880s. As Collini has written of the divide between jurisprudence and the broad culture of late Victorian England: "The development of legal education in the late nineteenth century, which promised at first to help bridge this gulf, came eventually to drive a deeper wedge between the legal and the wider intellectual worlds."[99] Where they had hoped to emulate the influence of a Blackstone or a Bentham, they found that their heralded new approaches to legal study satisfied academic trendiness but not the general public: "The direct and immediate influence of the classical law dons over the legal profession was relatively slight. The vast majority of lawyers continued to learn their law beyond rather than within the academy. The ancient prejudices against the academic lawyer seem to have survived."[100] Holland enjoyed considerable success, but this was framed by the nature of academic law itself. *The Elements of Jurisprudence,* the classic example of English analytical jurisprudence, had the unintended consequence of virtually exhausting the potential of that school and rendering it incapable of sustaining its former creativity:

> Holland's jurisprudence was in a crucial respect a very impoverished version of the theory which Bentham had developed a century before. For Bentham the purpose of jurisprudence had been the reform of the existing law; Holland excluded this notion altogether from its subject-matter: he elevated logical analysis, the instrument to this end, into the end itself. This produced a jurisprudence which was avowedly apolitical—one

which had developed, via Austin, from Bentham's methodology, but which had rejected his critical utilitarianism and the demands for reform which that implied.[101]

The result of the efforts of legal academicians was deleterious, for it fostered an intellectual ghetto that stifled attempts to return to the earlier issues of English jurisprudence. The fragmentation of jurisprudence was complete, for new academic disciplines staked claims for the scientific study of society.[102] By the turn of the twentieth century, the eclipse of jurisprudence as broad social interpretation was fully realized.

Chapter Seven

H. L. A. Hart
Law and Morality Reconsidered

In the first half of the twentieth century, as the generation of academic lawyers at Oxford who had matured in the 1880s eventually retired, their successors found little room for creativity. The paths into which Holland had turned jurisprudence now required learned commentaries on previous writings without concern for the discipline's potential, and certainly far removed from the censorial role that Bentham had defined for himself. Scholars such as John W. Salmond, Paul Vinogradoff, William Holdsworth, and Carleton Allen earned solid reputations, and their careers do not deserve cavalier dismissal. Yet it must be said that their jurisprudence has never been mistaken, in quality or focus, for that of their more famous predecessors. Holdsworth, for example, spent much of his life on his monumental *History of English Law,* which reached seventeen volumes when it was completed by others in 1972 more than a quarter century after his death in 1944. His contributions to jurisprudence were sparse, except for his interesting appraisals of earlier figures. In the 1920s this situation contributed to a substantial diminution of respect for English jurisprudence; in 1922 American jurist Roscoe Pound penned a scathing assessment of the Oxford law faculty, calling Holdsworth "very mediocre" and terming the jurisprudence as "old line analytical-historical. It has no relation to anything existent."[1] Jurisprudence as the discipline to interpret social phenomena had come to rest on narrow foundations.

At the end of the decade the potential of the analytical tradition appeared at the point of exhaustion, and "by the late 1920s, if not before, there were clear signs of crisis."[2] Part of the problem resulted from the self-absorption that characterized a jurisprudence cut off from the philosophical roots inaugurated by Bentham: "Jurisprudence in the universities had become a routine reading and re-reading of a canon of texts and text-books. Excepting a handful of brilliant exceptions, the subject was moribund."[3] Sociological jurisprudence in the United States aroused little but intellectual scorn in England. The jurisprudential ferment known collectively as realism in the 1930s suffered massive disdain in English academic circles. Analytical jurisprudence, protected by the prejudice of decades, seemed to have reached an intellectual dead end.

By 1950 the role for the academic lawyer of commentator on legislation and on decided cases had become well established at the expense of broader concerns: "This, though parasitic on practice, is nonetheless the unmistakable, unchallenged province of academic law."[4] The original purpose to offer social commentary or even to uncover the principles embedded in the common law had given way to the learned gloss on a particular aspect of the law usually, though not always, of little interest to the judiciary or the bar. The attempt to make academic law the arbiter of the legal system had failed, and the status of the academic lawyer languished:

> The blame that is usually put on Austin and his more mediocre successors and interpreters should, rather, fall on Pollock and his less distinguished followers and imitators, who subordinated their original notion of law as something independent of judicial decisions to their recognition of the social and, in some cases no doubt, the intellectual superiority of counsel and judges, and therefore contented themselves with publishing student textbooks which did their best to expound and simplify the wisdom lodged in judicial decisions.[5]

Harold Laski, for example, described Holdsworth as looking as if he wanted to throw himself prostrate before a law lord. The loss of the censorial function had other consequences as well. Jurisprudence had lost its place in the law curriculum and little professional interest was apparent: "Jurisprudence in Britain was scarcely an exciting and burgeoning field of enquiry."[6] Focus remained on those practical subjects upon which practice would depend. Into this world of diminished expectations in 1952, however, came H. L. A. Hart by virtue of his election to the Corpus chair of jurisprudence at Oxford. His selection restored vitality and excitement to English jurisprudence.

Herbert Hart was born in 1907 and attended New College, Oxford, where he earned a first in classics in 1929. Three years later he was called to the bar and spent the next eight years in successful practice as a Chancery barrister in highly technical areas of the law such as taxation and trusts. In 1940 he began service for the duration of World War II as a civilian member of military intelligence. At the cessation of hostilities he returned to New College as fellow and tutor in philosophy. In 1952 he won election to the Corpus chair and held that post until 1968. For the next four years he was senior research fellow at University College, and then became the principal of Brasenose College from 1972 until his retirement in 1978.[7] In retirement Hart continued his scholarly writing, particularly his extensive writings on the jurisprudence of Jeremy Bentham. Hart remained a central pillar of the Bentham industry that flourished in the 1970s and 1980s until his death in 1992.

Although his academic career had been highly productive, Hart will always be identified with one book, *The Concept of Law* (1961), a work that will undoubtedly rank as the most influential on English jurisprudence published in the twentieth century.[8] MacCormick has described it correctly as a "work of international eminence which even its strongest critics have acknowledged as a masterpiece worth at least the compliment of careful refutation."[9] From its initial appearance *The Concept of Law* attracted attention because of its avowed attempt to return to basic questions of jurisprudence and perhaps provide new answers after the long period of intellectual dormancy. The book was an academic lawyer's dream, for it touched upon fundamental issues in a forthright fashion, and its economical, even sparse, style invited close reading. Hart's book rapidly became the center of protracted analysis and discussion (which continues to the present), most of it in the form of law review articles in all common-law jurisdictions. Arousing interest greater than any other work on English jurisprudence in this century, it revived the soporific field at a single stroke. Hart established a standing in legal philosophy that eclipsed those predecessors whose work fell mainly in this century: "H. L. A. Hart, more than perhaps any other theorist in the 20th century, has defined and clarified the debates over many of the major issues in contemporary legal philosophy."[10] For three decades, despite extensive critiques and the work of other jurists such as Ronald Dworkin, *The Concept of Law* has exercised a hegemony rarely accomplished in any academic field.

The Concept of Law derived part of its success from Hart's decision to ignore the accumulated detritus of the analytical tradition as it had developed historically. Refusing to be bound by the narrow confines that were the legacy of Holland and his successors, he bypassed Holland and other jurists who had served as the pilot fish of analytical jurisprudence, and returned to an examination of both Bentham and Austin. For historians in 1961 Bentham retained significance only as the progenitor of the academic controversy about the manner in which his ideas on legislation had acted to spur government reforms. The antecedents of the welfare state, thought in 1961 to be the culmination of Victorian reform movements, had spurred a debate in 1958 and 1960 by Oliver MacDonagh and Henry Parris in the pages of the *Historical Journal.* The "Nineteenth-Century Revolution in Government" discussion kept Bentham's name before historians, but rarely did this attention include any reference to his stature as a jurist. Hart's work, at the minimum, demonstrated that Bentham amounted to much more in intellectual history than the *eminence grise* of the welfare state.

Since 1914 Austin had continued in the role of straw man for academic lawyers. His work served primarily as a convenient corpus of ideas against which to teach because his doctrines were known almost exclusively through depiction by unsympathetic critics such as Pollock. Reconsiderations of Austin had virtually disappeared, and his status as token target obscured the primacy of Bentham in the formation of the analytical tradition. Hart reversed this customary denigration, and despite his own trenchant criticisms acknowledged that Austin had asked the right questions even if he had given the wrong answers. Hart gave the work of both Bentham and Austin a respect that the two jurists had not enjoyed for decades. He freed them from the ritual condemnation that had been their lot and restored them to the prominence they deserved.

Hart began *The Concept of Law* by noting that law as a discipline suffered from the seemingly insoluble problem that jurists could not even agree on a basic definition of their subject; this circumstance led to the diffuse nature of legal speculation. In his first chapters Hart drew new definitions from a critical reading of Bentham and Austin to serve as tools for the resolution of knotty questions such as the nature of command. Hart actually read Bentham and Austin instead of what later jurists had written about them and what their jurisprudence meant; the result was, at least for Austin, that "both Austin's philosophy and his specific theory of law were squarely examined and perceptively assessed, while many aspects of the Austinian myth which had developed were dissected and attacked."[11] Where Hart found Austin wanting, he stated his differences in a tone that indicated true respect for the long-neglected jurist. Hart now became the primary medium for dissemination of Austin's work, and his account did not initially arouse opposition.[12] Whether Hart's reading of Austin was correct has remained open to debate; Moles, for example, has argued that Hart's version of Austin "bore little resemblance to the real thing."[13] This issue has not been resolved, but the central fact that Hart brought both Bentham and Austin in the original back into the mainstream of English jurisprudence is beyond dispute.

In his examination of Austin on sovereignty, for example, Hart found him on the right track but too simplistic in his analysis. Hart argued that two elements of Austin's argument required special attention. The first concerned Austin's idea of a habit of obedience and what exactly this meant. The second was the notion of continuity—"the *continuity* of the authority to make law possessed by a succession of different legislators, and the *persistence* of laws long after their maker and those who rendered him habitual obedience have perished."[14] Though he did not pursue the point in historical detail, Hart sought an explanation that would hold for Austin's era as well as for his own. For him a doctrine of sovereignty must propound fundamental qualities that defined a legal system and were not bound by the conditions of a specific age. In the end, therefore, Hart wrote that sovereignty "involves the substitution, for the too simple notion of habits of obedience to a sovereign person, of the notion of currently accepted fundamental rules specifying a class or line of persons whose word is to constitute a standard of behaviour for the society, i.e. who have the *right* to legislate."[15] Austin did not need refutation, but rather explication and refinement.

After the review of the difficulties that Bentham and Austin had not resolved, in the second half of the book Hart focused more specifically on his own conclusions about the nature of law, which might be summarized in his concentration on the concept of a legal system rather than law. This focus discussed the role that legal rules played in a general system of law. On this topic there were many antecedents, notably the skepticism about legal rules characteristic of American realism in the 1930s. Austin had argued that law was a species of command, but Hart indicated that this was clearly untrue, for not every legal rule entailed a command or prohibition. In this context Hart used the metaphor of the gunman's version of command to illustrate the failings of Austin's analysis. Austin had viewed law only as a species of coercion, whereas law had other variations of obligation.

In perhaps his most famous phrase, Hart postulated a rule of recognition that acted as the instrument for the identification of a valid law. Hart explained that a legal system was composed of primary rules of legal obligation and secondary rules that regulated change and continuity in the law itself.[16] He saw the union of primary and secondary rules, with the accompanying rule of recognition, as constituting the essence of a legal system, although he admitted that his analysis could not provide an answer to every question of jurisprudence. Primary rules imposed duties upon the citizen, and secondary rules conferred power and explained the ways by which authority might be altered.[17] While this distinction between primary and secondary rules has received frequent criticism because Hart himself never resolved ambiguities in their application, it succeeded in becoming a focal point for subsequent discussion. In short, Hart disagreed with the Bentham/Austin doctrine that legal rules necessarily had sanctions to make them effective.[18]

Hart emphasized that legal obligation was not so much a matter of coercion as of social consensus. This assertion applied to those officials who operated the government's legal system as well as those citizens who obeyed the law without responsibility for its enforcement. Hart attempted to analyze a legal system from the standpoint of an individual responsible for the exercise of authority instead of the more traditional position of a neutral observer standing apart from the system.[19] Using this approach Hart reinterpreted the themes that had resonated in English jurisprudence from the time of Blackstone: sovereignty, law as command, and the necessity to separate law from morality. The historian's confidence in Hart's analysis would be greater if he had cited actual instances of legal controversy to illustrate his points, but he did not include such evidence. Thus *The Concept of Law* was truly an extended essay in legal theory.

In the construction of his jurisprudence Hart added to its appeal by the realization of a cherished goal for most academics: the synthesis of different disciplines to provide new insights into issues of long standing. Hart achieved this remarkable feat by drawing upon his training in philosophy, abetted by the then reigning academic orthodoxy of linguistic analysis, and uniting them to focus on language problems inherent in legal analysis. He had rehearsed this methodology in perhaps the most significant of his early publications when he had examined the problems associated with the definition of a word such as "right" so often used in different senses by jurists.[20] In the attempt to escape from the malaise that enveloped English jurisprudence, Hart relied on the philosophical discussion of language by such leading figures as Ludwig Wittgenstein, who dominated linguistic analysis in the 1950s. Wittgenstein, who published very little during his lifetime, had argued that problems in philosophy were chiefly linguistic; therefore one must begin with consideration of language's structure and theory. Colleagues of Hart at Oxford, notably the philosopher John L. Austin, had followed Wittgenstein's lead in making language the central focus of English philosophy. In looking to philosophy for support in his legal analysis, Hart could justify passing over more recent jurists as irrelevant to his concerns and his return to the basics proposed originally by Bentham and Austin. These two, Hart concluded, had at least confronted the relationship between law and language realistically, even if he could not agree with most of their results. As Hart wrote about the difficulty of perceiving these connections: "I at least could not see how much of this was visible in the works of our predecessors until I was taught how to look by my [philosophy] contemporaries."[21] Hart had discovered the instrument with which to reassess the legacy of English jurisprudence.

When Hart published *The Concept of Law,* therefore, part of its appeal arose from his examination of jurisprudential issues through the application of linguistic analysis. That lawyers and jurists could not agree on a satisfactory definition of law made it possible for Hart to concentrate on language as the key element in reviving substantial debate on the issues of legal philosophy with respect to the law and morality issue. Hart sought to resolve troubling questions through examination of the different meanings a word might convey, as in his explanation of the various meanings an imperative might have and its relation to the Austinian model of law as command.[22] Hart remedied the peculiar state of affairs in which the field of legal philosophy had forgotten that the discipline depended upon a marriage of its two components: "Lawyers had stopped being interested in philosophy, philosophers in law."[23] Hart's junction of linguistic philosophy with legal analysis produced a synthesis that revived interest in the grand tradition of English jurisprudence. Hart sought to make language the tool for access to the technical language of the law that often baffled laypeople.[24] The result was a Hartian theory of law heavily indebted to the philosophy of ordinary language. This emphasis has been summarized in the following manner:

> Law is essentially and irreducibly, though not only, linguistic. Laws are formulated and promulgated in words. Legal acts and decisions involve articulate thought and public utterance—often also public argument. A complicated conceptual framework and indeed a large and partly specialized vocabulary is essential to the structuring of the wide range of practices and activities which constitute a legal order. Hence the understanding of law requires elucidation and analysis of the complex conceptual framework involved.[25]

Perhaps more than any other aspect of *The Concept of Law,* Hart's use of linguistic analysis provided the dramatically innovative approach that gave the book much of its great impact. Hart had hit the academic jackpot in the sense that *The Concept of Law* soon became the book that dominated discussion among those interested in legal philosophy.

Among other conclusions that marked *The Concept of Law* as a special contribution to jurisprudence was Hart's argument that Bentham had been especially attuned to the crucial relationship between law and language. Hart corrected the traditional view that had credited Austin as the founder of analytical jurisprudence and restored Bentham to the honor he deserved. This revision of the historical record that arose from the insights offered by linguistic philosophy gave Hart the ability to set Austin in proper perspective. In the long run, therefore, Hart's synthesis of the analytical tradition with the modern emphasis on the philosophy of language to form a distinctive interpretation of legal philosophy constituted his foremost contribution.[26] Hart's unique position as an icon of legal philosophy and his claims on posterity have rested on the reunion of the two disciplines whose paths had diverged: "By his ingenious application and adaptation of such developments Hart sharpened methods of jurisprudential analysis, illuminated numerous outstanding issues, and made it possible to raise a wide range of new problems."[27] In the process Hart brought the history of English jurisprudence full cycle by the vindication of Bentham's achievements and a return to fundamental issues that had originated in the Blackstone-Bentham era. Few scholars have managed to restore the credibility of a formerly great field once it had been discredited, yet Hart performed this difficult task: "Hart certainly succeeded in regenerating excitement and interest in it. He did so, not by abandoning traditional areas of conceptual study as the American realists did in the Law Schools of the USA in the 1930s, but by re-defining and re-examining the traditional questions in the style and spirit of the new philosophy."[28] By daring to break with his immediate predecessors Hart had rejected inherited assumptions, and made a successful return to basic issues.

Hart's alliance of linguistic analysis with the rediscovery of Bentham (in the jurisprudential sense) had its own irony. Bentham, who abused the English language consistently through his prolix, virtually unreadable prose, hardly seems an apt model upon whom to base the virtues of clarity in the explanation of meaning in language. The tirades against obfuscation in the language of the law launched by Bentham seem almost comical given the invention of jargon so frequent in his writings. Yet, in spite of the obvious obstacles Bentham presented, Hart found in linguistic analysis a tie that made even Bentham valuable to legal philosophy: "This is best seen if it is appreciated how Bentham's analysis of powers makes contact with certain important themes of modern linguistic philosophy."[29] Through the focus on Bentham's essential doctrines, stripped of their verbal pretensions, Hart discovered an individual (even more than Austin) who had identified the fundamental issues affecting the analysis of law. By taking Bentham seriously Hart regarded "Bentham's thought not as the venerable product of a past master's mind to be displayed as a scholastic, historical decoration on one's intellectual mantelpiece, nor as the last word on the nature of law, but as a series of challenging insights to struggle with."[30] Hart's bold synthesis rehabilitated Bentham (in the eyes of many, but not all) and provided a major step forward in the continuing dialogue of English jurisprudence.

Since Blackstone, perhaps the most persistent issue in the English jurisprudential tradition, as this work has attempted to demonstrate, has been the debate about the relationship between law and morality. These spheres of conduct and contemplation, often regarded as mutually exclusive categories, have had as checkered a record as the vagaries of jurisprudence itself. Those who have insisted on the necessity to separate law from morality, initially in reaction to Blackstone, have in practice found some means by which to account for their constant interaction. To sustain an analysis of law without some hint of moral connection has proved impossible. Blackstone specifically endorsed the relationship, and this provided the pretext for some of Bentham's most vituperative attacks. For Bentham the principle of utility functioned as the moral touchstone upon which to construct his jurisprudential edifice, and for Austin "'law', 'morality' and 'ethics' were not separate 'things', but separate perspectives on the same thing, that is,—human activity."[31] Maine and Holland, in their own ways, paid homage to the distinction between law as it is and law as it ought to be, but this constituted part of the cult of law as science that triumphed in the second half of the nineteenth century. Whether the separation of law from morality was an elaborate hoax or a fruitful way to approach the study of law remained unresolved.

Hart, who reiterated this analytical tradition so brilliantly, continued the blurring of the lines between law and morality and yet repeated that legal obligation differed from moral obligation and that the legal system must enforce only legal obligations. At the same time he held that law and morality are "related social phenomena" that affect the behavior of individuals.[32] Three decades after the publication of *The Concept of Law,* commentaries on Hart have increasingly stressed his connections with, but not his endorsement of, the natural law tradition. According to one recent assessment, "Hartian law *is* natural law."[33] English jurisprudence has come full cycle when Hart, originally hailed as the fulfillment of English legal positivism and as an admirer of Bentham, in retrospect may be regarded as returning to at least some of Blackstone's assumptions. Even if this conclusion may be accepted only with substantial reservations, Hart's views merit additional consideration.

The apparent inconsistency in Hart's legal philosophy disappears under closer scrutiny. In the first place, Hart followed his predecessors in regarding the distinction between law and morality as an analytical tool, not as a fact demonstrable by historical example. While the verbal distinction has an important place in any account of English jurisprudence, the formula has always worked only on a theoretical level, never to be accepted as a description of how society has actually operated. What is more, Hart himself has never denigrated the natural law tradition; even though he disagrees with some of its major premises, he has never treated it with the automatic condescension characteristic of Holland and his contemporaries. Hart took natural law jurisprudence seriously and found "that there is much in natural law theory which any philosophically defensible theory of law must include."[34] Finally, Hart has had to face the dilemma that confronts those who attempt intellectual synthesis on a grand scale. Commentators have examined his work in microscopic detail, and proponents of other legal theories have invariably decried Hart's failure to adhere to what they regard as the appropriate dogmas. Glosses upon *The Concept of Law* have focused frequently upon the extent to which the book concurred with or departed from particular doctrines. Hart has gone his own way, and his treatment of law and morality has caused varying reactions.

One criticism of Hart, for example, argues that he has paid insufficient heed to the venerable injunction that law for conceptual purposes must be kept separate from morality. This critique has applied specifically to Hart's division of a legal system into sets of primary and secondary rules, and to an accompanying rule of recognition that regulates the process of continuing legal change. In Hart's work, the obligation to observe the forms for legal amendment, as opposed to arbitrary action, rests upon the notion of an internal morality. Obedience to the prescribed rules of recognition by those responsible for governing represented an internal moral imperative. Hart has thus been inconsistent because he has upheld the basic positivist argument for the separation of law and morality, and yet has specified that certain elements of any legal system must rest on moral ideas.[35]

In retrospect, therefore, his debate with Lon Fuller about the inner morality of law does not now seem to represent the yawning gulf between the two scholars as it once did. Fuller defined this inner morality as essential to the vision of a legal system: "Certainly there can be no rational ground for asserting that a man can have a moral obligation to obey a legal rule that does not exist, or is kept secret from him, or that came into existence only after he had acted, or was unintelligible, or was contradicted by another rule of the same system, or commanded the impossible, or changed every minute."[36] The Fuller-Hart positions showed how difficult in practice it had become to honor the positivist commandment about the separation of law and morality.

But it is only fair to add that Hart recognized rightly that legal analysis did not fit into neat compartments subsumed under mutually exclusive slogans. The complexity of a legal system precluded such simplistic choices: "Indeed, as Hart frankly acknowledges at the end of his book (C.L. ch. 9 pp. 206–7) the ultimate basis for adhering to the positivist thesis of the conceptual differentiation of law and morals is itself a moral reason."[37] To his credit

Hart did not permit semantic rigidity to curb the fertility of his intellect or to restrict unduly the province of his inquiries. His willingness to examine sympathetically the natural law tradition, for example, has received this explanation: "He has tried to establish some kind of rapprochement with the natural law tradition, in his attempts to extract a core of truth from theories of natural law."[38] Hart concluded that the separation of law and morality is a means, not an end, and legal theory must not allow this doctrine to impede speculation where warranted.

Other critics have charged Hart with too great a resistance to the allure of natural law theory. They have tried without success to portray him as an unrepentant positivist whose work suffered from its failure to return completely to the natural law tradition. In this interpretation Hart remained too committed to the attitudes of legal positivism, thus paying too little attention to the complexity of legal phenomena and the insights provided by natural law theory.[39] Hart attracted glosses in great profusion, and the price paid for academic fame was a minute scrutiny that few scholars ever receive. The attempt to state a theory of law based on a synthesis of the positivist and natural law traditions and a return to Bentham's questions gave ample opportunity to jurists of every viewpoint to debate Hart's work in immense detail.

In his last major contribution, a postscript to the second edition of *The Concept of Law* (1994), Hart responded to some of the criticisms of his arguments, especially those offered by his successor at Oxford, the American jurist Ronald Dworkin. Hart noted the phenomenon of the response to the original work as a stimulus to legal theory on both sides of the Atlantic, although legal theory has sometimes been interpreted as a waiver of the responsibility to present empirical evidence. Hart discharged this obligation with a civility too often rare in academic exchanges, and he readily conceded that elements of the original argument required clarification or even concessions to critics. In the end, however, Hart stood by the basics of the original work, especially the argument that judges are often called upon to make new law, no matter what rhetoric is employed to disguise this fact. The reader of the postscript, however, would find it difficult to understand what all the fuss was about. The issues discussed appear so far removed from ordinary experience that even attorneys might find the debate arcane. Hart did not extend his work in any degree that would broaden the appeal or make the arguments relevant to a wider audience.

Regardless of the controversy that swirled (and continues to swirl) around Hart's work, his career has demonstrated the extraordinary impact that the academy now has had in shaping the course of jurisprudence. It has represented the fulfillment of the dreams of the professoriate that matured in the 1880s, and yet the victory has in certain respects proven hollow. In no sense should this conclusion be taken as a denigration of Hart's achievement, but rather as a commentary on the nature of academic law and its divorce from the broader traditions of jurisprudence to which both Blackstone and Bentham belonged. Even Hart, whose stature has endured a generation of law review evaluations, has drawn the following comment: "Behind both American Legal Realism and the movement to broaden the study of law in this country lies the simple truism that the study of rules alone is not enough for the understanding of law. To date Oxonian legal philosophy, largely because it has taken too much for granted the criteria of relevance of Austinian analytical jurisprudence, has contributed almost nothing to the systematic and persistent exploration of the implications of this truism."[40] The most frequent dissents from Hart's approach have fixed on the problem that, no matter how elegant the analysis, the relevance to how most of society conceives of a legal system is slim because few actual examples are given in support of the argument.[41] Even Hart's strongest admirers would have to admit that his influence has not extended far beyond the academy. While Hart remains secure in his position as the major English jurist of this century, this has not brought him wider fame. At the center of discussion about jurisprudence for over three decades, Hart never gained recognition as a public intellectual nor is it easy to discern, for all the interest in legal systems he engendered, significant impact on the English legal system itself.

The best example of Hart's relative lack of influence came in the consequences of his participation in an extended public exchange with Lord Devlin, a judge of substantial reputation, in the wake of the Wolfenden committee report of 1957 that recommended decriminalization of homosexual practices between consenting adults in private. Devlin had, in fact, given evidence in favor of the Committee recommendation before its publication. That testimony notwithstanding, in 1958 Devlin delivered a lecture on jurisprudence to the British Academy in which he advanced the argument that use of the criminal law to enforce moral standards represented a legitimate exercise of state authority. Devlin compared moral deviance to treason and suggested that the government had the obligation to protect society from the former as much as the latter. In justification of this thesis Devlin put forth the hypothesis that society would disintegrate if a common bond of moral beliefs were not enforced by the law: "But if society has the right to make a judgement and has it on the basis that a recognized morality is as necessary to society as, say, a recognized government, then society may use the law to preserve morality in the same way as it uses it to safeguard anything else that is essential to its existence."[42] This reasoning soon became known as the "disintegration" theory, uncontaminated as it was by any specific example. Devlin's argument prompted a public reply from Hart.

After preliminary debate with Devlin in periodicals, Hart published *Law, Liberty, and Morality* in 1963 to address specifically the hallowed issue of the separation of law from morality. Hart conceded that law had always been influenced by morals, but he denied that this role was appropriate in the contemporary context: "What is crucial to the dispute in its modern form is the significance to be attached to the historical fact that certain conduct, no matter what, is prohibited by a positive morality. The utilitarian [Hart] denies that this has any significance sufficient to justify its enforcement; his opponent [Devlin] asserts that it has."[43] Despite the attention of both parties to the assumptions of legal theory, Hart scored his strongest point when he noted that no empirical evidence supported the allegation that conflict over moral standards doomed a society: "No evidence is produced to show that deviation from accepted sexual morality, even by adults in private, is something which, like treason, threatens the existence of society. No reputable historian has maintained this thesis, and there is indeed much evidence against it."[44] Although Devlin published a collection of essays in 1965 in reply to Hart, the verdict among legal academics was that Hart had made his case more convincingly: "Many, however, perhaps even most, think that Hart carried the day inasmuch as Devlin failed to meet his challenge to produce hard empirical evidence to show that the erosion of a society's dominant morality places that society in danger of collapse."[45] In summaries of the Hart-Devlin exchange, one lost sight of the fact that Devlin, by virtue of his seat on the bench, might accomplish more of practical substance.

As regards its impact on a public program, of course, the crucial point was that the Wolfenden Committee had proclaimed its guiding principle before Hart entered the lists against Devlin. However valuable, Hart's comments occurred after the public policy decision had already been made and thus had no influence on the original choice. Hart's participation did not contribute to the broad discussion of social policy; rather, it followed in the aftermath of the committee's recommendation. Time has diminished the relevance of the Hart-Devlin controversy, and one critic has written that it was fortunately not a source of public policy but represented academic theorizing in impractical form: "I conclude by proposing that the Hart-Devlin debate, in prescinding from strong and substantial philosophizing about human well-being, and in prescinding from the actual, concrete habits of particular legal cultures and traditions, is vacuous, pedantic, and instructive only insofar as it teaches us how not to conduct moral discourse."[46] Thirty years later there remains a majestically baroque aura around an argument conducted on a sophisticated philosophical level without reference to real situations, especially when the evidence for the use of the criminal law to improve moral standards abounds.[47] In the end, therefore, Hart's reputation rarely extended outside the boundaries of the academy.

Another remarkable dimension of the process by which academic culture has affected the development of English jurisprudence may be seen in the scholarly reception of *The Concept of Law.* Hart's selection as Corpus professor antedated by nine years the appearance of the work that made his reputation. His appointment in 1952 was on the basis of potential, not accomplishment. One might argue that this represented remarkable prescience on the part of the electors who chose so wisely, given the distinction that Hart undoubtedly attained. One might also suggest, however, that his academic position conferred substantial prestige in advance of *The Concept of Law* and ensured that the book would command widespread attention. Thus it has been noted that Hart's major work "would doubtless not have had so great an influence had it not been written by the Professor of Jurisprudence at the University of Oxford. That is not so much a fact about Hart and the nature of the book but about the nature of the British university system and British society."[48] Campbell has explored carefully how the work of Hart's pupils (especially

Joseph Raz and Neil MacCormick) have helped to sustain the reputation of the master. The tracing of the popularization of *The Concept of Law,* apart from the merits of its argument, showed how the external factors of academic culture helped to make it the famous treatise it became.[49] This perceptive observation touched the sensitive area of academic trendiness and the peculiar way in which academic reputations are secured. The changing nature of academic jurisprudence has made the way a book gains its stature a legitimate concern.

One's initial assumption, of course, is that a book gains influence because it treats an important subject within a discipline, one that excites the interest of a wide audience. Yet books that are acclaimed as influential just as often draw critical reviews from other specialists in a field, and often are judged so erroneous that a neutral observer might well wonder what the fuss is all about. The reception of the book is structured by what other experts praise or criticize about the work. Historians might well reflect on the many hostile commentaries directed against E. P. Thompson's *The Making of the English Working Class* (1963), a book that has also exercised a great influence both inside and outside its discipline. Regardless of the shortcomings attributed to a book, it acquires influence precisely because other scholars become parasitic off it. One might speculate, for example, on how many tenure articles *The Concept of Law* spawned on both sides of the Atlantic. Many academics find a particular work easier to teach against, and so they refer to it more often than those whose conclusions they endorse. The arguments in *The Concept of Law* have provided the basis for literally hundreds of scholarly discussions—and recently for books and symposia, the ultimate hallmarks of academic recognition: "There are interminable articles on Hart and Dworkin but they are cast, for the most part, in the commentary mode. They tidy up bits of the argument; they rarely pose questions which give other scholars something to go out and find out about."[50] In certain respects, then, Hart became the prisoner of lesser scholars eager to define and exploit his position as an academic superstar. This process may add to or subtract from the study of jurisprudence, but its importance to the evolution of the discipline itself cannot be ignored.

In addition, Campbell has argued that the influence of *The Concept of Law* has actually not been nearly so great as it appeared because its place as an "exciting work" caused it to acquire a degree of importance it did not merit. He asserted that its standing "has been exaggerated and magnified by the adoption of his approach as something of an orthodoxy by the self-styled Oxford School of Jurisprudence."[51] Hart became accepted as the one true way to do legal philosophy. The supremacy of Hart's work over three decades has demonstrated the extent to which the assumptions of academic culture have prevailed from within in the continuing evaluation of the book. Few critics at present would defend all or even major points of Hart's book, yet it retains a reputation in the field after many scholars have acknowledged its shortcomings. As a factor in the historical unfolding of English jurisprudence, therefore, the peculiar fashions of academic culture must be noted.

Every academic field in the twentieth century has had

to wrestle with the distinction between that questioning attitude without which legitimate inquiry vanishes, and the embrace of fashionable trends that prize provocative conclusions at the expense of more judicious but less "exciting" writings. In the United States one might cite the successive movements of sociological jurisprudence before World War I, realism in the 1930s, and contemporary critical legal studies. All have invoked the similar rhetoric of broadening understanding of law by proclaiming an agenda based on extralegal insights. In retrospect, however, despite the self-described innovations of each era, each trend has the distinct air of playing the academic game at its worst. Hart clearly wished to make his work synthetic, not revisionist in the trendy sense of the academy. It should be clear that he did not seek the role of academic icon, but in some respects had that position imposed upon him by virtue of his professorship at Oxford and by the efforts of individuals of lesser attainment. Hart rarely availed himself of the opportunities to answer critics, and when he has chosen to do so, as in his posthumous postscript, his manner was unfailingly courteous; he eschewed the polemics that too often adorn academic debate. The reader might well conclude that this work itself reflects the academic culture that has been so important to the analysis offered here. The influence of Hart, so symbolic of academic law, must be seen in the long perspective of developments since the 1880s. In a tribute to Hart recently, Ruth Gavison wrote: "Thus Hart has more than earned the rare compliment that, had we not had his presence and contribution, the field would not have looked the same."[52] This verdict was certainly merited, but it indicated at least as much about the evolving nature of the field itself as it did about the place of Hart within it.

Hart's reputation, whatever reservations individual critics may have, seems secure despite the threats of his position becoming outflanked on the left by critical legal studies or from the right by the renaissance of natural law theory. At one level, therefore, the unparalleled enthusiasm for Hart's work signaled a greater attention to jurisprudence and the goals it might seek. True, the audience for his writing has diminished, for its increasingly academic tone has removed it from general discourse about public policy. Any assessment of Hart must recognize his reinforcement of this fundamental alteration in the jurisprudential tradition since the 1880s, the return to Bentham notwithstanding. Hart declared in *The Concept of Law* that his purpose included a wish "to further the understanding of law, coercion, and morality as different but related social phenomena."[53] His attempt at a sociology of law was perhaps the weakest part of his book; a reader would be hard pressed to understand how a real society operates after studying Hart. The result had been well described: "The deep complicities between professional and academic conceptions of law produced an English jurisprudence that was peculiarly constrained, one that protected law from significant engagement with political and social issues."[54] While this process from 1880 on has had a political dimension, the demands of academic legal culture have shaped the course of English jurisprudence even more substantially.

Hart returned intellectual sophistication to jurisprudence and restored the discipline to an honored position within the academy. This accomplishment must be tempered, however, by the continued drift away from jurisprudence as an appropriate vehicle for the discussion of contemporary public issues. Even after Hart's attempt to restore jurisprudence to a discussion of social issues, this effort must still be judged a failure. By becoming an orthodoxy, *The Concept of Law* "has circumscribed jurisprudential discussion."[55] Other academic disciplines have endured a variant of this development over the last century, but jurisprudence has suffered most because its modern origins with Blackstone had offered such splendid hopes for its important role in intellectual discussion. Academic culture has shaped the direction of jurisprudence more, perhaps, than any other single factor. To make jurisprudence a subject of public debate clearly requires special qualities, yet it might be argued that, given the special place of the common law in the nation's history, no topic is more vital to English society. To understand the past goals and contributions of English jurisprudence is to perceive as well the changed nature of its role since the 1880s.

Chapter Eight

Conclusion

Twentieth-century historians of law and jurisprudence have altered dramatically the approach to their craft. The documentation of doctrinal evolution has given way to increased sophistication about the many influences that affect the study of law in its historical contexts. Increased emphasis on the importance of a wide range of extralegal factors added useful perspectives from areas such as economics, politics, and sociology. To the extent that these additions to traditional legal analysis provided new alternatives, legal history since 1960 has reasserted its claim as a fundamental field of historical inquiry as well as an important adjunct to the new social history. This transformation has had an uneven impact, for even the emphases of the new social history have not resulted in major revisions of the way in which the ordinary citizen experiences the legal system on a daily basis. Focus on the rarefied plane of legal theory simply has not attracted a large audience. One recent assessment of this phenomenon has noted:

> Legal history remains terra incognita to the ordinary reader of history and is shunned by the average historian. There is little legal history in our textbooks or our classrooms. The reason for indifference to legal history cannot be the inherent dullness or mystery of legal institutions, laws and litigation. They affect the world we live in profoundly, fill the morning news programs, and daily shape our expectations of others' conduct. On television, courts and lawyers appear regularly. Legal history should be very popular, but quite the reverse is true.[1]

The impact of a legal system upon the individual and the way that individual regards the culture of legality reveals much about the conditions of daily existence.

In the specific instance of modern British history, several factors in the twentieth century have contributed to the decline of legal history's claims. Foremost is the pervasive bromide that the events of the Glorious Revolution in 1688 and its aftermath somehow "settled" the constitution for the next three centuries. Legal and constitutional history were rarely distinguished, and the putative end of constitutional history implied the end of legal history as well. The manner in which modern branches of the common law such as torts has influenced the development of a commercial society has rarely received attention. In addition, the loss of great power status by Great Britain has no doubt made the study of its legal history less compelling than in the era of Victorian glory, when global supremacy gave to the topic an intellectual hegemony it no longer enjoys. Finally, the inward turn of jurisprudence from social analysis to legal theory since the 1880s gave to the subject a forbidding facade that has made scholars from outside the discipline wary of meeting its challenges. Academics had the more modest goals of establishing a reputation and seeking publication, so that changing the world or even one's discipline no longer was foremost. Over the past century, therefore, English legal and constitutional history, which had reigned supreme, has diminished in prestige as other subsets of historical inquiry have superseded it.

Other scholars have hinted at this transition in approach that altered the purposes of jurisprudence. Twining, for instance, has written:

> Subsequent developments can be broadly interpreted in terms of a Maine-like hypothesis: between 1850 and 1950 the movement of academic law in England was a progressive narrowing of general jurisprudence, broadly conceived, to particular expository jurisprudence, concerned almost exclusively with the exposition and analysis and application of English legal doctrine. This was illustrated not only by the content and scope of the professional examinations and the rise of the expository textbook, but also by the history of taught jurisprudence in that period. Bentham was side-lined; the followers of Austin used him selectively and developed a narrower and more particular conception of analytical jurisprudence; and Maine was marginalized. Like Maine's grand hypotheses, this is vulnerable to particularistic attack as being simplified and over-generalized. But

> it contains a core of truth sufficient to provide a plausible and coherent story about English academic law over a hundred years. General jurisprudence and legal science, as these were variously interpreted by Bentham, Austin and Maine, never took root in England—for fairly obvious reasons.[2]

This work has agreed substantially with Twining's interpretation, but the 1880s seem a much safer period to delineate the impact of academic legal culture, a minor quibble at best. The fundamental argument about the course of modern English jurisprudence retains its appeal.

The foundation of a jurisprudential tradition in academic culture has provided the opportunity to revise its history-of-ideas ancestry. The most recent attempt to provide a new interpretation of legal history in general has appeared in Alan Watson's concern for the effects of a legal tradition that "to a marked degree, is independent of social, political, and economic factors."[3] This self-contained lawyers' culture has looked inward, with few influences permitted to alter professional perspectives. With respect to jurisprudence, this argument suggests that legal philosophy itself, in its academic guise, has since the 1880s also adhered to an internal tradition, especially if Watson's argument is accepted, that is, "the very powerful role that the legal culture itself has on law making."[4] The development of an academic legal culture has been the most important determinant of legal philosophy during the past century. For jurisprudence the consequences of this process have included an increased abstraction, a reluctance to set law in its ordinary context, and a narrow specialization that has separated its purview ever more remotely from the concerns of lawyers. Within academic culture jurisprudence has become an autonomous discipline, driven by academic concerns in which the value of speculation is determined by intellectual elites. Scholarly battles over issues far removed from the experience of ordinary citizens have added to the ethereal atmosphere that pervades jurisprudence. Every scholarly discipline has to some extent fallen victim to this failing, but this conclusion reinforces the point that the modern university has spawned a unique culture, one whose implications must be considered in the writing of a particular discipline's intellectual history. While teaching obligations still stress the ideal of a liberal education, with emphasis upon a broad acquaintance with an academically defined field, the research duties of the professoriate may result in focus upon the esoterica of a given subject. Complaints about this trend in modern academic life have surfaced regularly, but seldom have such lamentations specified the consequences for the discipline involved.

Scholars of English jurisprudence have tended to embrace, as Hart's career demonstrated, the academic culture of the law in its modern guise. This judgment is not a condemnation, but rather a way to account for the path on which jurisprudence has embarked since the 1880s. In other words, jurisprudence has followed the internal dictates of academic culture as much as or more than the search for the nature of law. Interest in legal theory has supplanted consideration of what lawyers actually do. Jurisprudential speculation has never fallen into neat, mutually exclusive categories of motivation; yet the increased dominance of academic influences on jurisprudence is a relatively modern phenomenon. Professorial elites now operate in the realm of jurisprudence much as Watson's legal elites determined change without reference to outside influences.[5] The role of the jurist as social critic has continued to diminish, as evidence about the attitudes of the judiciary has indicated. Academic discussion has little influence on the law lords, who remain distinctly insulated from this quarter.[6] The achievement of professional status for the legal academic brought intellectual strength but little commensurate political or social influence.[7] Jurisprudence has created an academic culture of its own where, to paraphrase Watson, it follows its internal values with scant impact outside its boundaries and free from societal pressures.[8] Legal dialogue rarely attracts the general public any longer, nor is it supposed to, for the conventional form of discourse addresses other academics. What jurisprudence has gained in precision, it has lost in terms of its target audience.

Historians rely frequently on such categories as high and low culture to explain the nuances of learned and popular beliefs. In the context of this distinction, jurisprudence has become the high culture of the legal system, accessible to few and beyond the interest of most members of the bar. Legal systems are described in extended metaphors that often invoke French anthropology or the language of deconstruction to make their point. If a legal system cannot have post-something in its analysis, then the interpretation must look for another form of sophisticated language. From Holmes's use of the law as viewed by a bad man to Hart's famous utilization of the gunman, or even to a fast driver,[9] metaphors about the law have abounded. Add in enticing words and phrases like *bricolage*[10] and palm tree justice,[11] and the high culture of jurisprudence is extended. There is, of course, nothing untoward about such theorizing as long as its theoretical role is fully recognized.

What might be made, for example, of a fanciful comparison of a legal system to the scene at a British football match in the Premier Division? Because the spectators would outnumber the participants, this would surely account for the truism that most citizens rarely become entwined in the intricacies of the legal system. Most individuals spend their lives in blissful isolation from the legal system, never involved beyond a simple will or the odd traffic ticket. The referee, who commands habitual obedience, is aided in the exercise of authority by the linesmen. This authority is discretionary and not to be applied mechanically, for the use of the advantage rule helps to maintain match control and make the play more pleasing to the crowd. Serious criminal behavior merits a sending off (or perhaps sending to, as with prison), but status offenses may be overlooked, as in the case of the four-step rule on the part of the goalkeeper. Soccer is governed by rules, seventeen in all, rather slim when compared to the thick rulebooks for other sports. Many scholars in the twentieth century, including Hart, have put rules at the center of a legal system. The football metaphor might in some small way help to understand the criminal law, but surely is of little help in civil matters. That this metaphor is inexact may be readily conceded, but the use of metaphorical language to describe what individuals experience directly must surely fail as a matter of logic. Academic fascination with legal theory perpetuates the division that has arisen between public and academic discourse. Whereas practitioners carry on the daily toil of the law, secure in a distinctive culture of their own, jurists contemplate issues that seemingly have little connection with the practical world of the law. Speculation about law and legal theory has ceased to form a part of general intellectual culture and is usually restricted to a small coterie of academic specialists. Some individuals may move between both worlds, as did the Victorian jurist Sir Frederick Pollock or the contemporary Richard Posner, but this facility has become a rarity. The specialization of legal philosophy has acquired the status of high culture, as have many other academic disciplines, and in the process has failed to communicate its ideas to those outside its own caste.[12]

It may be the case, of course, that jurisprudence in its modern form should concern only the few, that its appropriate role encompasses only those philosophical issues that practitioners rarely have the opportunity to ponder. If, however, the end result of such musings asserts that "the essence of law is that it has no essence,"[13] those outside the academy may well wonder about the purposes of jurisprudence. This narrow conception of jurisprudence's place within the boundaries of academic culture has triumphed at the expense of its previous role as a primary source of social commentary. What Watson has termed the "failure of the legal imagination" has robbed English jurisprudence of that vital dedication to educating the public that produced Blackstone and Bentham as well as Austin and Maine.[14] For the century after Blackstone, jurisprudence enjoyed a primary place in English intellectual life: "On the face of it, only political economy could seem to rival jurisprudence as an established 'moral science' by the middle of the nineteenth century, and, more broadly, no other form of enquiry rested upon so entrenched and powerful a basis as that provided by the social and intellectual position of the law."[15] Since the 1880s, in the name of intensive legal analysis, English jurisprudence has defined itself in such a narrow fashion that even the work of Hart did not provide a fresh start. With the end of his career, academic law in England stands at a crossroads; only a restoration of the ideal of jurisprudence as a study of the place of law in English society will provide a catalyst for a return to its former glory.

Notes

Notes to Chapter One

1. Albert Venn Dicey to Oliver Wendell Holmes, 19 January 1880, Oliver Wendell Holmes Papers, Harvard Law School Library, Cambridge, Mass.

2. Morton J. Horwitz, "History and Theory," 1825.

3. Albert Venn Dicey, "Jurisprudence," 382.

4. A. L. Goodhart, *English Contributions to the Philosophy of Law,* 12.

5. Raymond Cocks, *Sir Henry Maine,* 39.

6. Knud Haakonssen, *The Science of a Legislator,* 1–2.

7. Neil MacCormick, *H. L. A. Hart,* 1.

8. Richard Posner, *The Problems of Jurisprudence,* xi.

9. A. W. B. Simpson, *Legal Theory and Legal History,* 307.

10. Richard Burdon Haldane, "Higher Nationality: A Study in Law and Ethics," 401–2.

11. W. Durnan to Leo Maxse, 14 December 1909, Leo Maxse Papers, West Sussex County Record Office, Chichester, U.K.

12. Recent exceptions to this generalization include David Lieberman, *The Province of Legislation Determined,* and Michael Lobban, *Common Law and English Jurisprudence, 1760–1850.*

13. William Twining, "Academic Law and Legal Philosophy," 556.

14. Geoffrey Samuel, "Science, Law and History," 1.

15. Harold Perkin, *The Rise of Professional Society,* 395.

16. Alan Watson, *The Evolution of Law,* 117–9.

17. Alan Watson, "Legal Change," 1134.

18. A. W. B. Simpson, "Legal Education and Legal History," 111.

19. Sir Frederick Pollock, "The Methods of Jurisprudence," 38.

20. David Millon, "Positivism in the Historiography of the Common Law," 670.

21. Sir Frederick Pollock, *English Opportunities and Duties,* 30.

22. Robert S. Summers, *Instrumentalism and American Legal Theory,* 268.

23. Perkin, *The Rise of Professional Society,* 395–96.

24. Horwitz, "History and Theory," 1835.

25. Roger Cotterrell, *The Politics of Jurisprudence,* 22.

Notes to Chapter Two

1. John U. Lewis, "Blackstone's Definition of Law," 336.

2. Michael Lobban, "Blackstone and the Science of Law," 312.

3. David Lockmiller, *Sir William Blackstone,* 5–28.

4. J. L. Barton, "Legal Studies," 601.

5. Lucy S. Sutherland, "William Blackstone and the Legal Chairs at Oxford," 230.

6. Gareth Jones, "Introduction," xix.

7. H. G. Hanbury, "Blackstone as a Judge," 27.

8. Dennis R. Nolan, "Sir William Blackstone and the New American Republic," 731–68.

9. A. V. Dicey, "Blackstone's *Commentaries,*" 674.

10. Ibid., 307.

11. Oliver Wendell Holmes to Harold Laski, 1 June 1922, in Mark DeWolfe Howe, ed., *Holmes-Laski Letters,* I, 329.

12. Sir William S. Holdsworth, "Some Aspects of Blackstone and His Commentaries," 284.

13. S. F. C. Milsom, "The Nature of Blackstone's Achievement," especially 12.

14. Lobban, *Common Law and English Jurisprudence 1760–1850,* 18.

15. John N. Finnis, "Blackstone's Theoretical Intentions," 163–64.

16. See Daniel Boorstin, *The Mysterious Science of the Law,* 50.

17. Sir William Blackstone, *Commentaries on the Laws of England,* I, 41.

18. Ibid., I, 42.

19. Ibid., I, 44.

20. Ibid., I, 46.

21. Paul Lucas, "*Ex Parte* Sir William Blackstone," 158.
22. Donald R. Kelley, *The Human Measure,* 183.
23. Blackstone, *Commentaries,* I, 49.
24. Lobban, *Common Law and English Jurisprudence 1760–1850,* 29.
25. Blackstone, *Commentaries,* I, 49.
26. Robert P. Burns, "Blackstone's Theory of the 'Absolute' Rights of Property," 84.
27. Joseph W. McKnight, "Blackstone, Quasi-Jurisprudent," 402.
28. Lieberman, *The Province of Legislation Determined,* 45.
29. Boorstin, *Mysterious Science of the Law,* 121.
30. Finnis, "Blackstone's Theoretical Intentions," 163–83.
31. Lewis, "Blackstone's Definition of Law," 347. Emphasis in the original.
32. Lobban, *Common Law and English Jurisprudence 1760–1850,* 12.
33. Lobban, "Blackstone and the Science of Law," 321.
34. Lieberman, *The Province of Legislation Determined,* 35.
35. H. T. Dickinson, *Liberty and Property,* 141.
36. Rupert Cross, "The First Two Vinerian Professors," 613.
37. Sir William Blackstone, *A Discourse on the Study of the Law,* 205.
38. Ibid., 205–6.
39. Lieberman, *The Province of Legislation Determined,* 63.
40. David Lieberman, "Blackstone's Science of Legislation," 141.
41. Anton-Herman Chroust, "Blackstone Revisited," 28.
42. Jeremy Bentham, *A Fragment on Government,* 407.
43. Chroust, "Blackstone Revisited," 34.
44. Boorstin, *Mysterious Science of the Law,* 187–88.
45. Duncan Kennedy, "The Structure of Blackstone's Commentaries," 211.
46. Ibid., 217.
47. Ibid., 255.
48. H. L. A. Hart, "Blackstone's Use of the Law of Nature," 169.
49. Cross, "The First Two Vinerian Professors," 617.
50. H. G. Hanbury, *The Vinerian Chair and Legal Education,* 37.
51. J. C. D. Clark, *English Society 1688–1832,* 204.
52. Lockmiller, *Blackstone,* 167.
53. I. G. Philip, *William Blackstone and the Reform of the Oxford University Press,* passim.
54. Alan Watson, "The Structure of Blackstone's Commentaries," 795.

55. John W. Cairns, "Blackstone, an English Institutist," 351. Emphasis in the original.

56. See Watson, "The Structure of Blackstone's Commentaries," 802, n. 29, where other defects in Kennedy's article were enumerated.

57. Robert Willman, "Blackstone and the 'Theoretical Perfection' of English Law in the Reign of Charles II," 68–69.

58. John W. Cairns, "Blackstone, the Ancient Constitution and the Feudal Law," 717.

59. A. W. B. Simpson, *Legal Theory and Legal History,* 296.

60. Cairns, "Blackstone, an English Institutist," 321.

61. Ibid., 357.

62. R. J. Smith, *The Gothic Bequest,* 91.

63. Kendall L. Vick, "Sir William Blackstone's Commentaries on the Laws of England," 79.

64. Cairns, "Blackstone, an English Institutist," 353.

65. I. G. Doolittle, "Sir William Blackstone and His *Commentaries,*" 101.

66. Blackstone, *A Discourse on the Study of Law,* 220.

67. Watson, "The Structure of Blackstone's Commentaries," 810; see also H. G. Hanbury, "Blackstone in Retrospect," 321.

68. Paul Lucas, "Blackstone and the Reform of the Legal Profession," 460.

69. J. C. D. Clark, *Revolution and Rebellion* and *English Society 1688–1832.*

70. Clark, *English Society 1688–1832,* ix–x.

71. See Joanna Innes, "Jonathan Clark, Social History and England's 'Ancien Regime'," 165–200; and the reply, J. C. D. Clark, "On Hitting the Buffers," 195–207. See also the fall 1989 number of *Albion:* James E. Bradley, "The Anglican Pulpit, the Social Order, and the Resurgence of Toryism during the American Revolution," 361–88; John Money, "Provincialism and the English 'Ancien Regime,' " 389–425; John A. Phillips, "The Social Calculus," 426–49; and the response by Clark, "England's Ancien Regime as a Confessional State," 450–74.

72. Julian S. Waterman, "Mansfield and Blackstone's Commentaries," 558.

73. Ibid., 557.

74. Linda Colley, *Britons: Forging the Nation 1707–1837,* at p. 52, where the author comments on the role played by Parliament as a primary institutional element of the new British nation.

75. William Twining, *Theories of Evidence,* vii.
76. Lieberman, *The Province of Legislation Determined,* 31.
77. Barton, "Legal Studies," p. 603.
78. Lieberman, "Blackstone's Science of Legislation," 118.

Notes to Chapter Three

1. H. L. A. Hart, *Essays on Bentham,* 17–18.
2. Richard Posner, "Blackstone and Bentham," 570; see also Lobban, "Blackstone and the Science of Law," 312.
3. Sir William Holdsworth, "Gibbon, Blackstone and Bentham," 52.
4. Bentham, *A Fragment on Government,* 394, 413.
5. Shirley Letwin, *The Pursuit of Certainty,* 131.
6. Martin Wiener, "The Unloved State," 298.
7. Janet Semple, *Bentham's Prison,* especially 152–55.
8. For example, "The *Introduction to the Principles of Morals and Legislation* after many delays appeared in 1789. It did not, however, attract public attention to any great extent." Elie Halevy, *The Growth of Philosophic Radicalism,* 75.
9. Chroust, "Blackstone Revisited," 34.
10. Bentham, *A Fragment on Government,* 498.
11. Ibid., 441.
12. Jeremy Bentham, *A Comment on the Commentaries,* 200.
13. Posner, "Blackstone and Bentham," 596.
14. Bentham, *A Comment on the Commentaries,* 11.
15. Hanbury, *The Vinerian Chair and Legal Education,* 23.
16. Lieberman, *The Province of Legislation Determined,* 286–87.
17. Bentham, *A Fragment on Government,* 433.
18. Gertrude Himmelfarb, "Bentham versus Blackstone," 99. Bentham took the phrase "everything is now as it should be" and applied it to Blackstone's general attitude; it referred only to the law of heresy.
19. Hart, *Essays on Bentham,* 10.
20. Twining, *Theories of Evidence,* 62.
21. M. H. James, "Bentham and the Individuation of Laws," 359.
22. James E. Crimmins, *Secular Utilitarianism,* 46.
23. Thomas Horne, *Property Rights and Poverty,* 146.
24. Letwin, *The Pursuit of Certainty,* 155.
25. William Thomas, *The Philosophic Radicals,* 146.
26. Semple, *Bentham's Prison,* 14.

27. Horne, *Property Rights and Poverty,* 160.
28. Thomas, *The Philosophic Radicals,* 23.
29. Lieberman, "Blackstone's Science of Legislation," 149.
30. Himmelfarb, "Bentham versus Blackstone," 101–3.
31. John V. Orth, "Jeremy Bentham," 715.
32. Gerald Postema, *Bentham and the Common Law Tradition,* 313.
33. L. J. Hume, *Bentham and Bureaucracy,* 57.
34. Postema, *Bentham and the Common Law Tradition,* 160. Emphasis in the original.
35. Douglas Long, *Bentham on Liberty,* 92.
36. Crimmins, *Secular Utilitarianism,* 23.
37. Halevy, *The Growth of Philosophic Radicalism,* 6.
38. Long, *Bentham on Liberty,* 164.
39. Kelley, *The Human Measure,* 225.
40. James Steintrager, *Bentham,* 12.
41. Letwin, *The Pursuit of Certainty,* 5.
42. Philip Schofield, "Jeremy Bentham and Nineteenth-Century English Jurisprudence," 58.
43. Postema, *Bentham and the Common Law Tradition,* 167.
44. D. J. Manning, *The Mind of Jeremy Bentham,* 5.
45. Postema, *Bentham and the Common Law Tradition,* 295.
46. Bentham, *A Fragment on Government,* 416, 446–48, 482, 491.
47. Bentham, *A Comment on the Commentaries,* 27–28.
48. Jeremy Bentham, *Of Laws in General,* 32.
49. Jeremy Bentham, *Introduction to the Principles of Morals and Legislation,* 1.
50. Ibid., 3.
51. Ibid.
52. Postema, *Bentham and the Common Law Tradition,* 403.
53. Ibid., 441. Emphasis in the original.
54. Martin J. Packer, "Hermeneutic Inquiry in the Study of Human Conduct," 1085.
55. Martin Sicker, "Jeremy Bentham on Law and Jurisprudence," 282.
56. Semple, *Bentham's Prison,* 62.
57. Paul Kelly, *Utilitarianism and Distributive Justice,* 19.
58. John R. Dinwiddy, *Bentham,* 21. Emphasis in the original.
59. John Plamenatz, *The English Utilitarians,* 168.
60. Lieberman, *The Province of Legislation Determined,* 231.

61. Letwin, *The Pursuit of Certainty,* 173.
62. Posner, "Blackstone and Bentham," 600.
63. A. J. M. Milne, "Bentham's Principle of Utility and Legal Philosophy," 285.
64. Gertrude Himmelfarb, "On Reading Bentham Seriously," 180.
65. Rupert Cross, "Blackstone v. Bentham," 527; see also Sir William S. Holdsworth, "Blackstone," 239.
66. Himmelfarb, "Bentham versus Blackstone," 109.
67. Thomas, *The Philosophic Radicals,* 452–53.
68. Manning, *The Mind of Jeremy Bentham,* 111.
69. Richard A. Cosgrove, *The Rule of Law,* 181–90.
70. P. S. Atiyah and Robert S. Summers, *Form and Substance in Anglo-American Law,* 223.
71. H. L. A. Hart, "Bentham and the Demystificaiton of the Law," 4.
72. Atiyah and Summers, *Form and Substance in Anglo-American Law,* 244.
73. David Lyons, *In the Interest of the Governed,* vii.
74. H. L. A. Hart, "Bentham on Legal Powers," 806.
75. Semple, *Bentham's Prison,* 247.
76. Gertrude Himmelfarb, "The Haunted House of Jeremy Bentham," 78.
77. H. L. A. Hart, "Introduction," 1–16.
78. J. H. Burns, "Bentham on Sovereignty," 404–5.
79. Frederick Rosen, *Jeremy Bentham and Representative Democracy,* 44.
80. Plamenatz, *The English Utilitarians,* 65.
81. Ross Harrison, *Bentham,* 24.
82. Bentham, *A Comment on the Commentaries,* 58.
83. Hart, "Bentham and the Demystification of the Law," 7.
84. Lieberman, *The Province of Legislation Determined,* 219.
85. John R. Dinwiddy, "Bentham's Transition to Political Radicalism, 1809–10," 688.
86. Dinwiddy, *Bentham,* 59.
87. Letwin, *The Pursuit of Certainty,* 177.
88. Lobban, *Common Law and English Jurisprudence 1760–1850,* 222.
89. H. L. A. Hart, "Bentham and the United States of America," 547.
90. Atiyah and Summers, *Form and Substance in Anglo-American Law,* 242.

91. Lyons, *In the Interest of the Governed,* 1.

92. Dinwiddy, *Bentham,* 56. Emphasis in the original.

93. Shirley Letwin, "Justice, Authority and Jurisprudence," 412.

94. Ibid.

95. H. F. Jolowicz, *Lectures on Jurisprudence,* 101.

96. Milne, "Bentham's Principle of Utility and Legal Philosophy," 275.

97. Sicker, "Bentham on Law and Jurisprudence," 284.

98. Letwin, *The Pursuit of Certainty,* 142.

99. H. G. Jolowicz, "Was Bentham a Lawyer?" 11–12.

100. Dinwiddy, *Bentham,* 117.

101. S. E. Finer, "The Transmission of Benthamite Ideas 1820–1850," 11–32.

102. Thomas, *The Philosophic Radicals,* 447.

103. Helen Beynon, "Mighty Bentham," 69.

104. Anthony Brundage, *England's "Prussian Minister,"* 2–3.

105. Stephen Conway, "Bentham and the Nineteenth-Century Revolution in Government," 72: "The primary aim of this essay is to argue the case for considering the ideas of Jeremy Bentham as an important influence."

106. Twining, "Academic Law and Legal Philosophy," 559.

107. Schofield, "Jeremy Bentham and Nineteenth-Century English Jurisprudence," 85.

108. Hart, *Essays on Bentham,* 108; see also Lyons, *In the Interest of the Governed,* 1, 107; and Postema, *Bentham and the Common Law Tradition,* 327.

109. W. Friedmann, "Bentham and Modern Legal Thought," 234.

110. Frederick Rosen, "The Origin of Liberal Utilitarianism," 61.

Notes to Chapter Four

1. R. C. van Caenegem, *Judges, Legislators and Professors,* 99.

2. See W. L. Morison, *John Austin* (1982); Pohlman, *Justice Oliver Wendell Holmes and Utilitarian Jurisprudence* (1984); Lotte and Joseph Hamburger, *Troubled Lives* (1985); Wilfrid E. Rumble, *The Thought of John Austin* (1985); Robert N. Moles, *Definition and Theory in Legal Theory* (1987); and Lobban, *Common Law and English Jurisprudence 1760–1850* (1991).

3. Lotte and Joseph Hamburger, *Contemplating Adultery,* 32–33.

4. Quoted in ibid., 48.

5. For the importance of this German sojourn, see the recent discussion in Lobban, *Common Law and English Jurisprudence 1760–1850,* 227–34.

6. Van Caenegem, *Judges, Legislators and Professors,* 99.

7. Hamburger and Hamburger, *Contemplating Adultery,* 47.

8. Leslie Stephen, *The English Utilitarians,* III, 318. About the failure of the lecturer and the lectures, one auditor wrote: "His private conversation was as overbearing and ill-tempered as were his lectures. He seemed to say: 'If you don't agree with me, you must be the biggest fool that ever was.' " The student and old reporter was Richard Davis Craig. See Courtney Kenny, "What an Old Reporter Told Me," 355.

9. Hamburger and Hamburger, *Troubled Lives,* 61.

10. Sir William S. Holdsworth, *Some Makers of English Law,* 256.

11. Hamburger and Hamburger, *Troubled Lives,* x.

12. Wilfrid E. Rumble, "Nineteenth Century Perceptions of John Austin: A Study of the Reviews of *The Province of Jurisprudence Determined,* 1832–1865," paper presented at the Pacific Coast Branch meeting of the American Historical Association, Hawaii, August 1991.

13. Hamburger and Hamburger, *Contemplating Adultery,* 65.

14. John Austin, *Lectures on Jurisprudence,* IV–V.

15. Hamburger and Hamburger, *Contemplating Adultery,* 55.

16. John Austin, *The Province of Jurisprudence Determined,* 9.

17. Jolowicz, *Lectures on Jurisprudence,* 3.

18. Rumble, *The Thought of John Austin,* 1.

19. Austin, *The Province of Jurisprudence Determined,* 104.

20. John V. Orth, "Casting the Priests Out of the Temple," 239. In *Common Law and English Jurisprudence 1760–1850,* Lobban has argued (at 246) that Austin on utility was irrelevant to Austin's jurisprudence, "for they show fundamentally different methodologies and attitudes to the task he was engaged in." This conclusion about what Austin intended ignores the considerable space Austin devoted to utility and how he attempted, originally at least, to make the principle of utility as much a foundation of his jurisprudence as Bentham had done for his work. See also S. E. Stumpf, "Austin's Theory of the Separation of Law and Morals," 148.

21. Austin, *The Province of Jurisprudence Determined,* 113.

22. Ibid., 13.

23. Ibid., 143.

24. Hamburger and Hamburger, *Troubled Lives,* 182.

25. Morison, *John Austin,* 68.

26. Hamburger and Hamburger, *Troubled Lives,* 191.

27. Lobban, *Common Law and English Jurisprudence 1760–1850,* 223.

28. Hamburger and Hamburger, *Troubled Lives,* 10.

29. Rumble, *The Thought of John Austin,* 16.

30. Wilfrid E. Rumble, "Divine Law, Utilitarian Ethics, and Positivist Jurisprudence," 147.

31. Hamburger and Hamburger, *Troubled Lives,* 170.

32. Rumble, "Divine Law, Utilitarian Ethics, and Positivist Jurisprudence," 147.

33. Lobban, "Blackstone and the Science of Law," 335; Vick, "Sir William Blackstone's Commentaries on the Laws of England," 88.

34. Lobban, *Common Law and English Jurisprudence 1760–1850,* 225–26.

35. Morison, *John Austin,* 141.

36. W. L. Morison, "Some Myth about Positivism," 230.

37. Wilfrid E. Rumble, "The Legal Positivism of John Austin," 1004.

38. Stumpf, "Austin's Theory of the Separation of Law and Morals," 120.

39. John Stuart Mill, "Austin on Jurisprudence," 439, 445.

40. Harrison, "The English School of Jurisprudence," 478.

41. Sir Frederick Pollock, "Law and Command," 191.

42. Rumble, "Divine Law, Utilitarian Ethics, and Positivist Jurisprudence," 173.

43. Geoffrey Marshall, *Constitutional Theory,* 6.

44. Hart, *Essays on Bentham,* 222–23.

45. Harrison, "The English School of Jurisprudence," 492.

46. Rumble, "Divine Law, Utilitarian Ethics, and Positivist Jurisprudence," 180.

47. See Dinwiddy, "Bentham's Transition to Political Radicalism, 1809–10," 683–700.

48. Lobban, *Common Law and English Jurisprudence 1760–1850,* 14.

49. Eira Ruben, "John Austin's Political Pamphlets 1824–1859," 38.

50. Postema, *Bentham and the Common Law Tradition,* 327–28; see also Stefan Collini, *Public Moralists,* 260: "As Sarah Austin recalled of her husband's relations with Bentham: 'My husband used vainly to

represent to him that the ignorance and wrongheadedness of the people were fully as dangerous to good government as the "sinister interests" of the governing classes.' "

51. Hamburger and Hamburger, *Troubled Lives,* 181.

52. Rumble, *The Thought of John Austin,* 193.

53. Stumpf, "Austin's Theory of the Separation of Law and Morals," 145.

54. Sheldon Amos, *The Science of Law,* 4.

55. Sir Frederick Pollock, *A First Book of Jurisprudence,* 33.

56. R. M. Pankhurst, "The Study of Jurisprudence," 749.

57. B. R. Wise, *Outlines of Jurisprudence,* 5.

58. Richard A. Cosgrove, "The Reception of Analytic Jurisprudence," 55–56.

59. Schofield, "Jeremy Bentham and Nineteenth-Century English Jurisprudence," 65.

60. Robert N. Moles, "Law and Morality—How to Do Things with Confusion," 29.

61. Wilfrid E. Rumble, "John Austin and His Nineteenth Century Critics," 144.

62. Raymond Cocks, *Foundations of the Modern Bar,* 49.

63. Collini, *Public Moralists,* 259. Collini does not include Austin among his public moralists: "He did not attempt to present his special study as bearing directly upon the absorbing cultural and political issues of the day, nor did he deploy any of the seductive arts of the reviewer and essayist." The word "directly" is operative here because Austin's purpose was certainly to address fundamental social questions through jurisprudence.

64. John M. Kelly, *A Short History of Western Legal Theory,* 314.

65. John E. Stannard, "A Tale of Four Codes," 293.

66. Atiyah and Summers, *Form and Substance in Anglo-American Law,* 404.

67. Orth, "Casting the Priests Out of the Temple," 236.

68. Postema, *Bentham and the Common Law Tradition,* 330.

69. Lobban, *Common Law and English Jurisprudence 1760–1850,* 223.

70. F. H. Lawson, *The Oxford Law School 1850–1965,* 214; see also Stefan Collini, Donald Winch, and John W. Burrow, *That Noble Science of Politics,* 341: Austin "had examination greatness thrust upon him retrospectively as a result of the growth of legal education and, not

altogether paradoxically, as a result of having been taken as the representative of the *ancien regime* by Maine when launching his methodological revolution." In addition, see Collini, *Public Moralists,* 258, 267.

71. Cosgrove, "The Reception of Analytic Jurisprudence," 49.

72. W. W. Buckland, *Some Reflections on Jurisprudence,* 2.

73. Frederic W. Maitland to Sir Frederick Pollock, 4 December 1899, in C. H. S. Fifoot, ed., *The Letters of Frederic William Maitland,* 253.

74. Rumble, "John Austin and His Nineteenth Century Critics," 133.

75. David Sugarman, "'A Hatred of Disorder,' " 46.

76. Albert Venn Dicey, *Can English Law Be Taught at the Universities?,* 26.

77. Sir William Markby, "Analytical Jurisprudence," 618, 628–29.

78. Pollock, *A First Book of Jurisprudence,* 29.

79. Watson, *The Evolution of Law,* 57–58; and "The Evolution of Law: Continued," 560: "Customary systems of law are very much disguised to borrow from a mature, detailed system in writing even when the latter is constructed on very different lines and was credited for very different social, economic and political conditions."

80. Sir Frederick Pollock, *Oxford Lectures,* 17.

81. Morison, *John Austin,* 136.

82. C. H. S. Fifoot, *Pollock and Maitland,* 13.

83. Morison, *John Austin,* 147.

84. Twining, "Academic Law and Legal Philosophy," 558. See also Sugarman, " 'A Hatred of Disorder,' " 46: "What happened to Bentham was also to befall Austin. Friend and foe alike tended to narrow his ideas."

85. Morison, *John Austin,* 178.

86. Rumble, *The Thought of John Austin,* 220.

Notes to Chapter Five

1. Rumble, "John Austin and His Nineteenth Century Critics," 129.
2. Kenneth E. Bock, "Comparison of Histories," 232.
3. George Feaver, *From Status to Contract,* 27.
4. Cocks, *Sir Henry Maine,* 2.
5. Rumble, "John Austin and His Nineteenth Century Critics," 133.
6. Collini, Winch, and Burrow, *That Noble Science of Politics,* 210.
7. Sir Paul Vinogradoff, "The Teaching of Sir Henry Maine," 121.

8. Bock, "Comparison of Histories," 237.

9. S. G. Utz, "Maine's *Ancient Law* and Legal Theory," 848. See also 827, 848, 850.

10. Feaver, *From Status to Contract,* 45.

11. Peter Stein, *Legal Evolution,* 122.

12. Cocks, *Sir Henry Maine,* 102, 111.

13. Rumble, "John Austin and His Nineteenth Century Critics," 119.

14. These other works were: *Village Communities* (1871); *Lectures on the Early History of Institutions* (1875); *Dissertations on Early Law and Custom* (1883); and *Popular Government* (1885).

15. Sir Henry Maine, *Ancient Law,* 165–70.

16. Cocks, *Sir Henry Maine,* 60–61.

17. Stein, *Legal Evolution,* 87.

18. Rumble, "John Austin and His Nineteenth Century Critics," 122.

19. George Feaver, "Victorian Values of Maine," 37.

20. Cocks, *Sir Henry Maine,* 149.

21. Kelley, *The Human Measure,* 266.

22. Maine, *Ancient Law,* 183.

23. Collini, *Public Moralists,* 272.

24. John W. Burrow, *Evolution and Society,* 11.

25. Collini, Winch, and Burrow, *That Noble Science of Politics,* 209.

26. Cocks, *Sir Henry Maine,* 203; Stein, *Legal Evolution,* 91, pointed out that Maine's own comparisons "were limited."

27. Feaver, *From Status to Contract* , 153.

28. Burrow, *Evolution and Society,* 155.

29. Collini, Winch, and Burrow, *That Noble Science of Politics,* 211.

30. Pollock, *English Opportunities and Duties in the Historical and Comparative Study of Law,* 7–8; "Sir Henry Maine and His Work," 270–71; and "Sir Henry Maine as a Jurist," 104.

31. Pollock, "Maine and His Work," 271.

32. Collini, Winch, and Burrow, *That Noble Science of Politics,* 214.

33. James Bryce, *Studies in History and Jurisprudence,* II, 619.

34. Sir William Holdsworth, *The Historians of Anglo-American Law,* 81.

35. Collini, Winch, and Burrow, *That Noble Science of Politics,* 210.

36. Cocks, *Sir Henry Maine,* 84.

37. Maine, *Lectures on the Early History of Institutions,* 368.

38. Feaver, *From Status to Contract,* 61.

39. Rumble, "John Austin and His Nineteenth Century Critics," 137.

40. Stein, *Legal Evolution,* 122.

41. Cocks, *Sir Henry Maine,* 64.

42. Sir Henry Maine, "The Conception of Sovereignty and Its Importance in International Law," 26–45.

43. Bock, "Comparison of Histories," 239–40.

44. Feaver, *From Status to Contract,* 27.

45. Cocks, *Sir Henry Maine,* 122.

46. Maine, *Lectures on the Early History of Institutions,* 51.

47. Maine, *Ancient Law,* 73.

48. Cocks, *Sir Henry Maine,* 73–75.

49. Rumble, "John Austin and His Nineteenth Century Critics," 122–23, and Collini, *Public Moralists,* 273. Maine resembled Bentham and Austin in the way he embraced moral arguments even as he denounced them in theory. Collini especially emphasizes the moral qualities that Maine used to explain the history of progressive societies.

50. John W. Burrow, "Henry Maine and Mid-Victorian Ideas of Progress," 56–57.

51. Cocks, *Sir Henry Maine,* 14–19.

52. Stein, *Legal Evolution,* 88.

53. Rumble, "John Austin and His Nineteenth Century Critics," 129.

54. Maine, *Popular Government,* 171.

55. Ibid., 77.

56. N. Pilling, "The Conservatism of Sir Henry Maine," 111; Maine, *Popular Government,* 157–58.

57. George Feaver, "The Political Attitudes of Sir Henry Maine," 300–301; Collini, *Public Moralists,* 272.

58. Maine, *Popular Government,* 92.

59. Hugh Tulloch, *James Bryce's American Commonwealth,* 116.

60. Cocks, *Sir Henry Maine,* 11.

61. Rumble, "John Austin and His Nineteenth Century Critics," 120–21.

62. Burrow, *Evolution and Society,* 164.

63. Raymond Cocks, "Maine, Progress and Theory," 72.

64. Cocks, *Sir Henry Maine,* 210; Collini, *Public Moralists,* 274.

65. Brian Smith, "Maine's Concept of Progress," 412.

66. Feaver, *From Status to Contract,* 153.

67. Cocks, *Sir Henry Maine,* 53. For other evidence about Maine's projected audience, see also 2, 4, 37, 62–63, 76, 108, 120, and 210–13.

68. Collini, *Public Moralists,* 276–77.

69. Burrow, "Maine and Mid-Victorian Ideas of Progress," 63.

70. Sir Frederick Pollock to Frederick Maitland, 28 December 1900 and 26 October 1902, Frederick Maitland Papers, Cambridge University Library, Cambridge, England.

71. Maitland to Pollock, 21 January 1901, in Fifoot, ed., *Letters of Maitland,* 222; see also Richard A. Cosgrove, *Our Lady the Common Law,* 169.

72. Holmes to Pollock, 4 March 1888, in Howe, ed., *Holmes-Pollock Letters,* II, 31.

73. Pollock, "Sir Henry Maine and His Work," 271.

74. Rumble, "John Austin and His Nineteenth Century Critics," 148.

75. Cocks, *Sir Henry Maine,* 146.

76. William Twining, "Maine and Legal Education," 215.

77. Feaver, "Victorian Values of Maine," 41.

78. Cocks, "Maine, Progress and Theory," 75.

79. Quotation from James Fitzjames Stephen cited in Rumble, "John Austin and His Nineteenth Century Critics," 148.

80. See Cocks, *Sir Henry Maine,* 101–2, 111, 119.

Notes to Chapter Six

1. J. L. Brierly, "Sir Thomas Erskine Holland," 476.

2. Lawson, *The Oxford Law School, 1850–1965,* 75. See also R. F. V. Heuston, *Essays on Constitutional Law,* 4–5.

3. Brierly, "Holland," 477.

4. James Bryce to A. V. Dicey, 28 January 1917, James Bryce Papers, Bodleian Library, Oxford.

5. Dicey to Bryce, 24 June 1907, Bryce Papers.

6. Dicey to Bryce, 16 January 1910, Bryce Papers.

7. Bryce to Dicey, 25 March 1918, Bryce Papers.

8. Brierly, "Holland," 475.

9. Minute book, Old Mortality Club, Ms. Top. Oxon. d. 242, f. 42, Bodleian Library, Oxford.

10. Dicey to Bryce, 9 December 1884, Bryce Papers.

11. Brierly, "Holland," 477.
12. Sir Thomas Erskine Holland to Melville Madison Bigelow, 15 April 1898, Melville Madison Bigelow Papers, Boston University Library, Boston, Mass.
13. Dicey to Bryce, 27 May 1902, Bryce Papers.
14. Bryce to Holland, n.d., 1910, in Sir William S. Holdsworth, *Professor Sir Thomas Erskine Holland 1835–1926,* 3.
15. Marian Bryce to A. Lawrence Lowell, 13 April 1922, A. Lawrence Lowell Papers, Harvard University Archives, Cambridge, Mass.; Sir Frederick Pollock, "Our Jubilee," 6.
16. Sir William S. Holdsworth, *A History of English Law,* XI, 316.
17. Sir Thomas Erskine Holland, "Codification," 349.
18. Ibid., 372–76.
19. Ibid., 347.
20. Schofield, "Jeremy Bentham and Nineteenth-Century English Jurisprudence," 73.
21. Sir Thomas Erskine Holland, *Essays Upon the Form of the Law,* 13.
22. Sir Thomas Erskine Holland, *The Elements of Jurisprudence,* vii.
23. Ibid., vi–vii.
24. Ibid., vii.
25. Ibid., viii.
26. Ibid., 1.
27. David Sugarman, "Legal Theory, the Common Law Mind and the Making of the Textbook Tradition," 26.
28. Holland to Holmes, 21 March 1888, Holmes Papers.
29. Gregory S. Alexander, "The Transformation of Trusts as a Legal Category, 1800–1914," 306. The emphasis on identification of basic principles provided the "founding myth" of academic law, the "noble dream" common to academic disciplines that would justify their existence. For a specific instance of a founding myth, the issue of objectivity in historical inquiry in the United States, see Peter Novick, *That Noble Dream.*
30. Holland, *Elements of Jurisprudence,* 9.
31. Ibid., 12–13.
32. Ibid., 26.
33. Morison, *John Austin,* 5.
34. Holland, *Elements of Jurisprudence,* 41.
35. Ibid., 52.
36. Brierly, "Holland," 477.

37. Sir Thomas Erskine Holland, *Lectures on International Law,* 6.

38. Holland, *Elements of Jurisprudence,* 386. Emphasis in the original.

39. Ibid., 135.

40. Arthur Tilley, "Professor Holland's 'Jurisprudence' and Codification," 51.

41. Postema, *Bentham and the Common Law Tradition,* 10.

42. Lawson, *Oxford Law School,* 75.

43. Sir Frederick Pollock, *History of the Science of Politics,* 63.

44. Sir Frederick Pollock, *Essays in Jurisprudence and Ethics,* 9.

45. Lawson, *Oxford Law School,* 75.

46. Goodhart, *English Contributions to the Philosophy of Law,* 42.

47. Pollock, *Essays in Jurisprudence and Ethics,* 7; see also James E. Herget, *American Jurisprudence 1870–1970,* 91.

48. Lawson, *Oxford Law School,* 75.

49. A. Pearce Higgins, "Sir Thomas Erskine Holland," 471.

50. Holmes to Harold Laski, 4 January 1925, in Howe, ed., *Holmes-Laski Letters,* II, 692.

51. Cosgrove, "The Reception of Analytical Jurisprudence," 54–55.

52. Holland to Holmes, 25 February 1897, Holmes Papers.

53. R. B. M. Cotterrell, "English Conceptions of the Role of Theory in Legal Analysis," 689.

54. Morison, *John Austin,* 152.

55. Sugarman, "Legal Theory," 44.

56. Collini, *Public Moralists,* 282.

57. Sugarman, "Legal Theory," 44.

58. Perkin, *The Rise of Professional Society.*

59. For the specifics of this process, especially the establishment of an Honours School in jurisprudence, see Collini, *Public Moralists,* 267.

60. Peter R. H. Slee, *Learning and Liberal Education,* 87.

61. Brian Abel-Smith and Robert Stevens, *Lawyers and the Courts,* 166.

62. Sheldon Rothblatt, *The Revolution of the Dons,* 227; Arthur Engel, "Emerging Concepts of the Academic Profession at Oxford 1800–1854," 322–28.

63. This development also had the important consequence of making the state "the chief employer of intellectuals, especially through institutions of higher learning." See Collini, *Public Moralists,* 37; and T. R. Gourvish, "The Rise of the Professions," 13–35.

64. Arthur Engel, *From Clergyman to Don,* 271.

65. Thomas W. Heyck, *The Transformation of Intellectual Life in Victorian England,* 183.

66. Sheldon Rothblatt, *Tradition and Change in English Liberal Education,* 168.

67. Engel, *From Clergyman to Don,* 265.

68. Ibid., 272.

69. Cosgrove, *Our Lady the Common Law,* 28–33.

70. Richard L. Abel, "The Rise of Professionalism," 87.

71. Rothblatt, *Revolution of the Dons,* 175.

72. Abel, "The Rise of Professionalism," 87.

73. Learned journals led the list of professional criteria for academics—later came such measures as "associations, standardized training in esoteric skills, leading to certification and controlled access to practice, heightened status, autonomy." See Novick, *That Noble Dream,* 47–48.

74. Simpson, *Legal Theory and Legal History,* 303. Pollock wrote that the law was "still sadly lacking in instruments both of exposition and of criticism." See "Our Jubilee," 5. Bryce had written to Holmes in 1879 that "no respectable magazine devoted to jurisprudence of law can be kept alive." Bryce to Holmes, 26 July 1879, Holmes Papers. See also Richard A. Cosgrove, "Victorian Legal Periodicals," 21–25, and "Law," 11–21.

75. Collini has listed the debut of learned journals to illustrate the appearance of modern academic disciplines in England: *Mind,* 1876; *Law Quarterly Review,* 1884; *English Historical Review,* 1886; *Proceedings of the Aristotelian Society,* 1887; *Classical Review,* 1887; and the *Economic Journal,* 1891. Collini also concluded that "the establishment of such specialized publications usually reflected (perhaps it always does) what one might call 'supply push' rather than 'demand pull': the dynamic came from those who wished to write in a more specialized idiom at least as much as from those who wished to have such material to read." Collini, *Public Moralists,* 213.

76. Lucy Markby, *Memoirs of Sir William Markby, K.C.I.E. By His Wife,* 77; Holdsworth, *Holland,* 2.

77. Pollock, "Our Jubilee," 6.

78. Neil Duxbury, "Deconstruction, History and the Uses of Legal Theory," 167.

79. See Philip Abrams, *The Origins of British Sociology, 1834–1914;* Collini, Winch, and Burrow, *That Noble Science of Politics;* Rosemary

Jann, *The Art and Science of Victorian History;* and George W. Stocking, *Victorian Anthropology.*

80. On the subject of audience, Novick has written: "Pre-professional work was directed outward, to the general reading public. Professional historical work was increasingly, though unlike other disciplines, never exclusively, directed to colleagues." The new culture of academic law soon dispensed with the attempt to reach the educated public.

81. Anthony Brundage, *The People's Historian,* 117.

82. A. H. Halsey and M. A. Trow, *The British Academics,* 362; see also Philippa Levine, *The Amateur and the Professional,* 36.

83. Cosgrove, *Our Lady the Common Law,* 2–5.

84. Levine, *The Amateur and the Professional,* 59.

85. Collini, *Public Moralists,* 268.

86. Morison, *John Austin,* 151.

87. Dicey, *Can English Law Be Taught at the Universities?*

88. P. S. Atiyah, *Pragmatism and Theory in English Law,* 3.

89. Cotterrell, "English Conceptions of the Role of Theory," 681.

90. Peter Allen, "A Victorian Intellectual Elite," 122.

91. Holdsworth, *Holland,* 3.

92. Christopher Harvie, *The Lights of Liberalism,* 213. Reba Soffer has made the same point about the history curriculum at the Oxbridge universities. Although the methodology of history, particularly the emphasis on archival research, was new, the purpose of inculcating the lessons of history remained the same: service to nation and empire. See Reba N. Soffer, *Discipline and Power,* 118.

93. Holland to Holmes, 8 November 1891, Holmes Papers.

94. Robert Stevens, *Law and Politics,* 194.

95. Peter Scott, *The Crisis of the University,* 67.

96. P. Goodrich, "Review of Roger Cotterrell, *The Politics of Jurisprudence,*" 148.

97. Scott, *The Crisis of the University,* 69.

98. Atiyah, *Pragmatism and Theory in English Law,* 35.

99. Collini, *Public Moralists,* 306.

100. Sugarman, "Legal Theory," 53.

101. Schofield, "Jeremy Bentham and Nineteenth-Century English Jurisprudence," 74–75.

102. Kelley, *The Human Measure,* 278.

Notes to Chapter Seven

1. Roscoe Pound to Felix Frankfurter, 6 June 1922, Felix Frankfurter Papers, Library of Congress, Washington, D.C.

2. Cotterrell, "English Conceptions of the Role of Theory in Legal Analysis," 689.

3. MacCormick, *H. L. A. Hart,* 18.

4. W. T. Murphy and Simon Roberts, "Introduction," 677.

5. Geoffrey Wilson, "English Legal Scholarship," 843.

6. Colin A. Campbell, "The Career of the Concept," 2.

7. Biographical details on Hart's life are taken from MacCormick, *Hart;* and from Michael Martin, *The Legal Philosophy of H. L. A. Hart.*

8. Kelly, *Short History of Western Legal Theory,* 403, describes *The Concept of Law:* "Neither very long nor very elaborate, it provoked an immense literature and must be reckoned, whatever faults may be found with it, one of the seminal works of twentieth-century jurisprudence."

9. MacCormick, *Hart,* 3. For Hart's central place in English jurisprudence, see also Twining, "Academic Law and Legal Philosophy," 557.

10. Adijare Oledasu, "H. L. A. Hart on Legal Obligation," 152.

11. Morison, *Austin,* 178.

12. Robert N. Moles, "The Decline and Fall of Dworkin's Empire," 111.

13. Ibid., 96.

14. H. L. A. Hart, *The Concept of Law,* 50. Emphasis in the original.

15. Ibid., 61. Emphasis in the original.

16. Ibid., 77–96.

17. Campbell, "The Career of the Concept," 9–10.

18. Oledasu, "H. L. A. Hart on Legal Obligation," 156.

19. Martin, *The Legal Philosophy of H. L. A. Hart,* 6.

20. H. L. A. Hart, "Definition and Theory in Jurisprudence."

21. Ibid., 60.

22. Hart, *The Concept of Law,* 18–25.

23. MacCormick, *Hart,* 12.

24. R. Birmingham, "Hart's *Definition and Theory in Jurisprudence* Again," 789.

25. MacCormick, *Hart,* 12.

26. Philip Milton, "H. L. A. Hart: Jurisprudence and Linguistic Philosophy," 751.

27. P. M. S. Hacker, "Hart's Philosophy of Law," 2; see also Martin Krygier, "*The Concept of Law* and Social Theory," 155.

28. MacCormick, *Hart,* 19.

29. Hart, "Bentham on Legal Powers," 820.

30. J. Raz, "Hart on Moral Rights and Legal Duties," 123–24.

31. Moles, *Definition and Rule in Legal Theory,* 15.

32. K. A. Warner, "The Concept of Legal Obligation and the Separation of Law and Morality," 69; see also Aidan O'Neill, "The Legal Philosophies of H. L. A. Hart," 32.

33. Daniel W. Skubik, *At the Intersection of Legality and Morality,* 187. Emphasis in the original.

34. William C. Starr, "Law and Morality in H. L. A. Hart's Legal Philosophy," 675.

35. Keith Lovin, "H. L. A. Hart and the Morality of Law," 131.

36. Lon Fuller, *The Morality of Law,* 40.

37. MacCormick, *Hart,* 24–25.

38. Twining, "Academic Law and Legal Philosophy," 58.

39. J. W. Van Doren, "Theories of Professors H. L. A. Hart and Ronald Dworkin," 307.

40. Twining, "Academic Law and Legal Philosophy," 571.

41. Moles, "The Decline and Fall of Dworkin's Empire," 81.

42. Patrick Devlin, *The Enforcement of Morals,* 11.

43. H. L. A. Hart, *Law, Liberty and Morality,* 23–24.

44. Ibid., 50.

45. Robert P. George, "Social Cohesion and the Legal Enforcement of Morals," 30.

46. R. Hittinger, "The Hart-Devlin Debate Revisited," 53.

47. See Stefan Petrow, "The Legal Enforcement of Morality in Late-Victorian and Edwardian England," 59–74.

48. Zenon Bankowski, "Review of Leith and Ingram, eds., *The Jurisprudence of Orthodoxy,*" 118.

49. Campbell, "The Career of the Concept," 22.

50. Murphy and Roberts, "Introduction," 683.

51. Campbell, "The Career of the Concept," 21.

52. Ruth Gavison, ed., *Issues in Contemporary Legal Philosophy,* 1.

53. Hart, *The Concept of Law,* vii.

54. Peter Fitzpatrick, "The Abstracts and Brief Chronicles of the Times," 28.

55. Campbell, "The Career of the Concept," 24.

Notes to Chapter Eight

1. Peter Charles Hoffer, "Text, Translation, Context, Conversation," 410.

2. Twining, "Maine and Legal Education," 215–16.

3. Alan Watson, *Failures of the Legal Imagination,* 107.

4. Watson, "The Evolution of Law: Continued," 569; see also idem, "Legal Change: Sources of Law and Legal Culture," 1154.

5. Watson, "The Evolution of Law: Continued," 569.

6. Alan Paterson, *The Law Lords,* 14–15, 34; Cotterrell, *The Politics of Jurisprudence,* 221.

7. William C. Lubenow, "The Universities, the Professions, and British Society in the Nineteenth Century," paper delivered at the Western Conference on British Studies, Boulder, Colorado, October 1992, 25.

8. Alan Watson, *Joseph Story and the Comity of Errors,* 71.

9. Roger Shiner, *Norm and Nature,* 44–46.

10. N. E. H. Hull, "Networks and Bricolage," 317–19.

11. Wilfrid J. Waluchow, "Hart, Legal Rules and Palm Tree Justice," 41–70.

12. Perkin, *The Rise of Professional Society,* 397.

13. Neil Duxbury, "Post-Modern Jurisprudence and Its Discontents," 591.

14. Watson, *Failures of the Legal Imagination,* 124.

15. Collini, *Public Moralists,* 254.

Bibliography

Primary Works

Austin, *Lectures on Jurisprudence* (1863). 2 vols. New York: Burt Franklin, 1970.

———. *The Province of Jurisprudence Determined* (1832). London: Weidenfeld and Nicolson, 1954.

Bentham, Jeremy. *A Comment on the Commentaries.* London: Athlone Press, 1977.

———. *The Correspondence of Jeremy Bentham.* 8 vols. London: Athlone Press and Oxford University Press, 1968–88.

———. *A Fragment on Government* (1776). London: Athlone Press, 1977.

———. *Of Laws in General.* London: Athlone Press, 1970.

———. *Introduction to the Principles of Morals and Legislation* (1789). New York: Hafner Press, 1948.

Blackstone, Sir William. *Commentaries on the Laws of England.* 4 vols. Oxford: Clarendon Press, 1765–69.

———. *A Discourse on the Study of Law.* Oxford: Clarendon Press, 1758.

Hart, H. L. A. *The Concept of Law.* Oxford: Clarendon Press, 1961; 2d ed., 1994.

———. *Essays on Bentham: Studies on Jurisprudence and Political Theory.* Oxford: Clarendon Press, 1982.

———. *Essays in Jurisprudence and Philosophy.* Oxford: Clarendon Press, 1983.

———. *Law, Liberty and Morality.* Stanford, Calif.: Stanford University Press, 1963.

Holland, Sir Thomas Erskine. *The Elements of Jurisprudence.* Oxford: Clarendon Press, 1880.
———. *Essays Upon the Form of the Law.* London: Butterworth's, 1870.
———. *Lectures on International Law.* London: Sweet and Maxwell, 1898.
Maine, Sir Henry. *Ancient Law* (1861). New York: Henry Holt, 1864.
———. *Dissertations on Early Law and Custom* (1883). New York: Henry Holt, 1886.
———. *Lectures on the Early History of Institutions* (1875). New York: Henry Holt, 1886.
———. *Popular Government* (1885). New York: Henry Holt, 1886.
———. *Village Communities* (1871). New York: Henry Holt, 1889.

Secondary Works

Abel, Richard L. *The Legal Profession in England and Wales.* Oxford: Basil Blackwell, 1988.
Abel-Smith, Brian, and Robert B. Stevens. *Lawyers and the Courts: A Sociological Study of the English Legal System, 1760–1965.* Cambridge, Mass.: Harvard University Press, 1967.
Abrams, Philip. *The Origins of British Sociology, 1834–1914.* Chicago: University of Chicago Press, 1968.
Amos, Sheldon. *The Science of Law.* London: Stevens, 1874.
Atiyah, P. S. *Pragmatism and Theory in English Law.* London: Stevens and Sons, 1987.
Atiyah, P. S., and Robert S. Summers. *Form and Substance in Anglo-American Law: A Comparative Study of Legal Reasoning, Legal Theory, and Legal Institutions.* Oxford: Clarendon Press, 1987.
Bahmueller, Charles F. *The National Charity Company: Jeremy Bentham's Silent Revolution.* Berkeley and Los Angeles: University of California Press, 1981.
Barrow, Robin. *Utilitarianism: A Contemporary Statement.* Aldershot: Edward Elgar, 1991.
Bayles, Michael D. *Hart's Legal Philosophy: An Examination.* Dordrecht: Kluwer Academic Publishers, 1992.
Benditt, Theodore M. *Law as Rule and Principle: Problems of Legal Philosophy.* Stanford, Calif.: Stanford University Press, 1978.
Boorstin, Daniel J. *The Mysterious Science of the Law.* Cambridge, Mass.: Harvard University Press, 1941.

Brundage, Anthony. *England's "Prussian Minister": Edwin Chadwick and the Politics of Government Growth, 1832–1854*. University Park: Pennsylvania State University Press, 1988.

———. *The People's Historian: John Richard Green and the Writing of History in Victorian England*. Westport, Conn.: Greenwood Press, 1994.

Bryce, James. *Studies in History and Jurisprudence*. 2 vols. London: Oxford University Press, 1901.

Buckland, W. W. *Some Reflections on Jurisprudence*. Cambridge, Eng.: Cambridge University Press, 1945.

Burrow, John W. *Evolution and Society: A Study in Victorian Social Theory*. Cambridge, Eng.: Cambridge University Press, 1966.

———. *Whigs and Liberals: Continuity and Change in English Political Thought*. Oxford: Clarendon Press, 1988.

Campos Boralevi, Lea. *Bentham and the Oppressed*. Berlin: Walter de Gruyter, 1984.

Clark, J. C. D. *English Society 1688–1832: Ideology, Social Structure and Political Practice during the Ancien Regime*. Cambridge, Eng.: Cambridge University Press, 1985.

———. *Revolution and Rebellion: State and Society in England in the Seventeenth and Eighteenth Centuries*. Cambridge, Eng.: Cambridge University Press, 1986.

Cocks, Raymond. *Foundations of the Modern Bar*. London: Sweet and Maxwell, 1983.

———. *Sir Henry Maine: A Study in Victorian Jurisprudence*. Cambridge, Eng.: Cambridge University Press, 1988.

Colaiaco, James A. *James Fitzjames Stephen and the Crisis of Victorian Thought*. New York: St. Martin's Press, 1983.

Colley, Linda. *Britons: Forging the Nation 1707–1837*. New Haven: Yale University Press, 1992.

Collini, Stefan. *Public Moralists: Political Thought and Intellectual Life in Britain, 1850–1930*. Oxford: Clarendon Press, 1991.

Collini, Stefan, Donald Winch, and John W. Burrow. *That Noble Science of Politics: A Study in Nineteenth-Century Intellectual History*. Cambridge, Eng.: Cambridge University Press, 1983.

Cosgrove, Richard A. *Our Lady the Common Law: An Anglo-American Legal Community, 1870–1930*. New York and London: New York University Press, 1987.

———. *The Rule of Law: Albert Venn Dicey, Victorian Jurist*. Chapel Hill: University of North Carolina Press, 1980.

Cotterrell, Roger. *The Politics of Jurisprudence: A Critical Introduction to Legal Philosophy.* London: Butterworth's, 1989.

Crimmins, James E. *Secular Utilitarianism: Social Science and the Critique of Religion in the Thought of Jeremy Bentham.* New York: Oxford University Press, 1990.

Devlin, Patrick. *The Enforcement of Morals.* London: Oxford University Press, 1965.

Dicey, A. V. *Can English Law Be Taught at the Universities?* London: Macmillan, 1883.

Dickinson, H. T. *Liberty and Property: Political Ideology in Eighteenth-Century Britain.* London: Weidenfeld and Nicolson, 1977.

Dinwiddy, John. *Bentham.* New York: Oxford University Press, 1989.

Dube, Allison. *The Theme of Acquisitiveness in Bentham's Political Thought.* New York: Garland, 1991.

Ebenstein, Alan O. *The Greatest Happiness Principle: An Examination of Utilitarianism.* New York: Garland, 1991.

Engel, Arthur. *From Clergyman to Don: The Rise of the Academic Profession in 19th-Century Oxford.* Oxford: Clarendon Press, 1983.

Everett, C. W. *The Education of Jeremy Bentham.* New York: Columbia University Press, 1931.

Feaver, George. *From Status to Contract: A Biography of Sir Henry Sumner Maine 1822–1888.* London: Longmans, 1969.

Fifoot, Cecil H. S. *Judge and Jurist in the Reign of Victoria.* London: Stevens and Sons, 1959.

———. *Pollock and Maitland.* Glasgow: George Outram, 1971.

———, ed. *The Letters of Frederic William Maitland.* Cambridge, Mass.: Harvard University Press, 1965.

Finnis, John. *Natural Law and Natural Rights.* Oxford: Clarendon Press, 1980.

Fuller, Lon. *The Morality of Law.* New Haven: Yale University Press, 1964.

Garland, Martha M. *Cambridge before Darwin: The Ideal of a Liberal Education, 1800–60.* Cambridge, Eng.: Cambridge University Press, 1980.

Gavison, Ruth, ed. *Issues in Contemporary Legal Philosophy: The Influence of H. L. A. Hart.* Oxford: Clarendon Press, 1987.

Goodhart, A. L. *English Contributions to the Philosophy of Law.* Oxford: Oxford University Press, 1949.

Goodrich, Peter. *Languages of Law: From Logics of Memory to Nomadic Masks.* London: Weidenfeld and Nicolson, 1990.

Haakonssen, Knud. *The Science of a Legislator: The Natural Jurisprudence of David Hume and Adam Smith.* Cambridge, Eng.: Cambridge University Press, 1981.

Halevy, Elie. *The Growth of Philosophic Radicalism.* New York: Harcourt, Brace, 1926.

Halsey, A. H. *Decline of Donnish Dominion: The British Academic Professions in the Twentieth Century.* Oxford: Clarendon Press, 1992.

Halsey, A. H., and M. A. Trow. *The British Academics.* London: Faber and Faber, 1971.

Hamburger, Lotte and Joseph. *Contemplating Adultery: The Secret Life of a Victorian Woman.* New York: Fawcett Columbine, 1991.

———. *Troubled Lives: John and Sarah Austin.* Toronto: University of Toronto Press, 1985.

Hanbury, H. G. *The Vinerian Chair and Legal Education.* Oxford: Basil Blackwell, 1958.

Harrison, Ross. *Bentham.* London: Routledge and Kegan Paul, 1983.

Harvie, Christopher. *The Lights of Liberalism: University Liberals and the Challenge of Democracy 1860–1886.* London: Allen Lane, 1976.

Herget, James E. *American Jurisprudence, 1870–1970: A History.* Houston: Rice University Press, 1990.

Heuston, R. F. V. *Essays in Constitutional Law.* 2d ed. Oxford: Oxford University Press, 1964.

Heyck, Thomas W. *The Transformation of Intellectual Life in Victorian England.* London: Croom Helm, 1982.

Holdsworth, Sir William S. *The Historians of Anglo-American Law.* New York: Columbia University Press, 1928.

———. *A History of English Law.* 17 vols. Boston: Little, Brown, 1903–72.

———. *Professor Sir Thomas Erskine Holland 1835–1926.* London: Humphrey Milford, 1927.

———. *Some Makers of English Law.* Cambridge, Eng.: Cambridge University Press, 1938.

Horne, Thomas A. *Property Rights and Poverty: Political Argument in Britain, 1605–1834.* Chapel Hill: University of North Carolina Press, 1990.

Howe, Mark DeWolfe, ed. *Holmes-Laski Letters: The Correspondence of Mr. Justice Holmes and Harold J. Laski 1916–1935.* 2 vols. Cambridge, Mass.: Harvard University Press, 1953.

———. *Holmes-Pollock Letters: The Correspondence of Mr. Justice Holmes and Sir Frederick Pollock 1874–1932.* 2 vols. Cambridge, Mass.: Harvard University Press, 1942.

Hume, L. J. *Bentham and Bureaucracy.* Cambridge, Eng.: Cambridge University Press, 1981.

Jann, Rosemary. *The Art and Science of Victorian History.* Columbus: Ohio State University Press, 1985.

Jolowicz, H. F. *Lectures on Jurisprudence.* London: Athlone Press, 1963.

Kelley, Donald R. *The Human Measure: Social Thought in the Western Legal Tradition.* Cambridge, Mass.: Harvard University Press, 1990.

Kelly, John M. *A Short History of Western Legal Theory.* New York: Oxford University Press, 1992.

Kelly, Paul J. *Utilitarianism and Distributive Justice: Jeremy Bentham and the Civil Law.* New York: Oxford University Press, 1990.

Lawson, F. H. *The Oxford Law School, 1850–1965.* Oxford: Clarendon Press, 1968.

Letwin, Shirley R. *The Pursuit of Certainty.* Cambridge, Eng.: Cambridge University Press, 1965.

Levine, Philippa. *The Amateur and the Professional: Antiquarians, Historians and Archaeologists in Victorian England, 1838–1886.* Cambridge, Eng.: Cambridge University Press, 1986.

Lieberman, David. *The Province of Legislation Determined: Legal Theory in Eighteenth-Century Britain.* Cambridge, Eng.: Cambridge University Press, 1989.

Lobban, Michael. *Common Law and English Jurisprudence 1760–1850.* New York: Oxford University Press, 1991.

Lockmiller, David A. *Sir William Blackstone.* Chapel Hill: University of North Carolina Press, 1938.

Long, Douglas G. *Bentham on Liberty: Jeremy Bentham's Idea of Liberty in Relation to His Utilitarianism.* Toronto: University of Toronto Press, 1977.

Lyons, David. *In the Interest of the Governed: A Study in Bentham's Philosophy of Utility and Law.* Oxford: Clarendon Press, 1973.

MacCormick, Neil. *H. L. A. Hart.* London: Edward Arnold, 1981.

Mack, Mary P. *Jeremy Bentham: An Odyssey of Ideas 1748–1792.* London: Heinemann, 1962.

Manning, D. J. *The Mind of Jeremy Bentham.* London: Longmans, Green, 1968.

Markby, Lucy. *Memoirs of Sir William Markby, K.C.I.E. By His Wife.* Oxford: Clarendon Press, 1917.

Martin, Michael. *The Legal Philosophy of H. L. A. Hart: A Critical Appraisal.* Philadelphia: Temple University Press, 1987.

Marshall, Geoffrey. *Constitutional Theory.* Oxford: Clarendon Press, 1971.

McCulloch, Gary. *Philosophers and Kings: Education for Leadership in Modern England.* Cambridge, Eng.: Cambridge University Press, 1991.

Moles, Robert N. *Definition and Rule in Legal Theory: A Reassessment of H. L. A. Hart and the Positivist Tradition.* Oxford: Basil Blackwell, 1987.

Morison, W. L. *John Austin.* Stanford, Calif.: Stanford University Press, 1982.

Novick, Peter. *That Noble Dream: The "Objectivity Question" and the American Historical Profession.* Cambridge, Eng.: Cambridge University Press, 1988.

Ogden, C. K. *Bentham's Theory of Fictions.* London: Kegan Paul, 1932.

Parker, Christopher. *The English Historical Tradition since 1850.* Edinburgh: John Donald, 1990.

Paterson, Alan. *The Law Lords.* Toronto: University of Toronto Press, 1982.

Perkin, Harold. *The Rise of Professional Society: England since 1880.* London: Routledge, 1989.

Philip, I. G. *William Blackstone and the Reform of the Oxford University Press.* Oxford: Oxford Bibliographical Society Publications, 1957.

Plamenatz, John. *The English Utilitarians.* Oxford: Basil Blackwell, 1949.

Pohlman, Harry L. *Justice Oliver Wendell Holmes and Utilitarian Jurisprudence.* Cambridge, Mass.: Harvard University Press, 1984.

Pollock, Sir Frederick. *English Opportunities and Duties in the Historical and Comparative Study of Law.* London: Macmillan, 1883.

———. *Essays in Jurisprudence and Ethics.* London: Macmillan, 1882.

———. *A First Book of Jurisprudence for Students of the Common Law.* London: Stevens and Sons, 1896.

———. *History of the Science of Politics.* London: Macmillan, 1883.

———. *Oxford Lectures and Other Discussions.* London: Macmillan, 1890.

Posner, Richard A. *The Problems of Jurisprudence.* Cambridge, Mass.: Harvard University Press, 1990.

Postema, Gerald J. *Bentham and the Common Law Tradition.* Oxford: Clarendon Press, 1986.

Quinton, Anthony. *Utilitarian Ethics.* 2d ed. London: Duckworth, 1989.

Ringer, Fritz. *Fields of Knowledge: French Academic Culture in Comparative Perspective 1890–1920*. Cambridge, Eng.: Cambridge University Press, 1992.

Rosen, Frederick. *Jeremy Bentham and Representative Democracy: A Study of the Constitutional Code*. Oxford: Clarendon Press, 1983.

Rosenblum, Nancy L. *Bentham's Theory of the Modern State*. Cambridge, Mass.: Harvard University Press, 1978.

Rothblatt, Sheldon. *The Revolution of the Dons: Cambridge and Society in Victorian England*. New York: Basic Books, 1968.

———. *Tradition and Change in English Liberal Education: An Essay in History and Culture*. London: Faber and Faber, 1976.

Rumble, Wilfrid E. *The Thought of John Austin: Jurisprudence, Colonial Reform, and the British Constitution*. London: Athlone Press, 1985.

Scott, Peter. *The Crisis of the University*. London: Croom Helm, 1984.

Semple, Janet. *Bentham's Prison: A Study of the Panopticon Penitentiary*. Oxford: Clarendon Press, 1993.

Shiner, Roger. *Norm and Nature: The Movements of Legal Thought*. Oxford: Clarendon Press, 1992.

Simpson, A. W. B. *Legal Theory and Legal History: Essays on the Common Law*. London: Hambledon Press, 1987.

Skubik, Daniel W. *At the Intersection of Legality and Morality: Hartian Law as Natural Law*. New York: Peter Lang, 1990.

Slee, Peter R. H. *Learning and a Liberal Education: The Study of Modern History in the Universities of Oxford, Cambridge and Manchester, 1800–1914*. Manchester, Eng.: Manchester University Press, 1986.

Smith, K. J. M. *James Fitzjames Stephen: Portrait of a Victorian Rationalist*. Cambridge, Eng.: Cambridge University Press, 1988.

Smith, R. J. *The Gothic Bequest: Medieval Institutions in British Thought, 1688–1863*. New York: Cambridge University Press, 1987.

Soffer, Reba N. *Discipline and Power: The University, History, and the Making of an English Elite 1870–1930*. Stanford, Calif.: Stanford University Press, 1994.

Stein, Peter. *Legal Evolution: The Story of an Idea*. Cambridge, Eng.: Cambridge University Press, 1980.

Steintrager, James. *Bentham*. London: Allen and Unwin, 1977.

Stephen, Leslie. *The English Utilitarians*. 3 vols. New York: G. P. Putnam's Sons, 1900.

Stevens, Robert B. *The Independence of the Judiciary: The View from the Lord Chancellor's Office*. Oxford: Clarendon Press, 1993.

———. *Law and Politics: The House of Lords as a Judicial Body, 1800–1976*. Chapel Hill: University of North Carolina Press, 1978.

Stocking, George W. *Victorian Anthropology*. New York: Free Press, 1987.

Summers, Robert S. *Instrumentalism and American Legal Theory*. Ithaca, N.Y.: Cornell University Press, 1982.

Thomas, William. *The Philosophic Radicals: Nine Studies in Theory and Practice 1817–1841*. Oxford: Clarendon Press, 1979.

Tulloch, Hugh. *James Bryce's American Commonwealth: The Anglo-American Background*. Woodbridge, Eng.: Royal Historical Society, 1988.

Twining, William. *Theories of Evidence: Bentham and Wigmore*. London: Weidenfeld and Nicolson, 1985.

Van Caenegem, R. C. *Judges, Legislators and Professors: Chapters in European Legal History*. Cambridge, Eng.: Cambridge University Press, 1987.

Watson, Alan. *The Evolution of Law*. Baltimore: Johns Hopkins University Press, 1985.

———. *Failures of the Legal Imagination*. Edinburgh: Scottish Academic Press, 1988.

———. *Joseph Story and the Comity of Errors: A Case Study in Conflict in Laws*. Athens: University of Georgia Press, 1992.

Wise, B. R. *Outlines of Jurisprudence*. Oxford: Oxford University Press, 1881.

Zweiben, Beverly. *How Blackstone Lost the Colonies: English Law, Colonial Lawyers, and the American Revolution*. New York: Garland, 1990.

Articles

Abel, Richard L. "The Rise of Professionalism." *British Journal of Law and Society* 6 (Summer 1979): 82–98.

Alexander, Gregory S. "The Transformation of Trusts as a Legal Category, 1800–1914." *Law and History Review* 5 (Fall 1987): 303–50.

Allen, Peter. "A Victorian Intellectual Elite: Records of the Cambridge Apostles, 1820–77." *Victorian Studies* (Autumn 1989): 99–123.

Anon. "Austin's Comments on Blackstone's Commentaries." *Law Magazine and Review,* New Series 2 (October 1873): 922–31.

———. "Hart, Austin, and the Concept of a Legal System: The Primacy of Sanctions." *Yale Law Journal* 84 (January 1975): 584–607.

Bankowski, Zenon. "Review of Philip Leith and Peter Ingram, eds., *The Jurisprudence of Orthodoxy.*" *Legal Studies* 9 (March 1989): 116–18.

Barton, J. L. "Legal Studies." In L. S. Sutherland and L. G. Mitchell, eds., *The History of the University of Oxford: The Eighteenth Century,* pp. 593–605. Oxford: Clarendon Press, 1986.

Beynon, Helen. "Mighty Bentham." *Journal of Legal History* 2 (May 1981): 62–76.

Birmingham, Robert. "Hart's *Definition and Theory in Jurisprudence* Again." *Connecticut Law Review* 16 (Summer 1984): 775–801.

Bock, Kenneth E. "Comparison of Histories: The Contribution of Henry Maine." *Comparative Studies in Society and History* 16 (March 1974): 232–62.

Bradley, James E. "The Anglican Pulpit, the Social Order, and the Resurgence of Toryism during the American Revolution." *Albion* 21 (Fall 1989): 361–88.

Brierly, J. L. "Sir Thomas Erskine Holland." *Law Quarterly Review* 42 (October 1926): 475–77.

Burkholder, L. "Tarlton on Bentham's *Fragment on Government.*" *Political Studies* 21 (December 1973): 523–26.

Burns, J. H. "Bentham on Sovereignty: An Exploration." *Northern Ireland Legal Quarterly* 24 (Autumn 1973): 399–416.

Burns, Robert P. "Blackstone's Theory of the 'Absolute' Rights of Property." *University of Cincinnati Law Review* 54, no. 1 (1985): 67–86.

Burrow, John W. "Henry Maine and Mid-Victorian Ideas of Progress." In Alan Diamond, ed., *The Victorian Achievement of Sir Henry Maine: A Centennial Reappraisal,* pp. 55–69. Cambridge, Eng.: Cambridge University Press, 1991.

Cairns, John. "Blackstone, the Ancient Constitution and the Feudal Law." *Historical Journal* 28 (December 1985): 711–17.

———. "Blackstone, an English Institutist: Legal Literature and the Rise of the Nation State." *Oxford Journal of Legal Studies* 4 (Winter 1984): 318–60.

Campbell, Colin M. "The Career of the Concept." In Philip Leith and Peter Ingram, eds., *The Jurisprudence of Orthodoxy: Queen's University Essays on H. L. A. Hart,* pp. 1–25. London: Routledge, 1988.

Chroust, Anton-Herman. "Blackstone Revisited." *University of Kansas City Law Review* 17 (December–February 1949): 24–34.

Clark, J. C. D. "England's Ancien Regime as a Confessional State." *Albion* 21 (Fall 1989): 450–74.

———. "On Hitting the Buffers: The Historiography of England's Ancien Regime. A Response." *Past and Present* 117 (November 1987): 195–207.

Cocks, Raymond. "Maine, Progress and Theory." In Alan Diamond, ed., *The Victorian Achievement of Sir Henry Maine: A Centennial Reappraisal,* pp. 70–75. Cambridge, Eng.: Cambridge University Press, 1991.

———. "Sir Henry Maine: 1822–1888." *Legal Studies* 8 (November 1988): 247–57.

Conway, Stephen. "Bentham and the Nineteenth-Century Revolution in Government." In Richard Bellamy, ed., *Victorian Liberalism: Nineteenth Century Political Thought and Practice,* pp. 71–90. London: Routledge, 1990.

Cosgrove, Richard A. "Law." In J. Don Vann and Rosemary T. Van Arsdel, eds., *Victorian Periodicals and Victorian Society,* pp. 11–21. Toronto and Buffalo: University of Toronto Press, 1994.

———. "The Reception of Analytic Jurisprudence: The Victorian Debate on the Separation of Law and Morality." *Durham University Journal* 74 (December 1981): 47–56.

———. "Victorian Legal Periodicals." *Victorian Periodicals Newsletter* 8 (March 1975): 21–25.

Cotterrell, Roger. "English Conceptions of the Role of Theory in Legal Analysis." *Modern Law Review* 46 (November 1983): 681–99.

Cross, Rupert. "Blackstone v. Bentham." *Law Quarterly Review* 92 (October 1976): 516–27.

———. "The First Two Vinerian Professors: Blackstone and Chambers." *William and Mary Law Review* 20 (Summer 1979): 602–24.

Dicey, A. V. "Blackstone's *Commentaries.*" *National Review* 54 (December 1909): 653–74.

———. "The Study of Jurisprudence." *Law Magazine and Review,* Fourth Series 5 (August 1880): 382–401.

Dickinson, H. T. "The Eighteenth Century Debate on the Sovereignty of Parliament." *Transactions of the Royal Historical Society,* Fifth Series 26 (1976): 189–210.

Dinwiddy, John R. "Bentham's Transition to Political Radicalism, 1809–10." *Journal of the History of Ideas* 36 (October–December 1975): 683–700.

Doolittle, I. G. "Sir William Blackstone and His *Commentaries on the Laws of England* (1765–69): A Biographical Approach." *Oxford Journal of Legal Studies* 3 (Spring 1983): 99–112.

Duncanson, I. W. "The Strange World of English Jurisprudence." *Northern Ireland Legal Quarterly* 30 (Autumn 1979): 207–24.

Duxbury, Neil. "Deconstruction, History and the Uses of Legal Theory." *Northern Ireland Legal Quarterly* 41 (Summer 1990): 167–75.

———. "Making Legal History." *Modern Law Review* 52 (November 1989): 856–67.

———. "Post-Modern Jurisprudence and Its Discontents." *Oxford Journal of Legal Studies* 11 (Winter 1991): 589–97.

———. "Struggling with Legal Theory." *University of Toronto Law Journal* 43 (Fall 1993): 889–908.

Edgeworth, B. "H. L. A. Hart, Legal Positivism and Post-War British Labourism." *University of Western Australia Law Review* 19 (December 1989): 275–300.

Engel, Arthur. "Emerging Concepts of the Academic Profession at Oxford 1800–1854." In Lawrence Stone, ed., *The University in Society,* 2 vols., pp. 305–51. Princeton, N.J.: Princeton University Press, 1974.

Feaver, George. "The Political Attitudes of Sir Henry Sumner Maine." *Journal of Politics* 27 (May 1965): 290–317.

———. "The Victorian Values of Sir Henry Maine." In Alan Diamond, ed., *The Victorian Achievement of Sir Henry Maine: A Centennial Reappraisal,* pp. 28–52. Cambridge, Eng.: Cambridge University Press, 1991.

Finer, S. E. "The Transmission of Benthamite Ideas 1820–1850." In Gillian Sutherland, ed., *Studies in the Growth of Nineteenth Century Government,* pp. 11–32. London: Routledge and Kegan Paul, 1972.

Finnis, John N. "Blackstone's Theoretical Intentions." *Natural Law Forum* 12 (1967): 163–83.

Fitzpatrick, Peter. "The Abstracts and Brief Chronicles of the Times: Supplementary Jurisprudence." In Peter Fitzpatrick, ed., *Dangerous Supplements: Resistance and Renewal* in *Jurisprudence,* pp. 1–33. London: Pluto Press, 1991.

Friedmann, W. "Bentham and Modern Legal Thought." In George W. Keeton and Georg Schwarzenberger, eds., *Jeremy Bentham and the Law,* pp. 233–44. London: Stevens and Sons, 1948.

George, Robert P. "Social Cohesion and the Legal Enforcement of Morals: A Reconsideration of the Hart-Devlin Debates." *American Journal of Jurisprudence* 35 (1990): 15–46.

Glasser, Cyril. "Radicals and Refugees: The Foundation of the Modern Law Review and English Legal Scholarship." *Modern Law Review* 50 (October 1987): 688–708.

Goodrich, P. "Review of Roger Cotterrell, *The Politics of Jurisprudence*." *Modern Law Review* 55 (January 1992): 145–48.

Gourvish, T. R. "The Rise of the Professions." In T. R. Gourvish and Alan O'Day, eds., *Later Victorian Britain 1867–1900,* pp. 13–35. London: Macmillan Education Ltd., 1988.

Greenleaf, W. H. "Blackstone and the Office of Government." In R. Schnur, ed., *Die Rolle der Juristen bei der Entstehung des Modernen Staates,* pp. 499–520. Berlin: Dunker und Hunblat, 1986.

Hacker, P. M. S. "Hart's Philosophy of Law." In P. M. S. Hacker and J. Raz, eds., *Law, Morality and Society: Essays in Honour of H. L. A. Hart,* pp. 1–21. Oxford: Clarendon Press, 1977.

Hagry, H. "Liberalism and Legal Moralism: The Hart-Devlin Debate and Beyond." *Ratio Juris* 4 (July 1991): 202–18.

Haldane, Richard Burdon. "Higher Nationality: A Study in Law and Ethics." *American Bar Association Reports* 38 (1913): 393–417.

Hanbury, H. G. "Blackstone as a Judge." *American Journal of Legal History* 3 (January 1959): 1–27.

———. "Blackstone in Retrospect." *Law Quarterly Review* 66 (July 1950): 318–47.

Harrison, Frederic. "The English School of Jurisprudence." *Fortnightly Review* 24 (October 1878): 475–92.

Hart, H. L. A. "Bentham and the Demystification of the Law." *Modern Law Review* 36 (January 1973): 2–17.

———. "Bentham on Legal Powers." *Yale Law Journal* 81 (April 1972): 799–822.

———. "Bentham and the United States of America." *Journal of Law and Economics* 19 (October 1976): 547–67.

———. "Blackstone's Use of the Law of Nature." *South African Law Review* (1956): 169–74.

———. "Definition and Theory in Jurisprudence." *Law Quarterly Review* 70 (January 1954): 37–60.

———. "Introduction." In H. L. A. Hart, ed., Jeremy Bentham, *Of Laws in General,* pp. xxxi–xlii. London: Athlone Press, 1970.

Higgins, A. Pearce. "Sir Thomas Erskine Holland." *Law Quarterly Review* 42 (October 1926): 471–74.

Hill, H. H. "H. L. A. Hart's Hermeneutic Positivism: On Some Methodological Difficulties in the Concept of Law." *Canadian Journal of Law and Jurisprudence* 3 (January 1990): 113–28.

Himmelfarb, Gertrude. "Bentham versus Blackstone." In Gertrude Himmelfarb, *Marriage and Morals among the Victorians and Other Essays,* pp. 94–110. New York: Random House, 1987.

———. "Bentham's Utopia: The National Charity Company." *Journal of British Studies* 10 (November 1970): 80–125.

———. "The Haunted House of Jeremy Bentham." In Gertrude Himmelfarb, *Victorian Minds,* pp. 32–81. New York: Harper and Row, 1970.

———. "On Reading Bentham Seriously." *Studies in Burke and His Time* 14 (Winter 1972–73): 179–86.

Hittinger, R. "The Hart-Devlin Debate Revisited." *American Journal of Jurisprudence* 35 (1990): 47–53.

Hoffer, Peter Charles. "Text, Translation, Context, Conversation: Preliminary Notes for Decoding the Deliberations of the Advisory Committee that Wrote the Federal Rules of Civil Procedure." *American Journal of Legal History* 37 (October 1993): 409–39.

Holdsworth, Sir William S. "Bentham's Place in English Legal History." *California Law Review* 28 (July 1940): 568–91.

———. "Blackstone." *North Carolina Law Review* 17 (February 1939): 233–41.

———. "Gibbon, Blackstone and Bentham." *Law Quarterly Review* 52 (January 1936): 46–59.

———. "Sir William Blackstone." *Oregon Law Review* 7 (February 1928): 155–63.

———. "Some Aspects of Blackstone and His Commentaries." *Cambridge Law Journal* 4, no. 3 (1932): 261–85.

Holland, Sir Thomas Erskine. "Codification." *Edinburgh Review* 126 (October 1867): 347–76.

Horwitz, Morton J. "History and Theory." *Yale Law Journal* 96 (July 1987): 1825–35.

Hull, N. E. H. "Networks & Bricolage: A Prolegomenon to a History of Twentieth-Century American Academic Jurisprudence." *American Journal of Legal History* 35 (July 1991): 307–22.

Innes, Joanna. "Jonathan Clark, Social History and England's 'Ancien Regime.' " *Past and Present* 115 (May 1987): 165–200.

James, M. H. "Bentham and the Individuation of Laws." *Northern Ireland Legal Quarterly* 24 (Autumn 1973): 357–82.

Jezierski, John V. "Parliament or People: James Wilson and Blackstone on the Nature and Location of Sovereignty." *Journal of the History of Ideas* 32 (January–March 1971): 95–106.

Jolowicz, H. F. "Was Bentham a Lawyer?" In George W. Keeton and Georg Schwarzenberger, eds., *Jeremy Bentham and the Law,* pp. 1–19. London: Stevens and Sons, 1948.

Jones, Gareth. "Introduction." In *The Sovereignty of the Law: Selections from Blackstone's Commentaries on the Laws of England,* pp. vii–xlvii. Toronto: University of Toronto Press, 1973.

Kaye, Judith S. "One Judge's View of Academic Law Review Writing." *Journal of Legal Education* 39 (September 1989): 313–21.

Kennedy, Duncan. "The Structure of Blackstone's Commentaries." *Buffalo Law Review* 28 (Fall 1979): 205–382.

Kenny, Courtney. "What an Old Reporter Told Me." *Law Quarterly Review* 43 (July 1927): 349–65.

Krygier, Martin. "*The Concept of Law* and Social Theory." *Oxford Journal of Legal Studies* 2 (Summer 1982): 155–80.

Letwin, Shirley. "Justice, Authority and Jurisprudence." *Historical Journal* 16 (June 1973): 411–19.

Lewis, A. D. E. "John Austin (1790–1859): Pupil of Bentham." *Bentham Newsletter* 2 (1979): 18–29.

Lewis, John Underwood. "Blackstone's Definition of Law and Doctrine of Legal Obligation as a Link Between Early Modern and Contemporary Theories of Law." *Irish Jurist* 3 (Winter 1968): 336–51.

Lieberman, David. "Blackstone's Science of Legislation." *Journal of British Studies* 27 (April 1988): 117–49.

———. "From Bentham to Benthamism." *Historical Journal* 28 (March 1985): 199–224.

Lobban, Michael. "Blackstone and the Science of Law." *Historical Journal* 30 (June 1987): 311–35.

Lovin, Keith. "H. L. A. Hart and the Morality of Law." *American Journal of Jurisprudence* 21 (1976): 131–43.

Lucas, Paul. "Blackstone and the Reform of the Legal Profession." *English Historical Review* 77 (July 1962): 456–89.

Lucas, Paul. "*Ex parte* Sir William Blackstone, 'Plagiarist': A Note on Blackstone and the Natural Law." *American Journal of Legal History* 7 (April 1963): 142–58.

Maine, Sir Henry. "The Conception of Sovereignty and Its Importance in International Law." *Papers Read before the Juridical Society of London 1855–58* 1 (16 April 1855): 26–45.

Markby, Sir William. "Analytical Jurisprudence." *Law Magazine and Review,* Fourth Series 1 (August 1876): 617–30.

McKnight, Joseph W. "Blackstone, Quasi-Jurisprudent." *Southwestern Law Journal* 13 (Fall 1959): 399–411.

Mill, John Stuart. "Austin on Jurisprudence." *Edinburgh Review* 118 (October 1863): 438–82.

Millon, David. "Positivism in the Historiography of the Common Law." *Wisconsin Law Review* (1989): 669–714.

Milne, A. J. M. "Bentham's Principle of Utility and Legal Philosophy." *Northern Ireland Legal Quarterly* 24 (Autumn): 275–304.

Milsom, S. F. C. "The Nature of Blackstone's Achievement." *Oxford Journal of Legal Studies* 1 (Spring 1981): 1–12.

Milton, Philip. "H. L. A. Hart: Jurisprudence and Linguistic Philosophy." *Modern Law Review* 47 (November 1984): 751–60.

Moles, Robert N. "The Decline and Fall of Dworkin's Empire." In Alan Hunt, ed., *Reading Dworkin Critically,* pp. 71–121. London: Berg, 1992.

———. "Hart's Critique of Austin." *Northern Ireland Legal Quarterly* 36 (Winter 1985): 283–313.

———. "John Austin Reconsidered." *Northern Ireland Legal Quarterly* 36 (Autumn 1985): 193–221.

———. "Law and Morality—How to Do Things with Confusion." *Northern Ireland Legal Quarterly* 37 (Spring 1986): 29–60.

Money, John. "Provincialism and the English 'Ancien Regime': Samuel Pipe-Wolferstan and the 'Confessional State,' 1776–1820." *Albion* 21 (Fall 1989): 389–425.

Morison, W. L. "Some Myth about Positivism." *Yale Law Journal* 68 (December 1958): 212–33.

Murphy, W. T., and Simon Roberts. "Introduction." *Modern Law Review* 50 (October 1987): 677–87.

Nolan, Dennis R. "Sir William Blackstone and the New American Republic: A Study of Intellectual Impact." *New York University Law Review* 51 (November 1976): 731–68.

Oldham, J. "From Blackstone to Bentham: Common Law versus Legislation in Eighteenth-Century Britain." *Michigan Law Review* 89 (May 1991): 1637–60.

Oledasu, Adijare. "H. L. A. Hart on Legal Obligation." *Ratio Juris* 4 (July 1991): 152–76.

Olivecrona, Karl. "Will of the Sovereign: Some Reflections on Bentham's Concept of 'A Law.'" *American Journal of Jurisprudence* 20 (1975): 95–110.

O'Neill, Aidan. "The Legal Philosophies of H. L. A. Hart." *Juridical Review,* New Series 34 (June 1989): 32–48.

Orth, John V. "Casting the Priests Out of the Temple: John Austin and the Relation between Law and Religion." In John Witte, Jr., and Frank S. Alexander, eds., *The Weightier Matters of the Law: Essays in Law and Religion—A Tribute to Harold J. Berman,* pp. 229–49. Atlanta: Scholars Press, 1988.

———. "Jeremy Bentham: The Common Law's Severest Critic." *American Bar Association Journal* 68 (June 1982): 710–15.

———. "Sir William Blackstone: Hero of the Common Law." *American Bar Association Journal* 66 (February 1980): 155–59.

———. "Thinking about Law Historically." *North Carolina Law Review* 70 (November 1991): 287–95.

Packer, Martin J. "Hermeneutic Inquiry in the Study of Human Conduct." *American Psychologist* 40 (October 1985): 1081–93.

Pankhurst, R. M. "The Study of Jurisprudence." *Law Magazine and Review,* New Series 4 (July 1875): 730–51.

Petrow, Stefan. "The Legal Enforcement of Morality in Late-Victorian and Edwardian England." *University of Tasmania Law Review* 11 (1992): 59–74.

Phang, A. B. L. "Jurisprudential Oaks from Mystical Acorns: The Hart-Dworkin Debate Revisited." *Ratio Juris* 3 (December 1990): 385–98.

Phillips, John A. "The Social Calculus: Deference and Defiance in Later Georgian England." *Albion* 21 (Fall 1989): 426–49.

Pilling, N. "The Conservatism of Sir Henry Maine." *Political Studies* 18 (March 1970): 107–20.

Pollock, Sir Frederick. "Law and Command." *Law Magazine and Review,* New Series 1 (April 1872): 189–205.

———. "The Methods of Jurisprudence." *Law Magazine and Review,* Fourth Series 8 (November 1882): 25–53.

Pollock, Sir Frederick. "Sir Henry Maine and His Work." *Contemporary Review* 55 (February 1889): 265–76.

———. "Sir Henry Maine as a Jurist." *Edinburgh Review* 178 (July 1893): 100–21.

———. "Our Jubilee." *Law Quarterly Review* 51 (January 1935): 5–10.

Posner, Richard. "Blackstone and Bentham." *Journal of Law and Economics* 19 (October 1976): 569–606.

Raz, Joseph. "Hart on Moral Rights and Legal Duties." *Oxford Journal of Legal Studies* 4 (Spring 1984): 123–31.

Rosen, Frederick. "Bentham and Mill on Liberty and Justice." In Frederick Rosen and George Feaver, eds., *Lives, Liberties and the Public Good: New Essays in Political Theory for Maurice Cranston,* pp. 121–38. London: Macmillan, 1987.

———. "The Origin of Liberal Utilitarianism: Jeremy Bentham and Liberty." In Richard Bellamy, ed., *Victorian Liberalism: Nineteenth-Century Political Thought and Practice,* pp. 58–70. London: Routledge, 1990.

Ruben, Eira. "John Austin's Political Pamphlets 1824–1859." In Elspeth Attwooll, ed., *Perspectives in Jurisprudence,* pp. 20–41. Glasgow: University of Glasgow Press, 1977.

Rumble, Wilfrid E. "Divine Law, Utilitarian Ethics, and Positivist Jurisprudence: A Study of the Legal Philosophy of John Austin." *American Journal of Jurisprudence* 24 (1979): 139–80.

———. "John Austin and His Nineteenth Century Critics: The Case of Sir Henry Sumner Maine." *Northern Ireland Legal Quarterly* 39 (Summer 1988): 119–49.

———. "The Legal Positivism of John Austin and the Realist Movement in American Jurisprudence." *Cornell Law Review* 66 (1981): 986–1031.

Samuel, Geoffrey. "Science, Law and History: Historical Jurisprudence and Modern Legal Theory." *Northern Ireland Legal Quarterly* 41 (Spring 1990): 1–21.

Schofield, Philip. "Jeremy Bentham and Nineteenth-Century English Jurisprudence." *Journal of Legal History* 12 (May 1991): 58–88.

Sherwin, R. K. "Opening Hart's Concept of Law." *Valparaiso University Law Review* 20 (Spring 1986): 385–411.

Sicker, Martin. "Jeremy Bentham on Law and Jurisprudence." *Modern Age* 22 (Summer 1978): 277–84.

Simpson, A. W. B. "Legal Education and Legal History." *Oxford Journal of Legal Studies* 11 (Spring 1991): 106–13.

Smith, Brian. "Maine's Concept of Progress." *Journal of the History of Ideas* 24 (July–September 1963): 407–12.

Stannard, John E. "A Tale of Four Codes: John Austin and the Criminal Law." *Northern Ireland Legal Quarterly* 41 (Winter 1990): 293–314.

Starr, William C. "Law and Morality in H. L. A. Hart's Legal Philosophy." *Marquette Law Review* 67 (Summer 1984): 673–89.

Stumpf, S. E. "Austin's Theory of the Separation of Law and Morals." *Vanderbilt Law Review* 14 (December 1960): 117–49.

Sugarman, David. " 'A Hatred of Disorder': Legal Science, Liberalism and Imperialism." In Peter Fitzpatrick, ed., *Dangerous Supplements: Resistance and Renewal in Jurisprudence,* pp. 34–67. London: Pluto Press, 1991.

———. "Legal Theory, the Common Law Mind and the Making of the Textbook Tradition." In William Twining, ed., *Legal Theory and the Common Law,* pp. 26–61. Oxford: Basil Blackwell, 1986.

Summers, Robert S. "Professor H. L. A. Hart's Concept of Law." *Duke Law Journal* (1963): 629–70.

Sutherland, Lucy S. "William Blackstone and the Legal Chairs at Oxford." In Rene Wellek and Alvaro Ribeiro, eds., *Evidence in Literary Scholarship: Essays in Memory of James Marshall Osborn,* pp. 229–40. Oxford: Clarendon Press, 1979.

Tarlton, C. D. "The Overlooked Strategy of Bentham's *Fragment on Government.*" *Political Studies* 20 (December 1972): 397–406.

Taylor, E. H. "H. L. A. Hart's Concept of Law in the Perspective of American Legal Realism." *Modern Law Review* 35 (November 1972): 606–20.

Tilley, Arthur. "Professor Holland's 'Jurisprudence' and Codification." *Law Magazine and Review,* New Series 6 (November 1880): 44–67.

Twining, William. "Academic Law and Legal Philosophy: The Significance of Herbert Hart." *Law Quarterly Review* 95 (October 1979): 557–80.

———. "Maine and Legal Education," In Alan Diamond, ed., *The Victorian Achievement of Sir Henry Maine: A Centennial Reappraisal,* pp. 209–216. Cambridge, Eng.: Cambridge University Press, 1991.

Utz, Stephen G. "Maine's *Ancient Law* and Legal Theory." *Connecticut Law Review* 16 (Summer 1984): 821–52.

Van Doren, J. W. "Theories of Professors H. L. A. Hart and Ronald Dworkin." *Cleveland State Law Review* 29 (1980): 279–309.

Vick, Kendall L. "Sir William Blackstone's Commentaries on the Laws of England: Rebuttal of the Criticism Leveled against Them by Jeremy Bentham and John Austin." *Loyola Law Review* 13 (1967): 71–92.

Vinogradoff, Sir Paul. "The Teaching of Sir Henry Maine." *Law Quarterly Review* 20 (April 1904): 119–33.

Waluchow, Wilfrid J. "Hart, Legal Rules and Palm Tree Justice." *Law and Philosophy* 4 (April 1985): 41–70.

Warner, K. A. "The Concept of Legal Obligation and the Separation of Law and Morality." *Juridical Review* (June 1985): 69–84.

Waterman, Julian S. "Mansfield and Blackstone's Commentaries." *University of Chicago Law Review* 1 (March 1934): 549–71.

Watson, Alan. "The Evolution of Law: Continued." *Law and History Review* 5 (Fall 1987): 537–70.

———. "Legal Change: Sources of Law and Legal Culture." *University of Pennsylvania Law Review* 131 (April 1983): 1121–57.

———. "The Structure of Blackstone's *Commentaries*." *Yale Law Journal* 97 (April 1988): 795–821.

Wiener, Martin J. "The Unloved State: Twentieth-Century Politics in the Writing of Nineteenth-Century History." *Journal of British Studies* 33 (July 1994): 283–308.

Willman, Robert. "Blackstone and the 'Theoretical Perfection' of English Law in the Reign of Charles II." *Historical Journal* 26 (March 1983): 39–70.

Wilson, Geoffrey. "English Legal Scholarship." *Modern Law Review* 50 (October 1987): 818–54.

Index